LISA BARNARD

YOU ONLY LOOK ONCE

HARTMANN BOOKS

AFTER NATURE
ULRIKE CRESPO
PHOTOGRAPHY PRIZE **25**

GRUSSWORT

Christiane Riedel, Mitglied des Vorstands, Crespo Foundation

In der zweiten Runde des internationalen *After Nature. Ulrike Crespo Photography Prize* werden die Künstlerinnen Lisa Barnard und Isadora Romero ausgezeichnet. Ihre künstlerischen Herangehensweisen sind sehr unterschiedlich und doch eint sie, dass sie mit ihren innovativen Projekten unser Bewusstsein dafür schärfen, wie sehr sowohl Technologien als auch gemeinschaftliches Handeln unsere Beziehung zur Welt prägen. Wie können wir im Zeitalter des Anthropozäns eine ganzheitliche Verantwortung für unseren Planeten entwickeln, wenn sich unsere Erkenntnisse immer mehr in die Sphären von High-Tech und künstlicher Intelligenz verlagern? Und wo verbinden sich unsere gegenwärtigen technischen Möglichkeiten mit dem Wissen, das lokale Gemeinschaften seit Generationen pflegen und in die Zukunft tragen?

Lisa Barnards künstlerische Recherche behandelt die Prinzipien der Objekterfassung und erweiterte Systeme der Wahrnehmung aus einer durch die Kameratechnik informierten Perspektive. Ihr Projekt ist in Kalifornien angesiedelt und stellt überraschende Verbindungen zwischen dem strapazierten Ökosystem des Saltonsees, dem US-Militär, Rohstoffgewinnung, Fledermäusen und autonomen Fahrsystemen her. Isadora Romero hat über viele Monate hinweg mit den Bewohner:innen des Mache-Chindul-Reservats und der Gemeinde Yunguilla in den Nebelwäldern von Ecuador gearbeitet. Ihre Fotografien gewähren Einblick in ein Zusammenleben mit dem Wald, das ebenso von indigenem Wissen wie von alten und neuen Technologien geprägt ist.

Lange Zeit orientierte sich die Kunst primär an den Dingen, die sich mit dem bloßen Auge erfassen ließen. Die Wissenschaft entwickelte jedoch Instrumente, mit denen sie zu den zuvor unzugänglichen *res invisibiles* des Mikro- und Makrokosmos vordringen konnte. Zunehmend arbeiten Wissenschaft und Kunst mit denselben Werkzeugen, Methoden und Programmen – und erweitern die Rezeption und Perzeption der menschlichen Sinne und Erkenntnisse multidimensional. Beide Preisträgerinnen reflektieren die Kamera als ein Instrument, das verschiedenste Zugänge zur Welt (re-)produziert – auch solche, die über das menschliche Sehvermögen hinausweisen.

Durch den jährlich vergebenen *After Nature Prize* fördern die Crespo Foundation und die C/O Berlin Foundation je zwei fotografie- oder filmbasierte Projekte, die Verflechtungen zwischen Mensch, Umwelt und technischen Bildern sichtbar machen und so neue Perspektiven auf ein sich wandelndes Verständnis von Natur eröffnen. Der Preis ist Ulrike

GREETINGS

Christiane Riedel, Member of the Board, Crespo Foundation

Artists Lisa Barnard and Isadora Romero are the winners of the second edition of the international *After Nature: Ulrike Crespo Photography Prize*. Although their artistic approaches are very different, a common feature of their innovative projects is that they heighten our awareness of the degree to which our relationship to the world is informed both by technology and by collaborative action. In the age of the Anthropocene, how can we develop a holistic responsibility for our planet when our knowledge is increasingly shifting into the realms of high tech and artificial intelligence? And where do the technical capabilities we are now fostering join up with the knowledge that local communities have cultivated for generations and are carrying forward into the future?

Lisa Barnard's artistic research deals with the principles of object detection and wider systems of perception looked at from a perspective informed by camera-based technology. Located in California, her project establishes unexpected connections between the overtaxed ecosystem of the Salton Sea, the US military, resource extraction, bats, and autonomous driving systems. Isadora Romero has spent many months working with the people living on the Mache-Chindul Reserve and the Yunguilla community in the cloud forests of Ecuador. Her photographs afford insights into a way of living with the forest that is defined as much by Indigenous knowledge as by old and new technologies.

For a long time, art was primarily geared to things that could be seen with the naked eye. However, science developed instruments that could be used to probe the *res invisibiles* of the microcosm and macrocosm, which had hitherto been inaccessible. Science and art have long been working more and more with the same tools, methods, and programs – extending the reception and perception of the human senses and understanding into multiple dimensions. The two prizewinners reflect on the camera as an instrument that (re)produces all kinds of different approaches to the world – including those that transcend the human faculty of sight.

The Crespo Foundation and the C/O Berlin Foundation's annual award of the *After Nature Prize* provides support, each year, for two photography- or film-based projects that make visible the web of connections linking humans, the environment, and technical images, offering new perspectives on our shifting understanding of nature. The prize is dedicated to photographer and garden designer Ulrike Crespo, who spent decades engaging intensively with nature. Current developments in the

Crespo gewidmet, die sich als Fotografin und Gartengestalterin über Jahrzehnte intensiv mit der Natur beschäftigt hat. Heute sind die Künstler:innen durch die aktuellen Entwicklungen in den Bereichen Technologie und Ökologie mehr denn je herausgefordert, das Verhältnis von Mensch und Natur mit ihren Apparaten neu zu reflektieren.

Der gemeinsame *After Nature Prize* wird in der Umsetzung von C/O Berlin gestaltet. Die dazugehörige Ausstellung wird zunächst im Amerika Haus und anschließend im Open Space der Crespo Foundation in Frankfurt gezeigt. Unser großer Dank gilt Stephan Erfurt, Louisa Seelis, Katharina Täschner und Boaz Levin von C/O Berlin sowie Ben Livne Weitzman, der die Crespo Foundation in diesem Projekt unterstützt, für die inspirierende Zusammenarbeit.

realms of technology and ecology are now presenting the artists with even more of a challenge in using their cameras to ponder anew the relationship between humans and nature.

The implementation of the joint *After Nature Prize* is organised by C/O Berlin. The associated exhibition will initially be shown at C/O Berlin, followed by a run at the Crespo Foundation's Open Space in Frankfurt am Main. We are immensely grateful to Stephan Erfurt, Louisa Seelis, Katharina Täschner, and Boaz Levin from C/O Berlin and to Ben Livne Weitzman, who supports the Crespo Foundation in this project, for the inspiring process of collaboration.

VORWORT

Stephan Erfurt, CEO, C/O Berlin Foundation

Die Frage, wie wir heute auf eine Natur blicken, die durch unser eigenes Handeln zunehmend verändert wird, steht im Zentrum des *After Nature. Ulrike Crespo Photography Prize*. Mit Lisa Barnard und Isadora Romero zeichnen wir zwei Künstlerinnen aus, die auf unterschiedliche Weise neue Perspektiven auf unser Verhältnis zur Umwelt eröffnen. Während Barnard sich mit Systemen der Wahrnehmung beschäftigt und zeigt, wie diese in globale Zusammenhänge eingebunden sind, setzt sich Romero mit dem Wissen, der Geschichte, den Technologien und der Spiritualität der Nebelwälder in Ecuador auseinander. Sie fragt nach den Formen eines funktionierenden Zusammenlebens mit dem Wald in Vergangenheit, Gegenwart und Zukunft.

Mit großer Freude führen wir dieses gemeinsame Projekt von C/O Berlin und der Crespo Foundation fort. Die zweite Ausgabe des Preises baut auf dem erfolgreichen Auftaktjahr auf, das mit der Preisträger:innen-Ausstellung bei C/O Berlin begann und mit der zweiten Station im neuen Crespo Open Space in Frankfurt am Main eine überregionale Auseinandersetzung mit den Themen Natur und Umwelt ermöglichte. Die diesjährige Doppelausstellung im Amerika Haus Berlin präsentiert erneut zwei herausragende fotografische Positionen und wird durch begleitende Publikationen ergänzt. Sie ist Ausdruck einer langfristigen Zusammenarbeit, die sich der kontinuierlichen Reflexion ökologischer Fragestellungen in der zeitgenössischen Fotografie und den visuellen Medien widmet.

Der *After Nature Prize* reagiert auf die Dringlichkeit unserer Gegenwart. In einer Zeit, in der die Klimakrise und ihre sozialen wie politischen Folgen das Leben weltweit beeinflussen, betont der Preis die Rolle der Fotografie als Medium der Reflexion, der Kritik und des künstlerischen Handelns. Er fördert Projekte, die neue Perspektiven auf das Zusammenspiel von Gesellschaft, Umwelt und Technologie eröffnen und über vertraute Erzählungen hinausdenken.

Dabei ist der Preis mehr als eine klassische Auszeichnung, er ist eine Plattform für künstlerische Forschung und interdisziplinären Dialog. Mit seiner gezielten thematischen Ausrichtung auf die »Fotografie nach der Natur« reagiert er auf eine der drängendsten Fragen unserer Zeit: Wie können Bilder dazu beitragen, ein neues Verständnis von Natur zu entwickeln, jenseits romantischer Vorstellungen, jenseits der Trennung von Natur und Kultur? Der Preis bietet nicht nur finanziellen Spielraum für die Realisierung ambitionierter Projekte, sondern schafft

FOREWORD

Stephan Erfurt, CEO, C/O Berlin Foundation

The *After Nature: Ulrike Crespo Photography Prize* foregrounds the question of how we look at nature today, in an age when our own actions are increasingly changing it. In presenting the awards to Lisa Barnard and Isadora Romero, we are honouring two artists who, in different ways, offer new perspectives on our relationship with the environment. While Barnard is concerned with systems of perception and shows how they are linked to global contexts, Romero focuses on the knowledge, history, technology, and spirituality associated with Ecuador's cloud forests, looking at past, present, and future scenarios to examine respectful and enduring ways of living with the forest.

We are delighted that C/O Berlin and the Crespo Foundation will be continuing this joint project. The second edition of the prize builds on the successful inaugural year, which kicked off with an exhibition of the award winners' work at C/O Berlin before moving on to the new Crespo Open Space in Frankfurt am Main, enabling an engagement with issues relating to nature and the environment at a transregional level. This year's double exhibition at Amerika Haus in Berlin, which is augmented by accompanying publications, once again presents two outstanding photographic positions. It is the fruit of a long-term collaborative venture centred on an ongoing process of reflection on ecological issues in contemporary photography and visual media.

The *After Nature Prize* is a response to the urgent concerns of the present we live in. At a time when the climate crisis and its social and political fallout are impacting life on a global scale, the prize highlights the role of photography as a medium of reflection, criticism, and artistic action. It supports projects that offer new angles on the interplay between society, the environment, and technology and are able to think outside the box beyond the limits of familiar narratives.

The prize is not just a typical award; it is a platform for artistic research and interdisciplinary dialogue. Its targeted focus on 'photography after nature' is a response to one of the most pressing questions of our time: how can images help us develop a new understanding of nature, beyond romantic notions and the split between nature and culture? The prize does not merely offer financial scope for realising ambitious projects, it also makes artistic positions visible that take an innovative approach to engaging with ecological, technological, and cultural upheavals. By bringing in international experts, providing thoughtful curatorial support, and leveraging the media and institutional

auch Sichtbarkeit für künstlerische Positionen, die sich innovativ mit ökologischen, technologischen und kulturellen Umbrüchen auseinandersetzen. Durch die Einbindung internationaler Expert:innen, die sorgfältige kuratorische Begleitung sowie die mediale und institutionelle Reichweite der Partnerinstitutionen trägt der Preis aktiv zur Etablierung neuer Erzählungen über Natur, Verantwortung und Zukunft bei.

Mein herzlicher Dank gilt der Crespo Foundation, insbesondere Christiane Riedel und ihrem Team, für die vertrauensvolle und anregende Zusammenarbeit. Ebenso danke ich den Mitgliedern der Jury, unserem engagierten Team bei C/O Berlin sowie ganz besonders Katharina Täschner, unserer Projektleiterin und Kuratorin, Boaz Levin, unserem Co-Programmleiter, und Louisa Seelis, Leitung Sponsoring und Fundraising.

Ich lade Sie herzlich ein, die Ausstellung zu besuchen und sich von den Arbeiten inspirieren zu lassen – als Einladung zum Sehen, Nachdenken und Weiterdenken.

reach of our partners, the prize plays an active part in establishing new narratives about nature, responsibility, and the future.

My heartfelt thanks to the Crespo Foundation – in particular, Christiane Riedel and her team – for the inspiring collaboration and spirit of trust they brought to the process. I would also like to thank the members of the jury and our dedicated team at C/O Berlin, with a special mention to Katharina Täschner, our project lead and curator; Boaz Levin, our co-head of programming; and Louisa Seelis, head of sponsoring and fundraising.

You are warmly invited to visit the exhibition – may the works be a source of inspiration, encouraging you to see, reflect, and keep on pondering.

SENSORIK, ODER: DAS ERFASSEN DER WELT

Katharina Täschner

Die Entwicklung verlässlicher Systeme zur Objekterkennung im Straßenverkehr ist ein milliardenschweres Unterfangen. Anders als Texte oder Bilder lässt sich eine Wahrnehmung der Welt, durch die wir uns bewegen – einschließlich ihres bisweilen chaotischen Straßenverkehrs – nicht ohne Weiteres auf Basis eines bestehenden Datenpools generieren. Autonome Fahrsysteme erfordern eine Vielzahl an Informationen, die durch Kameras und Sensoren in Echtzeit erfasst und ausgewertet werden müssen. Obwohl Unternehmen wie Waymo, deren elektrische, fahrerlose Taxis bereits die Straßen von San Francisco, Los Angeles, Phoenix und Austin bevölkern, kontinuierlich an der Verbesserung ihrer Systeme arbeiten, bleibt die Programmierung eines sich durch Raum und Zeit bewegenden Körpers – das Kreieren einer maschinellen Wahrnehmung, die ohne eigenes Bewusstsein Entscheidungen trifft – ein komplexes Unterfangen im Bereich der sogenannten künstlichen Intelligenz.

Gleichzeitig ist unser Verhältnis zur Umwelt selbst als Produkt technologischer Vermittlung zu begreifen. Die Übertragung der Welt in ein Bild mithilfe der Kamera ist dabei nur eines von vielen Verfahren, das Teil unseres alltäglichen Erfahrungsrepertoires geworden ist. In ihrer Funktion als Werkzeuge schreiben sich Technologien, wie James Bridle betont, in »die Gesellschaft, die Politik und zunehmend auch die Umwelt« ein. Genährt durch extraktiven Rohstoffabbau und das Wachstumsstreben großer Konzerne strukturieren sie heute nicht nur unser Denken, sondern auch unser Handeln. Angesichts der zerstörerischen Macht dieses Gefüges, so Bridle weiter, gelte es »Mittel und Wege [zu] finden, um unsere technologischen Fähigkeiten und unser Gefühl der Einzigartigkeit des Menschen mit einer erdverbundenen Sensibilität und Aufmerksamkeit für die Vernetzung aller Dinge in Einklang zu bringen.«[1]

Einen Schritt in Richtung einer solchen Dezentrierung unserer menschlichen Wahrnehmung geht Lisa Barnard mit ihrem Projekt *You Only Look Once*. Ihre in Kalifornien angesiedelte Recherche befasst sich mit Techniken der Objekterfassung in zivilen wie militärischen Anwendungen, der Echolokation von Fledermäusen sowie den ökologischen Ressourcen, die der Entwicklung zukünftiger Technologien zugrunde liegen. Durch die Verknüpfung verschiedener Untersuchungsstränge, die sie vom Saltonsee nahe Palm Springs über Sacramento bis auf die Straßen von San Francisco führen, schafft Barnard ein Bewusstsein für die Parallelen und Differenzen zwischen menschlichem, tierischem und maschinellem Bewusstsein sowie für die Momente, in denen das Erkennen von Welt in deren aktive Gestaltung

SENSING THE WORLD

Katharina Täschner

The task of developing reliable systems for detecting objects on roads is an endeavour worth billions. An awareness of the world we move through – including its sometimes chaotic traffic – cannot simply be generated on the basis of an existing data pool, as is possible for text and images. Autonomous driving systems require a huge amount of data that needs to be recorded and evaluated in real time by cameras and sensors. Although companies such as Waymo, whose electric, driverless taxis already crowd the streets of San Francisco, Los Angeles, Phoenix, and Austin, are constantly working to improve their systems, the job of programming a body that moves through space and time – creating a machine perception that can make decisions without having any inbuilt consciousness – remains a complex undertaking in the realm of so-called artificial intelligence.

Our relationship with the environment itself can also be seen as being mediated by technology. Using a camera to translate the world into an image is just one of many processes that has become part of our day-to-day repertoire of experiences. As James Bridle emphasises, technologies, operating as tools, 'affect society, politics and, increasingly, the environment'. Fed by extractive mining and the growth imperatives of large corporations, these technologies now structure both our thinking and our behaviour. Given the destructive power of this framework, Bridle goes on to argue that 'we must find ways to reconcile our technological prowess and sense of human uniqueness with an earthy sensibility and an attentiveness to the interconnectedness of all things.'[1]

Lisa Barnard's project *You Only Look Once* takes a step in this direction as it seeks to decentralise human perception. Based in California, the research she conducts deals with techniques for object detection in civilian and military applications, bat echolocation, and the ecological resources underpinning the development of future technologies. By weaving together different strands of study that take her from the Salton Sea near Palm Springs to Sacramento and the streets of San Francisco, Barnard makes us aware of the parallels and differences between human, animal, and machine consciousness, and of the moments when recognising the world devolves into an active way of shaping it. In the midst of the climate crisis, Barnard shows how closely questions of perception are linked to ideas of technological progress and the exploitation of ecological resources – and illustrates the importance of making the relationships between them visible.

übergeht. Inmitten der Klimakrise zeigt Barnard, wie eng Fragen der Wahrnehmung mit Vorstellungen von technologischem Fortschritt und der Ausbeutung ökologischer Ressourcen verknüpft sind – und wie notwendig es ist, diese Verflechtungen sichtbar zu machen.

SPEKULATIONEN IN DER WÜSTE

Lisa Barnards Untersuchung nimmt ihren Ausgangspunkt am Saltonsee, dem bis heute größten Binnengewässer Kaliforniens. Er entstand 1905, als der Damm eines mit dem Colorado River verbundenen Kanals brach und das Wasser über zwei Jahre hinweg die sogenannte Salton-Senke flutete. Seither bildet der See ein fragiles Ökosystem inmitten der Wüste, das Barnard als Matrix eines komplexen Wechselverhältnisses von technologischer Ambition und ökologischer Vernachlässigung zeigt. Ihre Recherche setzt am Ende des Zweiten Weltkriegs ein, als der See zum Schauplatz von Testflügen zur Vorbereitung der Atombombenabwürfe auf Hiroshima und Nagasaki wurde. In den Jahren 1944 und 1945 warfen mehrere B-29-Bomber Testkörper über dem See ab, die in Größe und Gewicht den Atombomben »Little Boy« und »Fat Man« entsprachen. Während die Bombenattrappen heute auf dem Grund des Sees ruhen und nur mithilfe von Sonartechnologien lokalisiert werden können, ragen die Plattformen, die den Bombern einst als Zielmarkierungen dienten, noch immer sichtbar aus dem Wasser. Als verwitternde Fragmente einer größeren Geschichte des militarisierten Blicks von oben verkörpern sie frühe Formen der Objekterkennung: Technologien, die unsere Vorstellungen von Sichtbarkeit, Kontrolle und geopolitischer Macht geprägt haben und in ihrer zivilen Fortentwicklung in unseren Alltag eingezogen sind.

Nach dem Ende des Zweiten Weltkriegs entwickelte sich der Saltonsee zu einem beliebten Naherholungsgebiet: ein kalifornischer Sehnsuchtsort, den auch Hollywoodstars und Celebrities wie die Beach Boys für sich entdeckten. Mit einem Foto badender Frauen im Colorado River, rund zwei Autostunden östlich des Sees aufgenommen, erinnert Barnard an diese einst florierenden Tage der Region, während das Bild eines ausgestopften Braunpelikans von der weit weniger glamourösen Situation der Gegenwart erzählt. Die Kombination aus stetig sinkendem Wasserpegel, steigendem Salzgehalt und zunehmender Schadstoffbelastung hat den See an den Rand des ökologischen Kollapses getrieben. Die Folgen: massives Fischsterben, eine damit einhergehende Dezimierung der Vogelpopulation und die Schließung touristischer Einrichtungen. Da der See über keinen natürlichen Abfluss verfügt und lediglich durch das Abwasser landwirtschaftlicher Betriebe gespeist wird, stellt der durch den Wind aufgewirbelte Staub des freiliegenden Seebetts ein erhebliches Gesundheitsrisiko für die lokale Bevölkerung dar.[2] Hinzu kommt die extraktive Industrie, die sich am Rand des Sees angesiedelt hat. Als hier in den

SPECULATION IN THE DESERT

Barnard's study takes as its starting point the Salton Sea, California's largest inland body of water to this day. It was created in 1905 when a canal bringing water from the Colorado River broke its dam, flooding the Salton Trough for two years. Since then, the lake has been a fragile ecosystem in the middle of the desert, which Barnard presents as a matrix of complex interrelationships involving technological ambition and ecological neglect. She began her research looking at the end of World War II, when the lake became a theatre of operations for test flights in preparation for the dropping of atomic bombs on Hiroshima and Nagasaki. In 1944 and 1945, several B-29s released test devices over the lake that corresponded in size and weight to the 'Little Boy' and 'Fat Man' bombs. While these dummy devices now lie at the bottom of the lake and can only be pinpointed with the help of sonar technology, the platforms that were once used to mark the target for the bombers can still be seen projecting above the water. Exposed to the elements, these fragments of a larger history of the militarised view from above embody early forms of object recognition: technologies that have shaped our ideas of visibility, control, and geopolitical power and have been absorbed – through their development outside the military context – into the fabric of our everyday lives.

After World War II, the Salton Sea developed into a popular area for local recreation: a dream destination for Californians that Hollywood stars and celebrities such as the Beach Boys also discovered for themselves. Barnard's photo of women bathing in the Colorado River, taken in a location about a two hours' drive east of the lake, recalls the region's halcyon days, while the picture of a stuffed brown pelican speaks of the far less glamorous situation today. The combination of steadily falling water levels, rising salinity, and an increasing pollutant load has driven the lake to the brink of ecological collapse. This has resulted in fish die-off on a massive scale, causing a decimation of the bird population and the closure of tourist facilities. Since the lake has no natural outlet and is fed solely by agricultural effluent, the dust that the wind blows up from the exposed lake bed constitutes a significant health risk for the local population.[2] This is exacerbated by the extractive industry that has established itself on the edge of the lake. When oil was being drilled for here in the 1960s, hot brine was located instead. This is now pumped out of the ground to generate electricity in large geothermal plants before being injected back into the earth. Barnard photographed these plants using a night vision camera, once again highlighting the fragile relationship between a vital piece of infrastructure and a gaze enhanced by military technology.

1960er-Jahren nach Öl gebohrt wurde, stieß man stattdessen auf heiße Sole. Diese wird heute in großen Geothermieanlagen aus der Erde gepumpt und zur Stromerzeugung genutzt, bevor sie zurück in den Untergrund geleitet wird. Lisa Barnard hat diese Anlagen mit einem Nachtsichtgerät fotografiert und verweist so abermals auf das fragile Verhältnis zwischen kritischer Infrastruktur und einem durch militärische Technologie verstärkten Blick.

Das in der Sole gelöste Lithium macht den Saltonsee zu einem Ort neuer ökonomischer Begehrlichkeiten. Lithium gilt nahezu weltweit als kritischer Rohstoff und ist unter anderem essenziell für die Herstellung von Speichersystemen im Energiesektor, Batterien in Elektroautos und die Entwicklung autonomer Fahrsysteme. Die Einstufung als »kritisch« orientiert sich dabei gleichermaßen an der wirtschaftlichen Bedeutung des Rohstoffs wie an den Risiken eines möglichen Versorgungsengpasses.[3] Aller Voraussicht nach wird der weltweite Bedarf an Lithium in den kommenden Jahren deutlich steigen. Die zentrale Rolle der Autoindustrie in diesem Prozess zeigt sich unter anderem daran, dass Kaliforniens Energiebehörde, die California Energy Commission, in ihrer Vision für das »Lithium Valley« das am Saltonsee verfügbare Lithium nicht in Tonnen, sondern anhand der 375 Millionen Autobatterien quantifiziert, die sich daraus produzieren ließen.[4] Doch bleiben zentrale Fragen bislang nur vage beantwortet, etwa jene nach den Auswirkungen des Lithiumabbaus auf den Wasserhaushalt des Sees oder nach der Beteiligung der einkommensschwachen Anrainerkommunen an den erwarteten Profiten. So wird der See nicht nur zur Ressource für neue Technologien, sondern auch zur Projektionsfläche für Narrative von Fortschritt, Sicherheit und »grüner« Transformation, die Barnard mit ihrem Projekt herausfordert.[5]

BAT RECOGNITION

1974 veröffentlichte der Philosoph Thomas Nagel den Aufsatz »What Is It Like to Be a Bat?«.[6] In seinem Text argumentiert er, dass subjektives Erleben durch rein objektive, physiologische Beschreibungen des Wahrnehmungsprozesses nicht vollständig zu erfassen sei. Um dies zu veranschaulichen, führt er das Beispiel der Fledermaus an: Obwohl deren Sinneswelt wissenschaftlich beschrieben werden kann, bliebe es uns Menschen unzugänglich, wie sich ihr Leben tatsächlich anfühlt – insbesondere, da ihre räumliche Orientierung mittels Echolokation an eine Sinnesebene geknüpft ist, die sich unserer Vorstellungskraft entzieht. Heute erfreut sich Nagels Aufsatz im Kontext aktueller Debatten über maschinelles Bewusstsein und künstliche Intelligenz neuer Aufmerksamkeit. Doch auch ganz praktisch dient Forschenden die Echolokation der Fledermaus als Inspiration bei der Entwicklung autonomer Navigationssysteme.[7]

The lithium dissolved in the brine makes the Salton Sea a highly coveted place in today's economy. Lithium, which is regarded as a critical mineral almost everywhere in the world, is essential in a variety of contexts, including in the manufacture of storage systems in the energy sector, in batteries for electric cars, and in the development of autonomous driving systems. Its 'critical' classification derives from both the economic importance of the raw material and the risks of a possible supply bottleneck.[3] In all likelihood, global demand for lithium will rise significantly in the coming years. One of the indicators of the key role that the automotive industry plays in this process is the fact that, in its vision for Lithium Valley, the California Energy Commission quantifies the lithium available at the Salton Sea not in tons but in terms of the 375 million car batteries that could be produced from it.[4] Yet the answers to some major questions remain vague, including the issue of the impact that lithium mining will have on the lake's water regime and the stake that the low-income communities located nearby will have in the expected profits. As a result, the lake is not only turning into a resource for new technologies; it is also becoming a projection screen for narratives of progress, security, and 'green' transformation of the kind that Barnard's project challenges.[5]

BAT RECOGNITION

In 1974, the philosopher Thomas Nagel published the essay 'What Is It Like to Be a Bat?', in which he argues that subjective experience cannot be fully accounted for by purely objective, physiological descriptions of the process of perception.[6] To illustrate this, he invokes the example of bats, claiming that although their sensory world can be described in scientific terms, it is impossible for humans to access what their lives actually feel like – especially since their spatial orientation, which relies on echolocation, is linked to a level of sensory activity that defies our powers of imagination. Today, Nagel's essay is receiving renewed attention in light of current debates about machine consciousness and artificial intelligence. There is, after all, a very practical aspect to the bat echolocation system, which has inspired the development of autonomous navigation systems.[7]

Against this backdrop, Barnard uses the motif of the bat as a means to examine the points at which perception coincides with technological modes of object recognition. Her research has led her, for example, to Daniel Kish, who, in the year 2000, founded the Los Angeles-based non-profit organisation World Access for the Blind, whose goal is to impart methods of navigation to blind people that will help them orient themselves in the world by themselves. Kish, who himself went blind in early childhood, draws on the principle of echolocation, using

Vor diesem Hintergrund nutzt Lisa Barnard die Fledermaus als Motiv, um den Berührungspunkten zwischen Wahrnehmung und technischer Objekterkennung nachzuspüren. Ihre Recherche führt sie unter anderem zu Daniel Kish, der im Jahr 2000 in Los Angeles die gemeinnützige Organisation World Access for the Blind gründete. Ziel der Organisation ist es, blinden Menschen Methoden zu vermitteln, die ihnen helfen, sich eigenständig in der Welt zu orientieren. Kish, der selbst seit seiner frühen Kindheit erblindet ist, bedient sich dabei des Prinzips der Echolokation: Durch Klickgeräusche sendet er Schallwellen aus, die von der Umgebung reflektiert werden. Über Jahrzehnte hinweg hat er sich darin geschult, diese auditiven Informationen differenziert auszuwerten und in ein mentales Bild zu übersetzen. Ohne Nagels Feststellung der Unzugänglichkeit subjektiven Erlebens infrage zu stellen, scheint Kish der Erfahrung einer Fledermaus so nahe zu kommen wie nur wenige andere Menschen auf der Welt.

Während es Kish gelingt, die Welt mit den Methoden der Fledermaus zu »sehen«, nutzt Barnard maschinelles Lernen, um den Blick zurück auf die Fledermaus selbst zu lenken. Westlich von Sacramento liegt der Yolo Causeway, eine Hochstraße, die ein Überschwemmungsgebiet des Sacramento River im Yolo County überquert. Jeden Sommer nisten unter dieser Brücke rund 250.000 migrierende Fledermäuse und beginnen in der Dämmerung auszuschwärmen. Barnard hat die Fledermäuse während ihres Flugs gefilmt und mit eintausend Bildern, die aus diesem Material extrahiert wurden, einen Algorithmus trainiert, um sie zu identifizieren und zu zählen. Hierfür hat sie ein You Only Look Once-System (kurz: YOLO) verwendet, das eine Objekterkennung in Echtzeit ermöglicht. Im Gegensatz zu anderen Systemen kann YOLO ein Bild in seiner Gesamtheit erfassen, anstatt es in einzelne Bereiche aufteilen und diese separat analysieren zu müssen. Das macht den Algorithmus besonders effizient für den Einsatz in autonomen Fahrsystemen und der Videoüberwachung. In ihrer Arbeit zeigt Barnard den Prozess des maschinellen Sehens als Markierung erkannter Fledermäuse im Overlay des Videomaterials. So entfaltet sich zwischen Echolokation und Echtzeiterkennung ein Nachdenken darüber, wie eng Prozesse der Wahrnehmung heute mit Technologien verknüpft sind – und darüber, wo technologische Systeme über uns bekannte sensorische Erfahrungen hinausweisen, ohne sie je vollständig erfassen zu können.

Die Bewegung der Fledermäuse, betrachtet durch Kamera und Algorithmus, führt Lisa Barnard schließlich in das Transportation Research Center in Atwater nahe San Francisco, wo selbstfahrende Autos getestet und trainiert werden. Ihre Fotografien zeigen dabei nicht die Fahrzeuge selbst, sondern Elemente der Straßenausstattung wie Schilder, Ampeln oder Zebrastreifen, an denen sich die autonomen Systeme orientieren. Inmitten dieser künstlichen Umgebung wirkt die Infrastruktur überraschend

clicking noises to emit sound waves that are reflected by the environment. Over the course of decades, he has trained himself to interpret the nuances of this auditory information and translate it into a mental image. Without challenging Nagel's assertion that subjective experience is inaccessible, Kish seems to have approximated the experience of a bat in a way that few other people in the world have managed.

While Kish manages to 'see' the world by applying the methods employed by bats, Barnard uses machine learning to refocus attention on the bat itself. To the west of Sacramento is the Yolo Causeway, an elevated highway running across one of the floodplains of the Sacramento River in Yolo County. Every summer, some 250,000 migrating bats nest under this bridge and begin to swarm out at dusk. Barnard filmed the bats in flight and then extracted a thousand images from this material, which were used to train an algorithm to identify and count them. To achieve this, she used a You Only Look Once (YOLO) system, which enables the real-time detection of objects. Unlike other systems, YOLO can capture the entirety of an image rather than having to divide it up into individual areas for separate analysis. This makes the algorithm particularly effective for deployment in autonomous driving systems and video surveillance. Barnard's work shows the process of machine vision by marking bats that have been detected in a video overlay. Combining the themes of echolocation and real-time detection gives her space to reflect on the close links that now exist between processes of perception and different technologies – and on the ways in which technological systems go beyond familiar sensory experiences without ever being able to fully apprehend them.

The bats' movement, as observed by camera and algorithm, ultimately leads Barnard to the Transportation Research Center in Atwater near San Francisco, where self-driving cars are tested and trained. Her photographs do not show the vehicles themselves but rather items of road equipment such as signs, traffic lights, and crosswalks, which the autonomous systems use to orient themselves. In this artificial environment, the infrastructure seems surprisingly banal, as if the idea were to identify one obstacle after another tentatively and with a maximum of caution. The pictures were taken at dusk for good reason, as this is when the bats swarm out and when driving systems are most prone to error. Under ideal conditions, functional systems have the potential to operate vehicles more safely and efficiently than human drivers, but it remains to be seen whether and when we will be prepared to actually surrender this responsibility. In tackling this question, Barnard engages in a self-experiment: she provides insight into what it is like to take one of Waymo's self-driving taxis, an experience that is both futuristic and mundane, while also turning herself into a road obstruction as part of

banal, als ginge es darum, tastend und mit größtmöglicher Vorsicht ein Hindernis nach dem anderen zu identifizieren. Nicht umsonst sind die Bilder in der Dämmerung entstanden, wenn Fledermäuse ausschwärmen und die Fahrsysteme am fehleranfälligsten sind. Unter idealen Bedingungen haben funktionierende Systeme das Potenzial, Fahrzeuge sicherer und effizienter zu steuern als menschliche Fahrer:innen, doch bleibt offen, ob und wann wir bereit sind, diese Verantwortung tatsächlich abzugeben. Dieser Frage nähert sich Barnard im Selbstversuch, indem sie einerseits einen Einblick in die ebenso futuristisch wie alltäglich daherkommende Erfahrung einer Fahrt mit einem selbstfahrenden Taxi der Firma Waymo gibt und andererseits im Rahmen eines performativen Eingriffs selbst zum Hindernis auf der Straße wird. Den Blicken in das Auto hinein und aus dem Auto heraus wird so die abstrakte Perspektive des Blicks des Autos selbst hinzugefügt, auch wenn die operativen Bilder der Bordkameras lediglich einen Datenpunkt unter vielen darstellen.

Lisa Barnards Projekt zeigt, dass automatisierte Systeme zur Objekterkennung nicht nur Werkzeuge zur Fortbewegung oder Orientierung sind, sondern neue Formen der Weltwahrnehmung hervorbringen. Was Maschinen erkennen, wie sie klassifizieren, priorisieren oder übersehen, verändert auch unsere eigenen Vorstellungen von Umwelt, Kontrolle und deren Bedeutung: »Je größer die ›Autonomie‹ der Maschinen, desto verworrener und kaputter scheint die Welt […]«,[8] schreibt Hito Steyerl im Hinblick auf den hohen Grad, in dem die globalen Multi-Krisen der Gegenwart miteinander verknüpft sind. Und so bleibt gerade in Zeiten der Klimakrise die Frage bestehen, wie sich Technologien entwickeln lassen, die nicht nur effizient, sondern auch sensibel für die Welt sind, die sie erfassen sollen.

KATHARINA TÄSCHNER ist Fotohistorikerin und Kuratorin. Als ehemalige Stipendiatin des Programms »Museumskurator:innen für Fotografie« der Alfried Krupp von Bohlen und Halbach-Stiftung hat sie an zahlreichen internationalen Ausstellungsprojekten in Deutschland, Frankreich und der Schweiz mitgewirkt. Bei C/O Berlin kuratiert sie den *After Nature. Ulrike Crespo Photography Prize.*

a performative intervention. The shots into the vehicle and those taken from it are complemented by the abstract perspective of the car's own view, albeit that the operational images from the on-board cameras are just one data point among many.

Barnard's project shows that automated systems for detecting objects are not simply tools that can be used to assist movement or orientation; rather they engender new ways of perceiving the world. What machines detect – and how they classify, prioritise, or disregard what they 'see' – also changes our own ideas about the environment and surveillance and what this signifies. Reflecting on the extent to which today's global multicrises are interconnected, Hito Steyerl writes, 'The more machine "autonomy", the more entangled and messed up the world seems to be.'[8] So, at a time when the climate is in crisis, we must ask how technologies can be developed that are not only efficient but also sensitive to the world they are intended to capture.

KATHARINA TÄSCHNER is a photography historian and curator. As a former fellow of the Alfried Krupp von Bohlen und Halbach-Stiftung's Museum Curators for Photography programme, she has been involved in numerous international exhibition projects in Germany, France, and Switzerland. She curates the *After Nature: Ulrike Crespo Photography Prize* at C/O Berlin.

1 James Bridle, *Die unfassbare Vielfalt des Seins. Jenseits menschlicher Intelligenz*, München: C.H. Beck 2016, S. 12 und 23.

2 Vgl. Iqbal Pittalwala, »Salton Sea Dust Triggers Lung Inflammation. UC Riverside Study Has Health Implications for People Living Around California's Largest Lake«, in: *UC Riverside News*, 8. Dezember 2022, https://news.ucr.edu/articles/2022/12/08/salton-sea-dust-triggers-lung-inflammation. Sämtliche in diesem Text zitierten Links wurden zuletzt am 28. Mai 2025 aufgerufen.

3 Vgl. U.S. Department of Energy, »What Are Critical Materials and Critical Minerals?«, https://www.energy.gov/cmm/what-are-critical-materials-and-critical-minerals und European Council, »An EU Critical Raw Materials Act for the Future of EU Supply Chains«, https://www.consilium.europa.eu/en/infographics/critical-raw-materials.

4 California Energy Commission, »Lithium Valley Vision«, https://www.energy.ca.gov/programs-and-topics/programs/lithium-valley-vision.

5 Siehe hierzu weiterführend Thea Riofrancos, »The Security-Sustainability Nexus: Lithium Onshoring in the Global North«, in: *Global Environmental Politics*, Bd. 23, Nr. 1, 2023, S. 20–41.

6 Thomas Nagel, *What Is It Like to Be a Bat? / Wie ist es, eine Fledermaus zu sein?* [1974], übersetzt, herausgegeben und mit einem Nachwort von Ulrich Diehl, Ditzingen: Reclam 2023.

7 Siehe beispielsweise Ralph Simon u. a., »Bioinspired Sonar Reflectors as Guiding Beacons for Autonomous Navigation«, in: *PNAS*, Bd. 117, Nr. 3, 2020, S. 1367–1374.

8 Hito Steyerl, Einführung zu *Medium Hot. Images in the Age of Heat*, London und New York: Verso 2025, S. 2.

1 James Bridle, *Ways of Being: Animals, Plants, Machines; The Search for a Planetary Intelligence* (Penguin Books, 2023), 2 and 11.

2 See Iqbal Pittalwala, 'Salton Sea Dust Triggers Lung Inflammation', *UC Riverside News*, 8 December 2022, https://news.ucr.edu/articles/2022/12/08/salton-sea-dust-triggers-lung-inflammation. All links cited in this essay were accessed on 28 May 2025.

3 See 'What Are Critical Materials and Critical Minerals?', US Department of Energy, https://www.energy.gov/cmm/what-are-critical-materials-and-critical-minerals; and 'An EU Critical Raw Materials Act for the Future of EU Supply Chains', European Council, https://www.consilium.europa.eu/en/infographics/critical-raw-materials.

4 'Lithium Valley Vision', California Energy Commission, https://www.energy.ca.gov/programs-and-topics/programs/lithium-valley-vision.

5 For more on this, see Thea Riofrancos, 'The Security–Sustainability Nexus: Lithium Onshoring in the Global North', *Global Environmental Politics* 23, no. 1 (February 2023).

6 Thomas Nagel, 'What Is It Like to Be a Bat?', *Philosophical Review* 83, no. 4 (1974): 435–50.

7 See, for example, Ralph Simon et al., 'Bioinspired Sonar Reflectors as Guiding Beacons for Autonomous Navigation', *PNAS* 117, no. 3 (21 January 2020), https://doi.org/10.1073/pnas.1909890117.

8 Hito Steyerl, introduction to *Medium Hot: Images in the Age of Heat* (Verso, 2025), 2.

Es gibt keinen direkten oder geradlinigen Weg in diesem Projekt, doch liegt eine Schönheit im Spiel der mäandernden Netzwerke. Wellen aus Licht und Klang strömen aus den Erinnerungen der Vergangenheit in eine ungewisse Zukunft. Ich höre Geschichten, begegne Menschen mit Freundlichkeit und Hingabe und entdecke dabei die verschlungenen Pfade, die das Menschliche, das Technologische und die natürliche Welt miteinander verbinden. Im Zentrum des Projekts stehen praktische und wissenschaftliche Lösungsansätze für den Klimawandel, verbunden mit einer Reflexion über den Einsatz moderner Technologien und deren Auswirkungen auf die Frage der Wahrnehmung. Wir müssen mit der gleichen Entschlossenheit vor- und zurückblicken: jenseits des chaotischen, unebenen Wegs, der vor uns liegt, denn die unvorhersehbare Zukunft eines »Superalignments« künstlicher Intelligenz wirft bereits ihre Schatten voraus. Nichts ist sicher, und wenn uns die Geschichte eines gelehrt hat, dann, dass Risikoabwägung und eine prognostizierte Wahrscheinlichkeit »nahe null« stets ein Akt des Glaubens sind. Wir müssen hoffen – und der Verzweiflung widerstehen. Lisa Barnard

There is no direct or straight path in this project, but there *is* a beauty in the meandering networks at play. Waves of light and sound flow from the memories of the past into the uncertain future. I listen to stories, interact with kindness and commitment, uncovering as I go the woven threads that link the human, the technological, and the natural world. The key components focus on the practical and scientific solutions to climate change, whilst addressing the use of technologies and the impact on wider issues of experience. We must look both ways with equal commitment and beyond the chaotic and uneven road ahead, as the unpredictable future of AI superalignment looms. Nothing is certain, and if history has taught us anything it is that risk and a ‘near zero’ prediction is an act of faith; we must hope and not give in to despair. Lisa Barnard

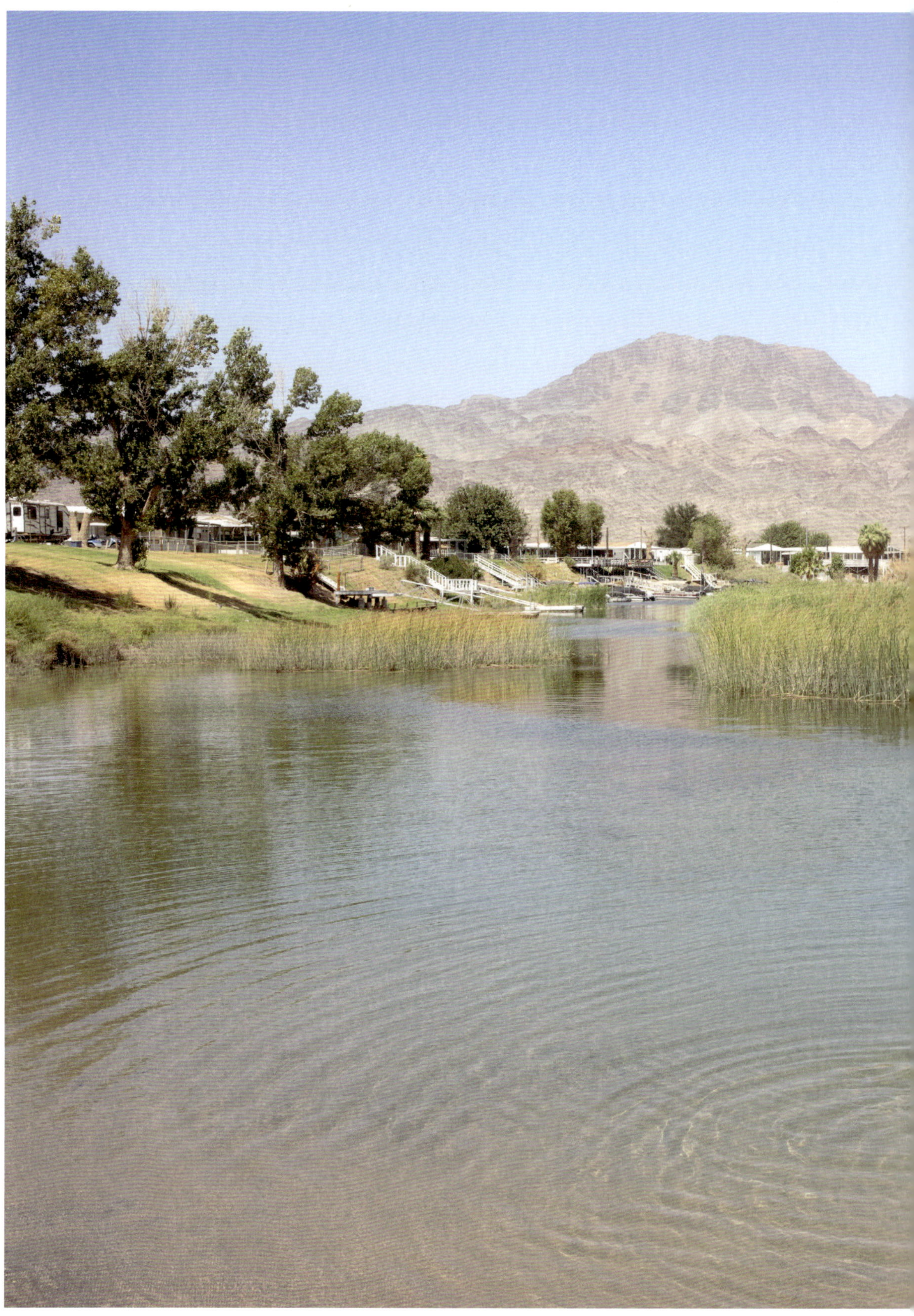

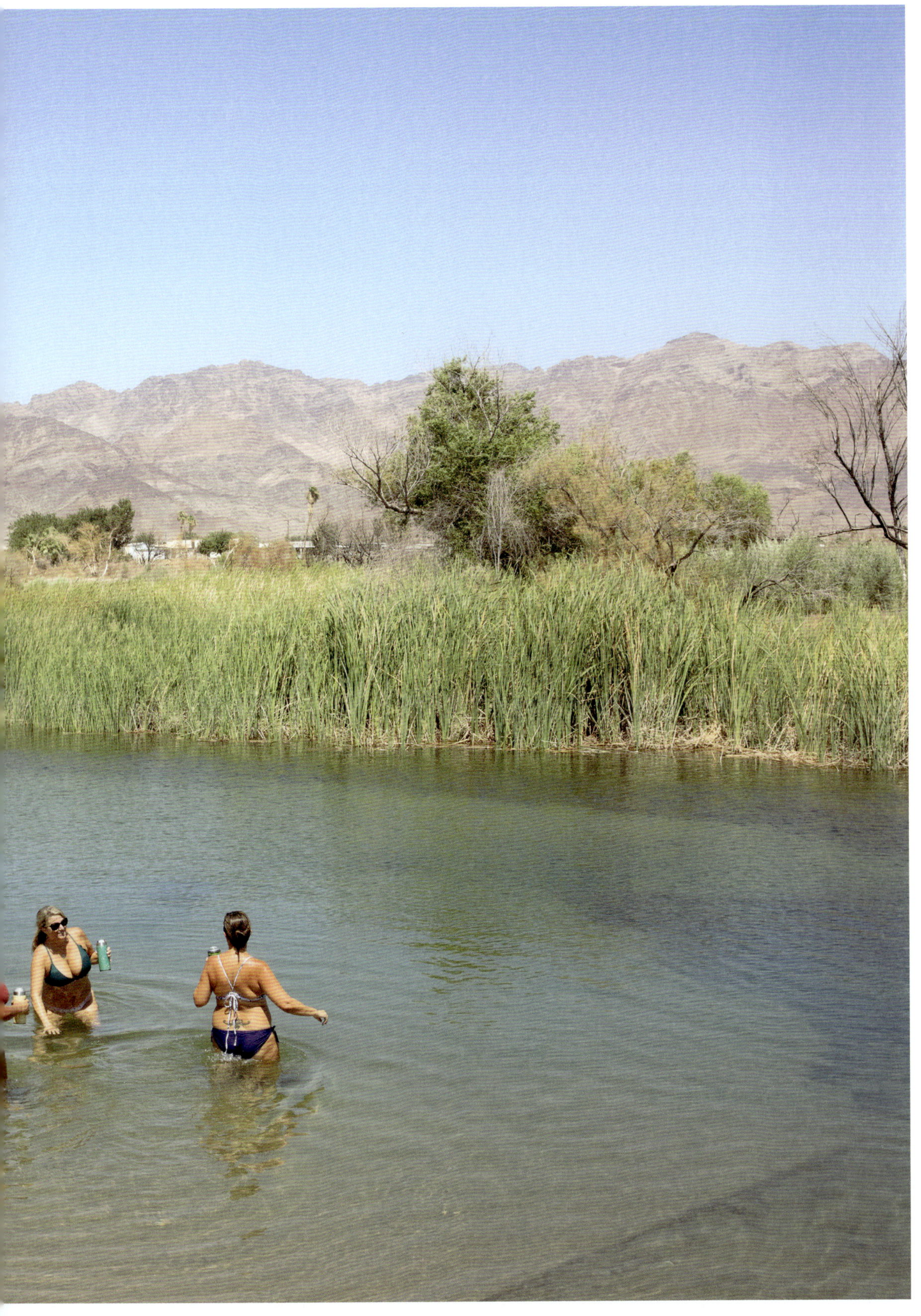

Colorado River, Lost Lake, Blythe, Kalifornien

Der Colorado River deckt etwa ein Drittel des gesamten Wasserbedarfs in Südkalifornien. Zwischen den Vereinigten Staaten und Mexiko herrscht ein anhaltender »Wasserstreit«, der sich im Wesentlichen um die jeweiligen Verbindlichkeiten aus dem Wasservertrag von 1944 dreht. Dieser verpflichtet beide Länder zur gemeinsamen Nutzung der Wasserressourcen aus dem Colorado River und dem Rio Grande. Der Konflikt wird durch schwere Dürren und die zunehmende Nachfrage in beiden Staaten verschärft.

Mexiko schuldet den USA beträchtliche Wassermengen aus dem Rio Grande, während die USA weiter Wasser aus dem Colorado River an mexikanische Grenzstädte wie Tijuana und Mexicali liefern. Der Colorado River versorgt außerdem eine bedeutende Agrarwirtschaft in den Bezirken Imperial und Riverside. Ein internationales Abkommen regelt die Wasserverteilung, doch die Übernutzung durch Landwirtschaft und städtische Gebiete bedroht einheimische Arten entlang des Flusses.

←

Colorado River, Lost Lake, Blythe, California

The Colorado River supplies roughly a third of all water for Southern California. The United States and Mexico are engaged in a 'battle for water' largely centred on their obligations under the 1944 Water Treaty, which mandates water sharing from the Colorado River and Rio Grande, a dispute intensified by severe droughts and increasing demand in both countries.

Mexico owes a significant amount of water from the Rio Grande to the US, while the US, in turn, continues to deliver water from the Colorado River to Mexican border cities such as Tijuana and Mexicali. The Colorado River also supports a large farming industry in Imperial and Riverside Counties and an international treaty govern its water allocation. Over-allocation to farms and cities has harmed native species along the river.

Saltonsee, Kalifornien

Der Saltonsee im Imperial County in Südkalifornien ist sowohl ein Ort ökologischer Fragilität als auch technologischer Ambitionen: ein Schauplatz, an dem das Zusammenspiel von Bewusstsein, Technologie und Ökologie überaus sichtbar ist. Unter seiner Oberfläche verbirgt sich ein gewaltiges geothermisches Reservoir, das jährlich bis zu 18 Millionen Tonnen Lithiumkarbonat liefern könnte – ein Rohstoff von zentraler Bedeutung für autonome Fahrsysteme und die KI-gesteuerte Wirtschaft im Allgemeinen. Das Gewinnungsverfahren gilt als umweltfreundlicher als der konventionelle Bergbau, dennoch gibt es Bedenken hinsichtlich des Wasserverbrauchs, seismischer Aktivität und der empfindlichen Ökosysteme rund um den Saltonsee.

Der Saltonsee entstand 1905 aufgrund von Dammbrüchen am Colorado River. Heute ist er ein Gewässer ohne Abfluss, das rund 73 Meter unter dem Meeresspiegel liegt und hauptsächlich durch landwirtschaftliches Abwasser aus dem Imperial Valley gespeist wird. Er ist Zeugnis des menschengemachten Klimawandels: Das Wasser ist hypersalin und enthält hohe Konzentrationen giftiger Chemikalien, insbesondere Ammoniumsulfat-Dünger. In der Folge haben sich die Fischbestände dezimiert, was sich erheblich auf die Vogelpopulationen entlang des Pacific Flyway auswirkt.

←

The Salton Sea, California

The Salton Sea in Southern California's Imperial County is a site of both environmental fragility and technological ambition, where the interplay between consciousness, technology, and ecology is starkly visible. Beneath its surface lies a vast geothermal reservoir of water capable of producing eighteen million tonnes of lithium carbonate annually – a resource critical for automated vehicles and the broader AI-driven economy. The process of extraction is arguably more eco-friendly than traditional mining, but there are concerns about water use, seismic activity, and the fragile ecosystem of the Salton Sea.

In 1905, levee failures on the Colorado River created the Salton Sea. Now an endorheic lake, at 240 feet below sea level and sustained by irrigation runoff from agriculture in Imperial Valley, the sea is evidence of anthropogenic change, being hypersaline with high concentrations of toxic chemicals, particularly ammonium sulphate fertiliser. Fish have subsequently disappeared, impacting the birds on the Pacific Flyway.

Tierpräparat eines Braunpelikans, Natural History Museum of Los Angeles County, Kalifornien

In der christlichen Kunst zeigt das Motiv des »Pelikans in seiner Frömmigkeit« ein Muttertier, das sich die eigene Brust aufreißt, um seine Jungen zu ernähren – der ultimative Akt der Fürsorge und Selbstaufopferung. Der Saltonsee beherbergte einst eine Population von Braunpelikanen, die sich von Tilapia-Fischen ernährten. Als die Fische verschwanden, ging folglich auch die Zahl der Braunpelikane stark zurück.

Brown Pelican Taxidermy Specimen, Natural History Museum of Los Angeles County, California

In Christian art, the 'Pelican in Her Piety' shows a mother piercing her breast to feed her young, the ultimate act of nurturing and self-sacrifice. The Salton Sea used to host a population of brown pelicans that fed on the tilapia fish. These fish have now disappeared and consequently the numbers of brown pelicans have declined.

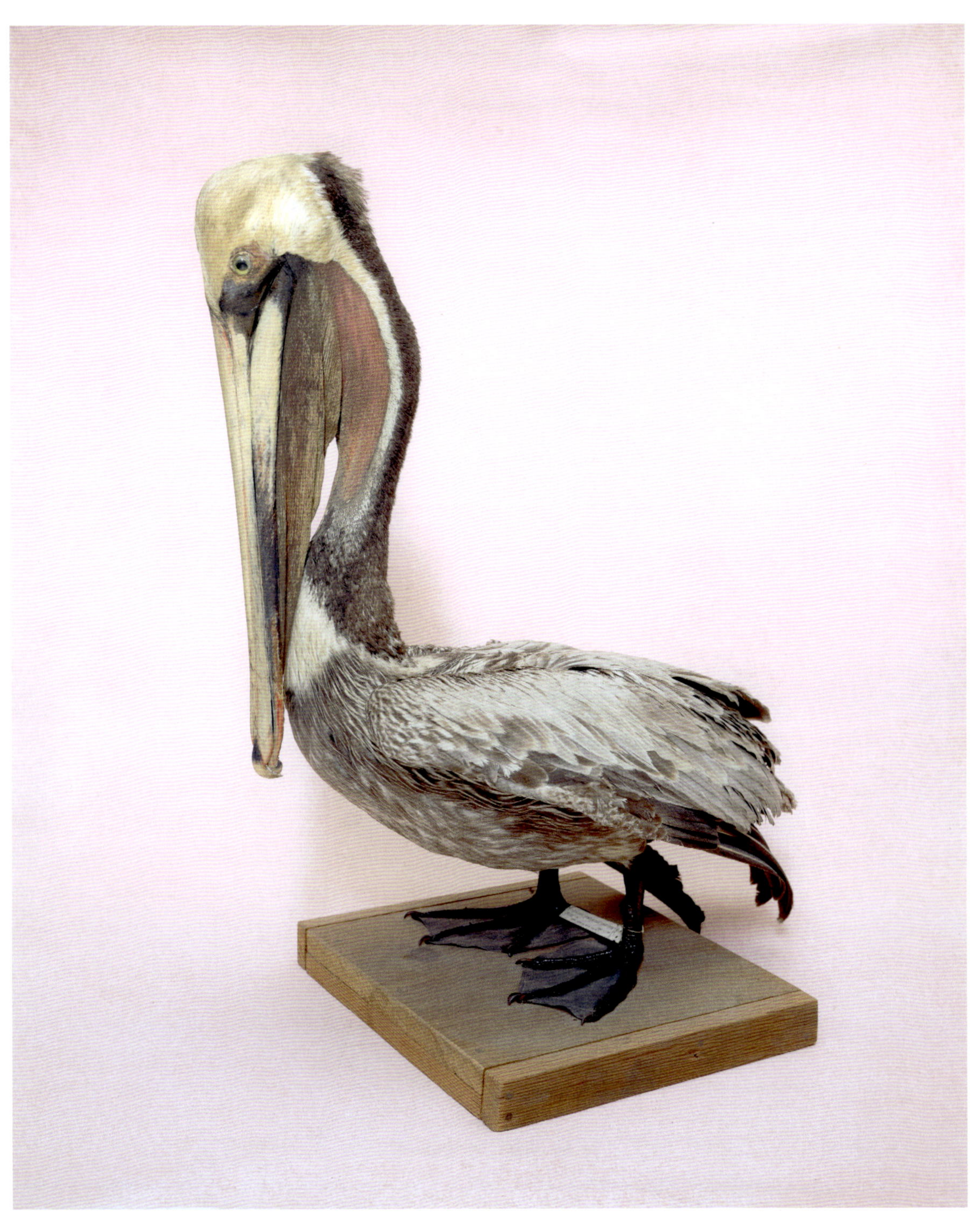

Kalifornische Washingtonpalme (Washingtonia filifera) und betonierter Bewässerungskanal, Niland, Kalifornien

Die Kalifornische Washingtonpalme ist ursprünglich in der Region des Colorado River beheimatet, nicht jedoch in trockenen Wüstenlandschaften. Sie wurde in Palm Springs und anderen Städten des Coachella Valley eingeführt und hat sich im Agrargebiet des Imperial Valley inzwischen selbst ausgesät. Heute bietet sie einen wichtigen Lebensraum für die Westliche Gelbfledermaus.

California Fan Palm (*Washingtonia filifera*) and Concrete Irrigation Channel, Niland, California

Washingtonia filifera fan palms are native in the area of the Colorado River and not of the arid environments of the desert. They were bought to Palm Springs and other towns in the Coachella Valley and have self-seeded in the farming district of Imperial Valley. They provide an important habitat for the western yellow bat.

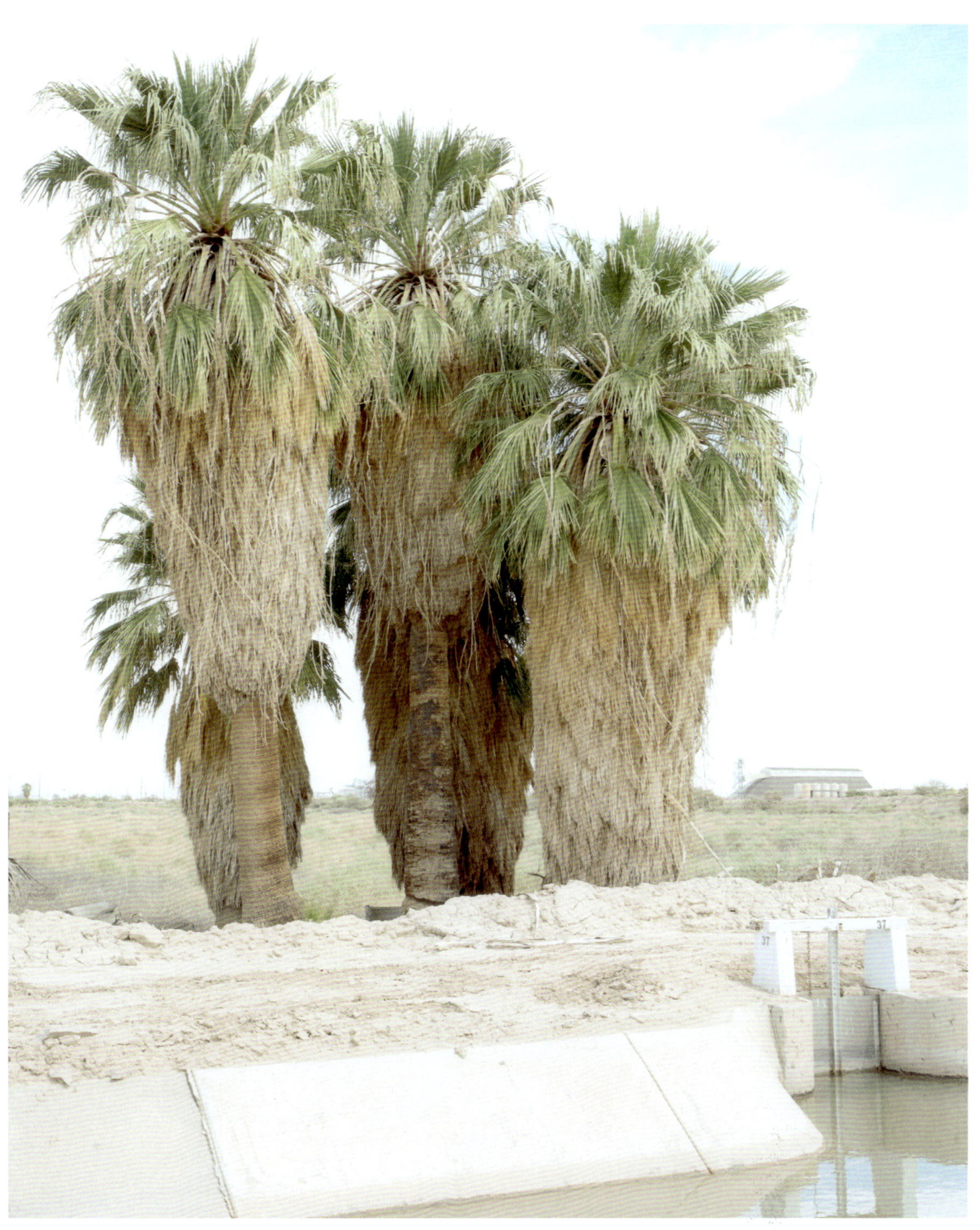

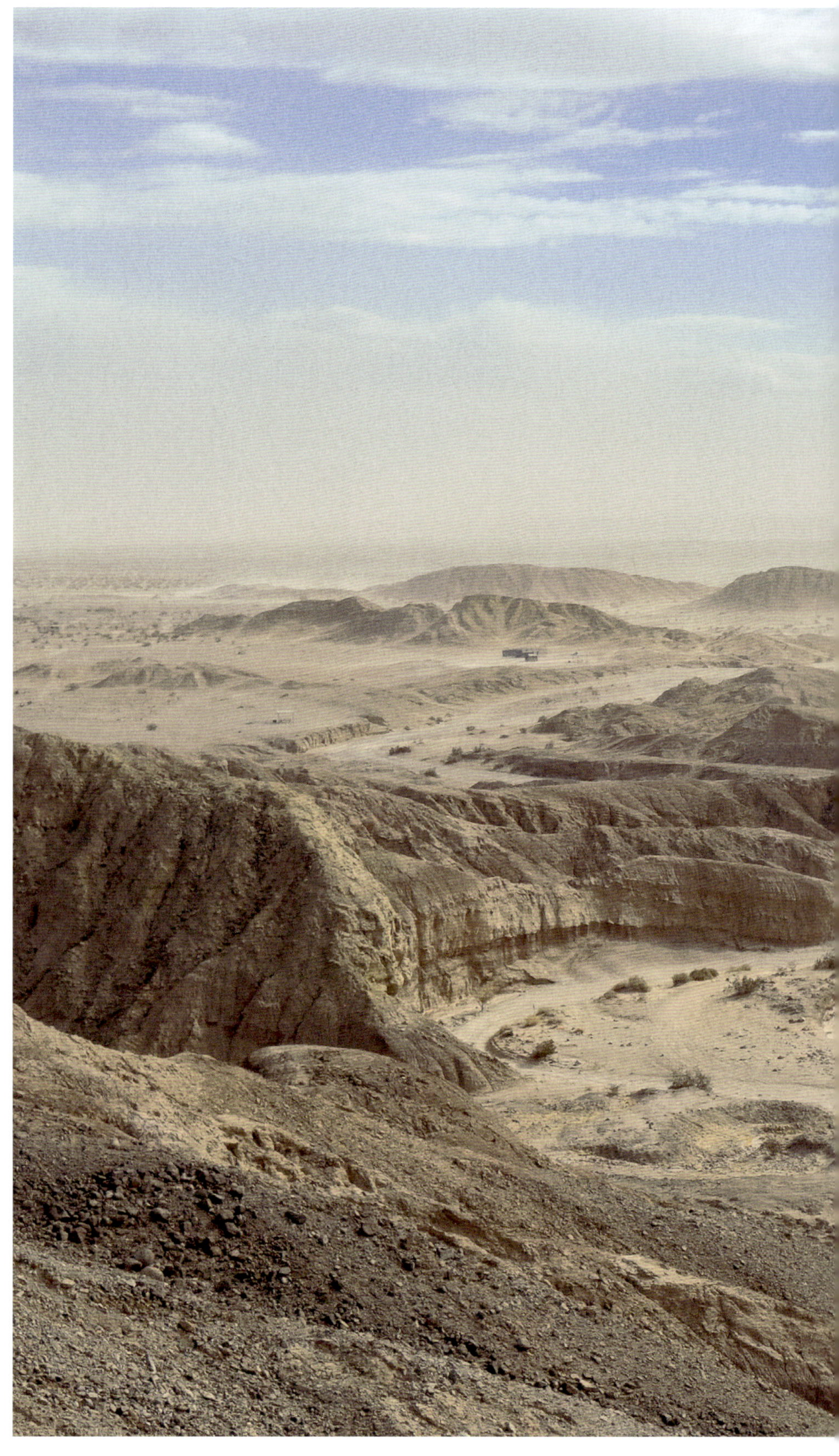

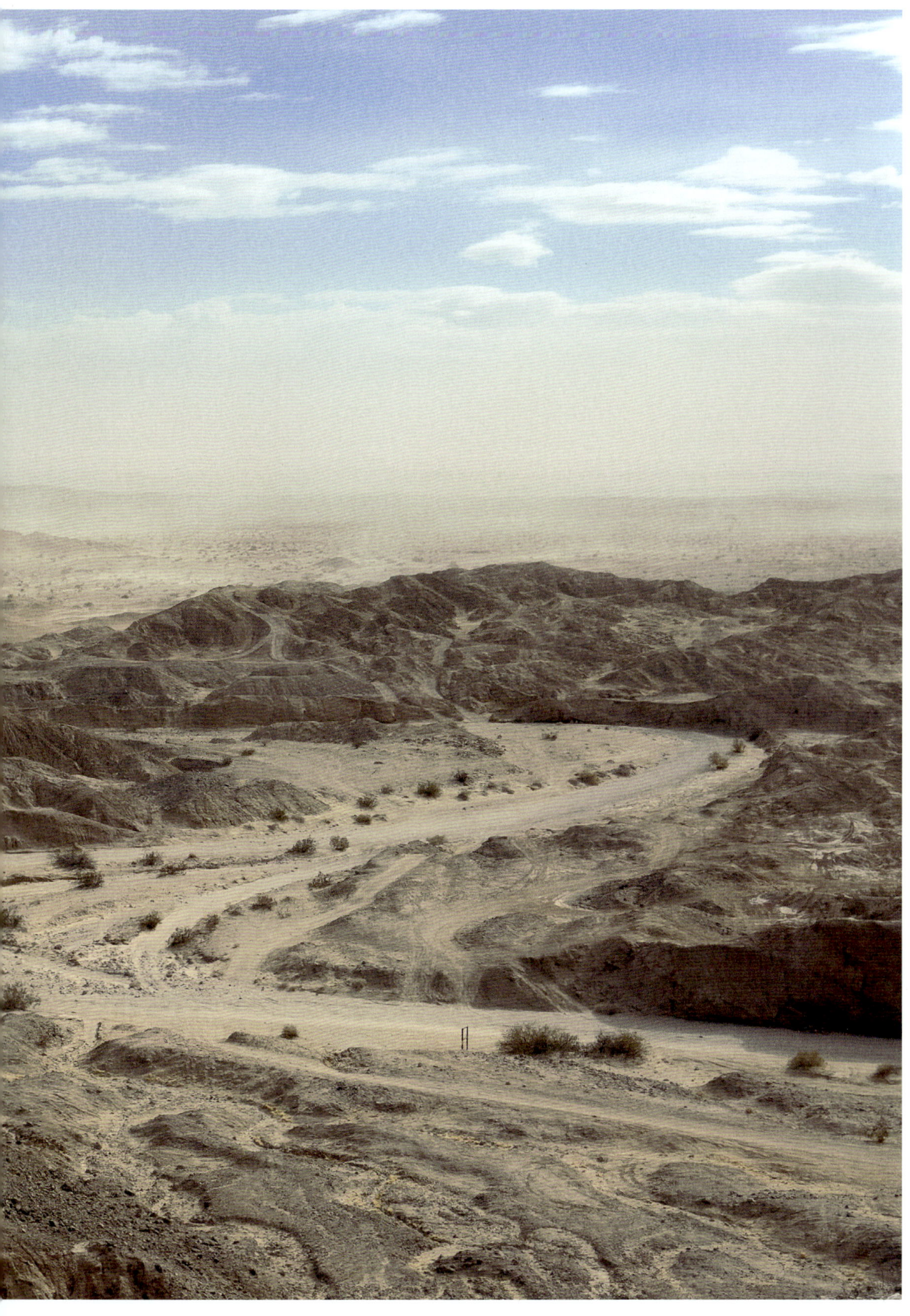

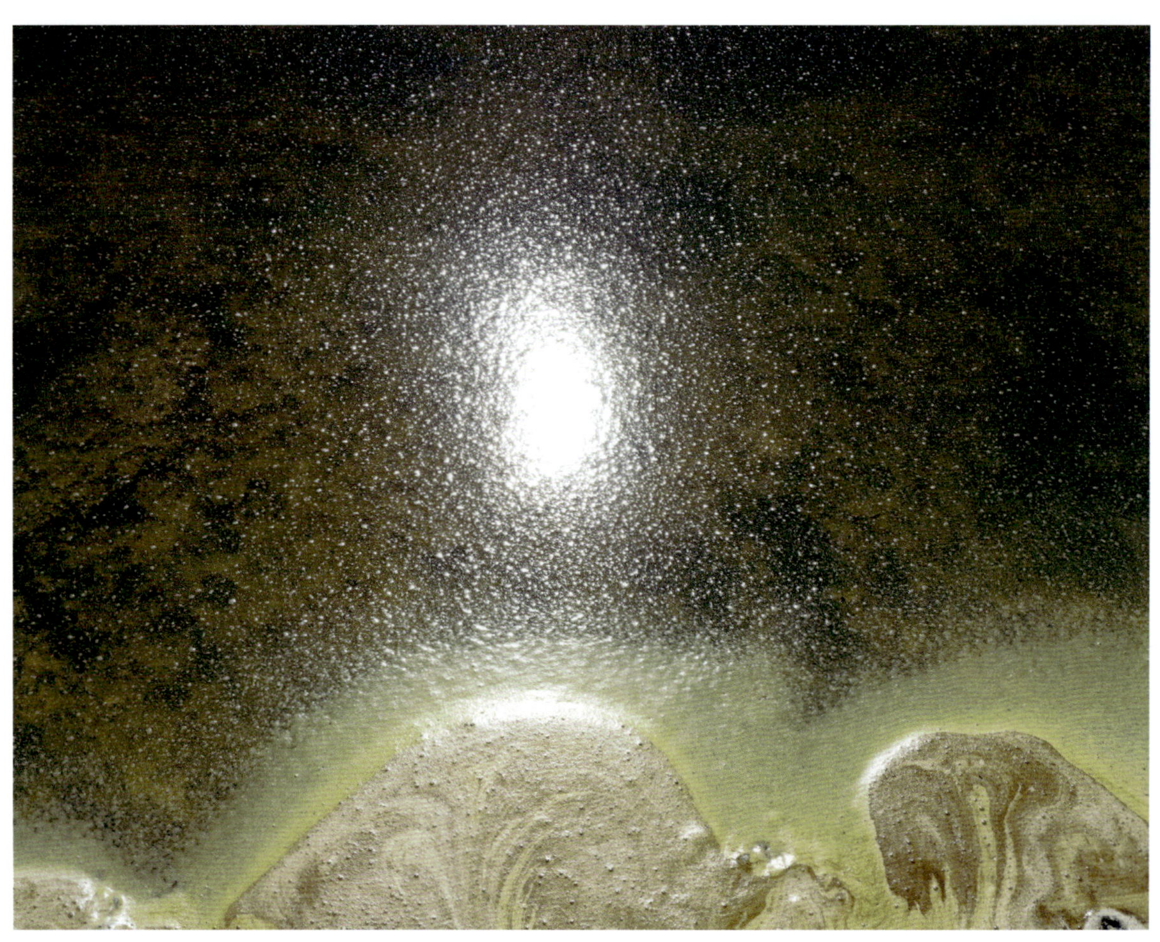

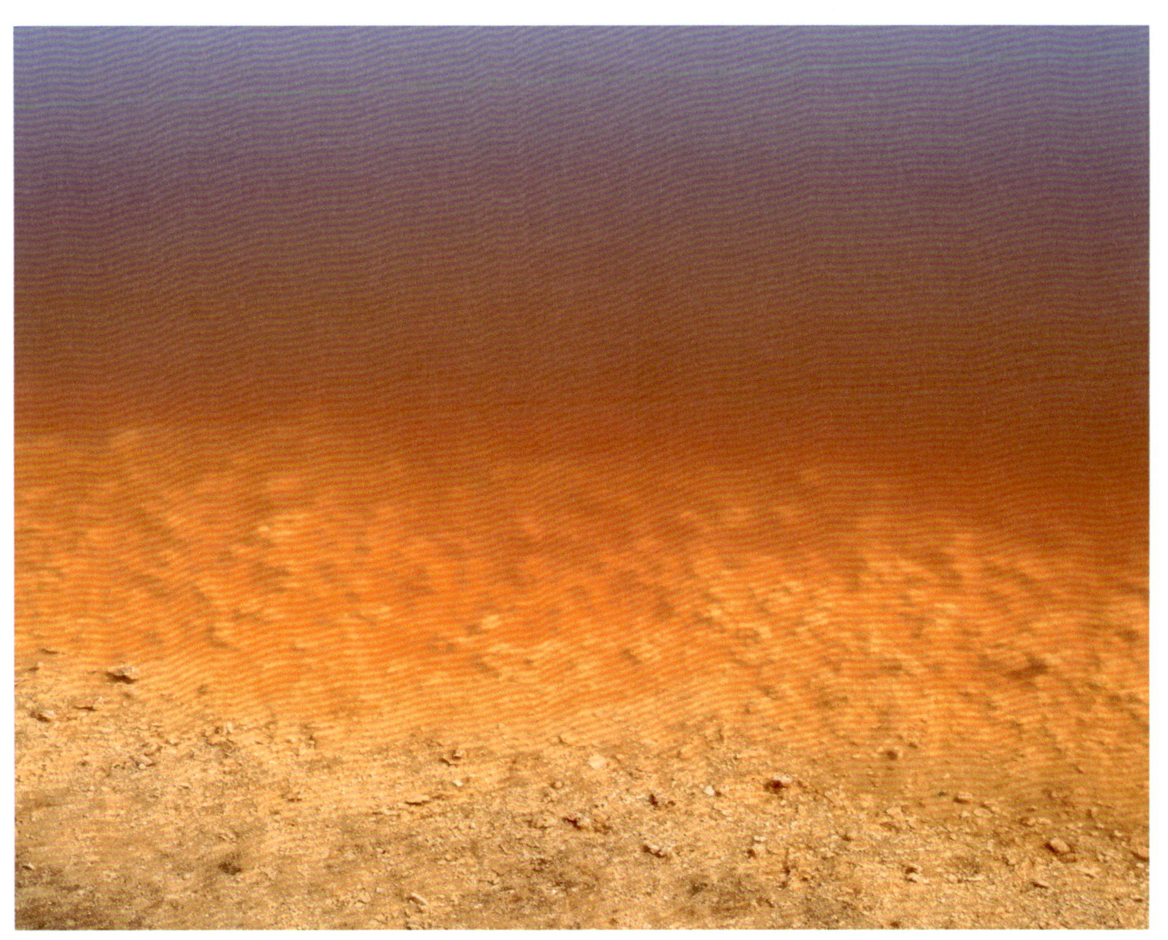

Brachland während der Santa-Ana-Winde im Januar 2025. Blick in Richtung des Saltonsees, Anza-Borrego State Park, Kalifornien

Zwischen 2017 und 2019 waren die Bewohner:innen des Imperial County einer Belastung von über 540 Kilogramm Pestiziden pro Quadratkilometer ausgesetzt – über die Luft, das Wasser und die Vegetation. Diese Expositionsrate liegt über 90 Prozent höher als im Rest Kaliforniens. Zudem ist die Region laut einem Bericht zu extremer Hitze aus dem Jahr 2022 die heißeste des Bundesstaates, mit mehr als 117 Tagen über 38 Grad Celsius pro Jahr.

Die Reduzierung des landwirtschaftlichen Abflusses hat die Situation zusätzlich verschärft: Durch das Schrumpfen des Sees und die Freilegung des Seebodens kommt es nun häufig zu Staubaufwirbelungen. Diese werden mit Atemwegserkrankungen in Verbindung gebracht (nirgendwo in den USA ist deren Häufigkeit höher), die besonders Mitglieder des indigenen Cahuilla-Stammes, ältere Menschen und Kinder betreffen. Der Lithiumabbau mag wirtschaftliche Perspektiven eröffnen, doch mit dem zunehmenden Schwerlastverkehr ist auch eine verstärkte Staubbelastung zu erwarten – was die Gesundheitssituation weiter verschärfen dürfte.

←

Badlands, During the Santa Ana Winds in January 2025. View Towards the Salton Sea, Anza-Borrego State Park, California

Imperial County residents were exposed to over 1,200 pounds of pesticides – via the air, water, and on the vegetation – per square mile from 2017 to 2019. That exposure rate is over ninety percent higher than the rest of California. On top of that, the region is the hottest in the state – with over 117 days over one hundred degrees Fahrenheit, according to a 2022 *Hazardous Heat* report.

By reducing irrigation run-off, the problem has been exacerbated. As the sea shrinks and the lake bed is exposed, dust events are now common and are linked to respiratory issues (the highest evidence of respiratory disease in the whole of the United States), especially in the local Cahuilla tribal members; the elderly and children are particularly affected. Lithium mining may promise more economic opportunities, but an increase in truck traffic is likely to create more dust and further aggravate respiratory health issues.

Algenblüte, Saltonsee, Kalifornien
Algenblüten sind ein typisches Phänomen am Saltonsee, besonders jene, die durch Cyanobakterien (auch als Blaualgen bekannt) verursacht werden. Unter bestimmten Bedingungen können sie nützlich sein, da sie vielfältige Lebensräume fördern. Schädliche Algenblüten (harmful algal blooms, kurz: HABs) entstehen jedoch, wenn sich Algen unkontrolliert vermehren und dabei giftige oder anderweitig schädliche Effekte auf Menschen, Fische und Vögel entwickeln. Das am Saltonsee vorkommende Phänomen des »roten Wassers« wird vermutlich durch eine Kombination mehrerer Faktoren verursacht: eine hohe Konzentration der Grünalge Dunaliella salina sowie Bakterien, die unter stark salzhaltigen und nährstoffreichen Bedingungen rote Pigmente bilden. Auch das Vorkommen von Gipskristallen spielt dabei eine Rolle.

←

Algal Blooms, Salton Sea, California
These are a common feature of the Salton Sea, particularly those caused by cyanobacteria (also known as blue-green algae). They can be beneficial, encouraging diverse habitats. Harmful algal blooms, or HABs, occur when algae grow out of control, producing toxic or harmful effects on people, fish, and birds. The ‘red water’ phenomenon at the Salton Sea is likely caused by a combination of factors, including high levels of *Dunaliella salina,* a cyanobacterium, and bacteria that produce red pigments in response to high salinity and nutrient levels, and the presence of gypsum crystals.

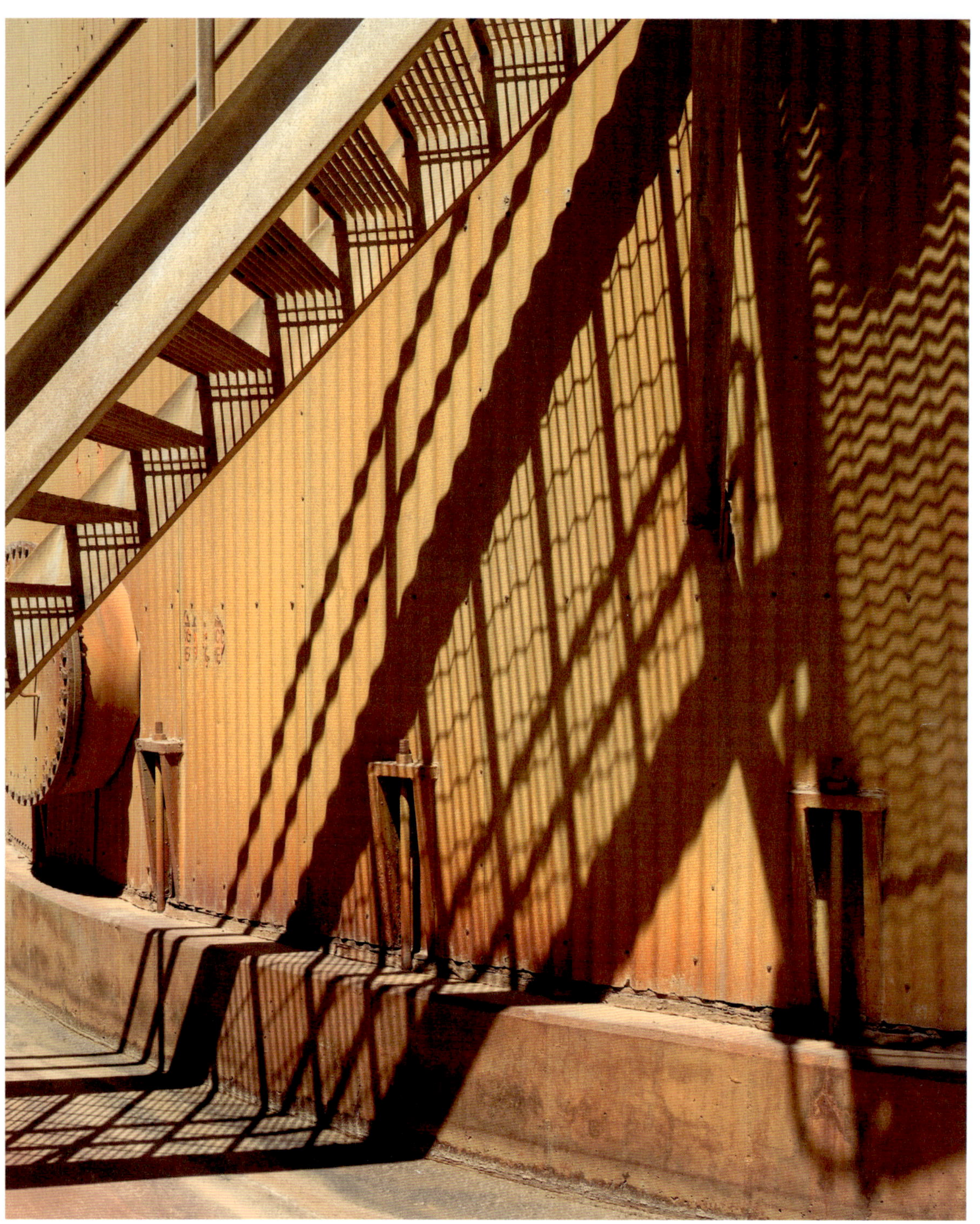

Wasserturm, Geothermieanlage der Firma EnergySource Minerals, Project ATLiS, Niland, Kalifornien

EnergySource entwickelt mit ILiAD eine Technologie zur direkten Lithiumextraktion (DLE), die eine kostengünstige Lithiumproduktion aus geothermischen Ressourcen in Kalifornien mit geringen Umweltauswirkungen und niedrigem Kohlenstoffausstoß ermöglichen soll. Das Unternehmen strebt eine jährliche Produktion von 20 Kilotonnen Lithiumhydroxid aus dem Solestrom eines bestehenden Geothermiekraftwerks am Saltonsee mit einer Leistung von 55 Megawatt an. EnergySource behauptet, dieses das Verfahren werde eines der Lithiumprojekte mit den geringsten CO_2-Emissionen weltweit sein, bei minimalem Einsatz von Reagenzien und Wasser.

Die Wärme der geothermischen Sole, die an die Oberfläche gepumpt wird, treibt zunächst eine Turbine zur Stromerzeugung an, womit eine effiziente und erneuerbare Methode der Energiegewinnung zum Einsatz kommt. Anschließend durchläuft die Sole ein Wärmerückgewinnungssystem und wird dort weiterverarbeitet. In diesem Schritt werden spezialisierte Technologien genutzt, um gezielt Mineralien wie Lithium zu extrahieren, die dann für Batterien von Elektrofahrzeugen und zur Speicherung erneuerbarer Energien verwendet werden.

Water Tower, Geothermal Plant, EnergySource Minerals' Project ATLiS in Niland, California

EnergySource is pioneering Direct Lithium Extraction (DLE) technology called ILiAD to create low-cost lithium production from geothermal resources in California, with low environmental impact and carbon footprint. The company is targeting an annual production of twenty kilotonnes of lithium hydroxide from brine flow from an existing fifty-five-megawatt geothermal power plant at the Salton Sea. EnergySource claim that the process will be one of the lowest CO_2-emitting lithium projects globally, with minimal reagent and water use.

The heat from the geothermal brines, pumped to the surface, drives a turbine-generator producing electricity. This is a highly efficient and renewable method of electricity generation. These brines are then directed to a heat recovery system, where they undergo further processing. In this stage, specialised technologies are employed to extract and recover specific minerals or elements, such as lithium, which is then used for electric vehicle batteries and renewable energy storage.

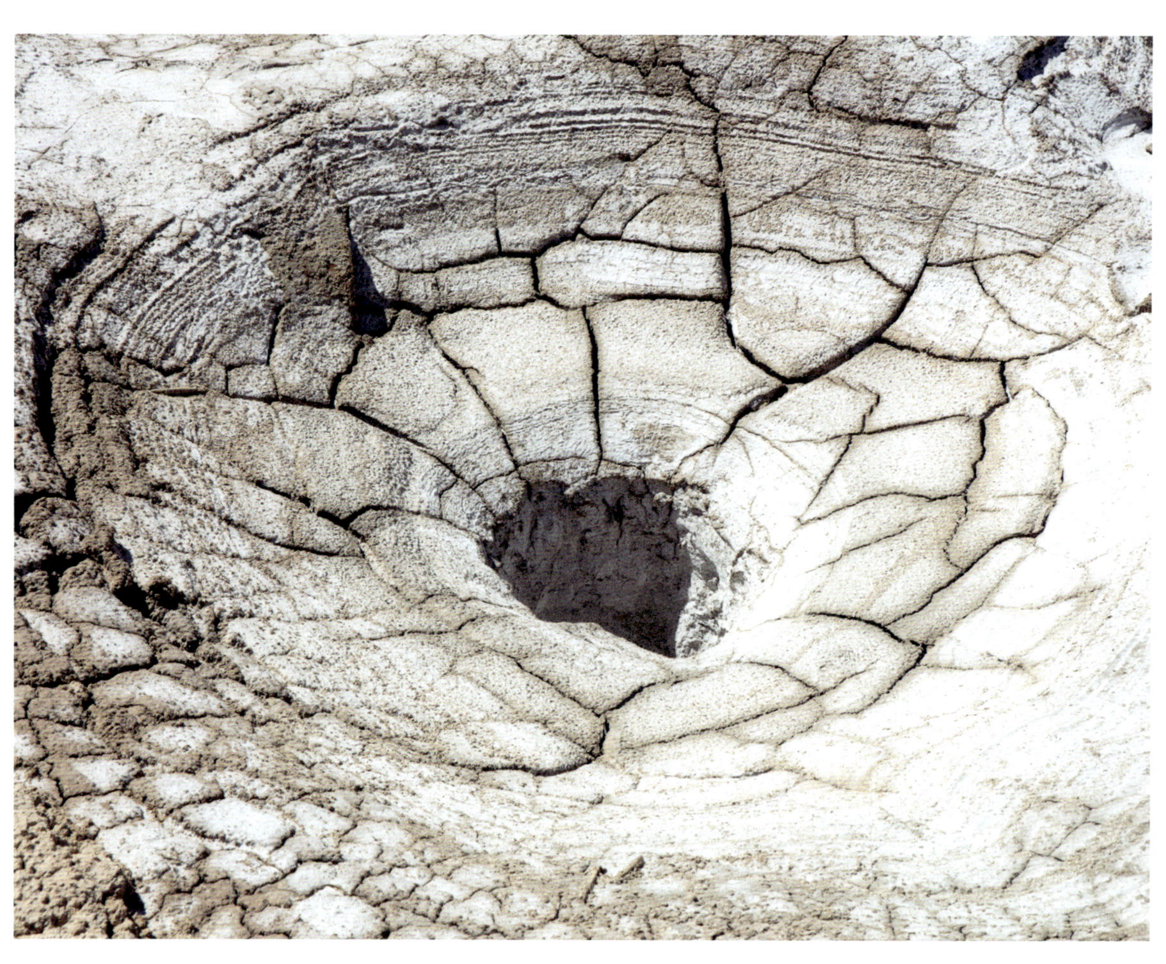

Geothermische Becken und Schlammtöpfe in der Nähe von EnergySource, Niland, Kalifornien / Geothermal Ponds and Mud Pots Next to EnergySource, Niland, California

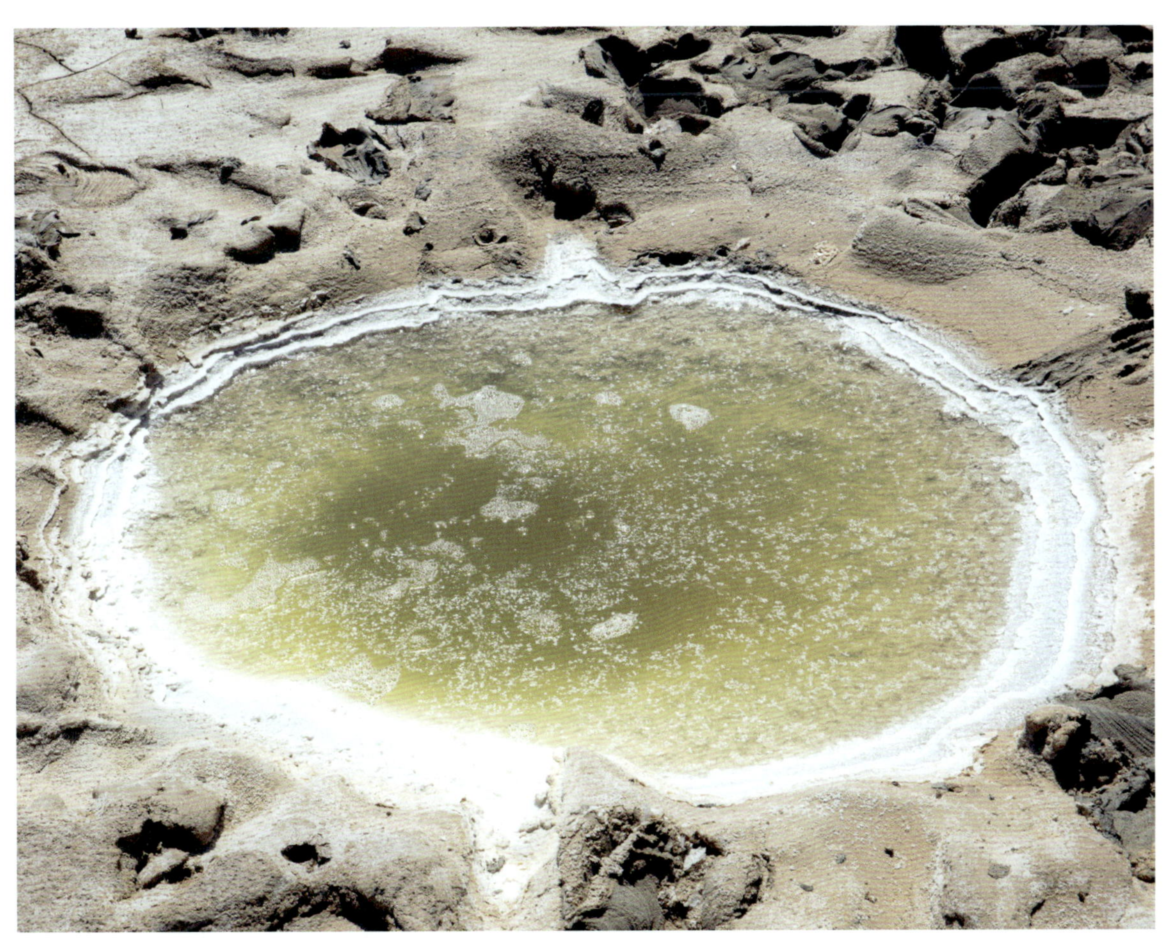

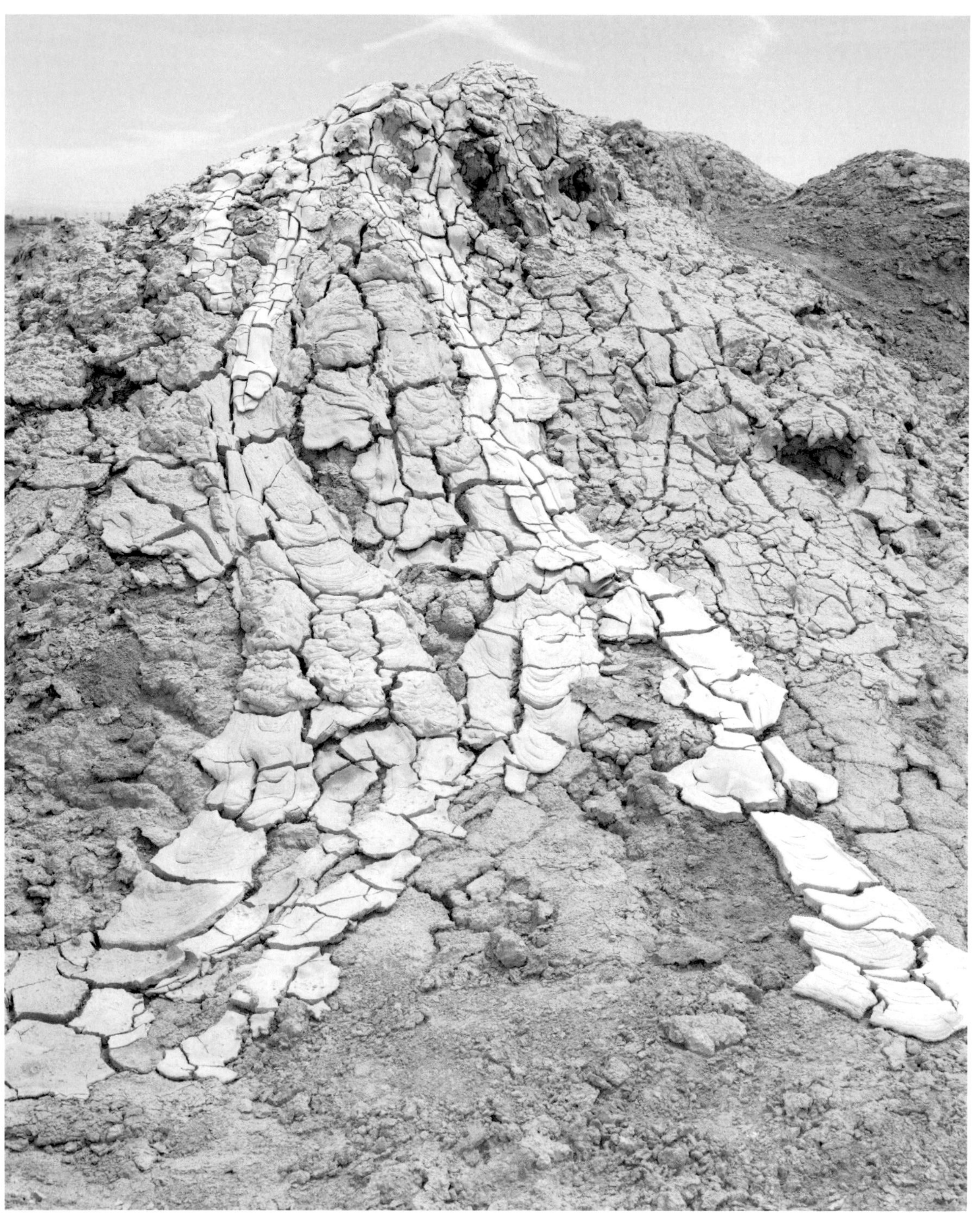

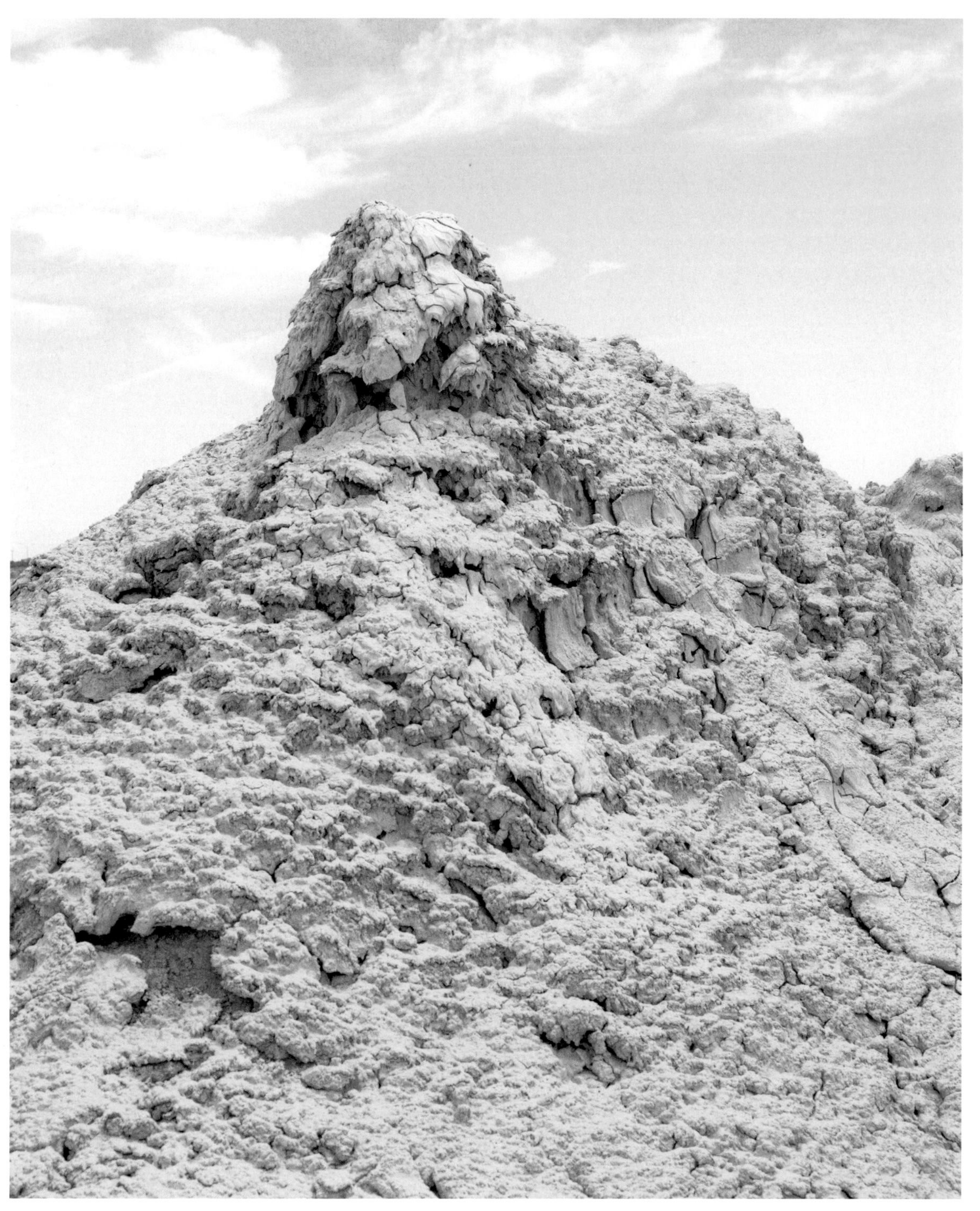

Salz und giftige Kristalle aus landwirtschaftlichen Abwässern, Salton City, Kalifornien /
Salt and Toxic, Agricultural Run-Off Crystals, Salton City, California

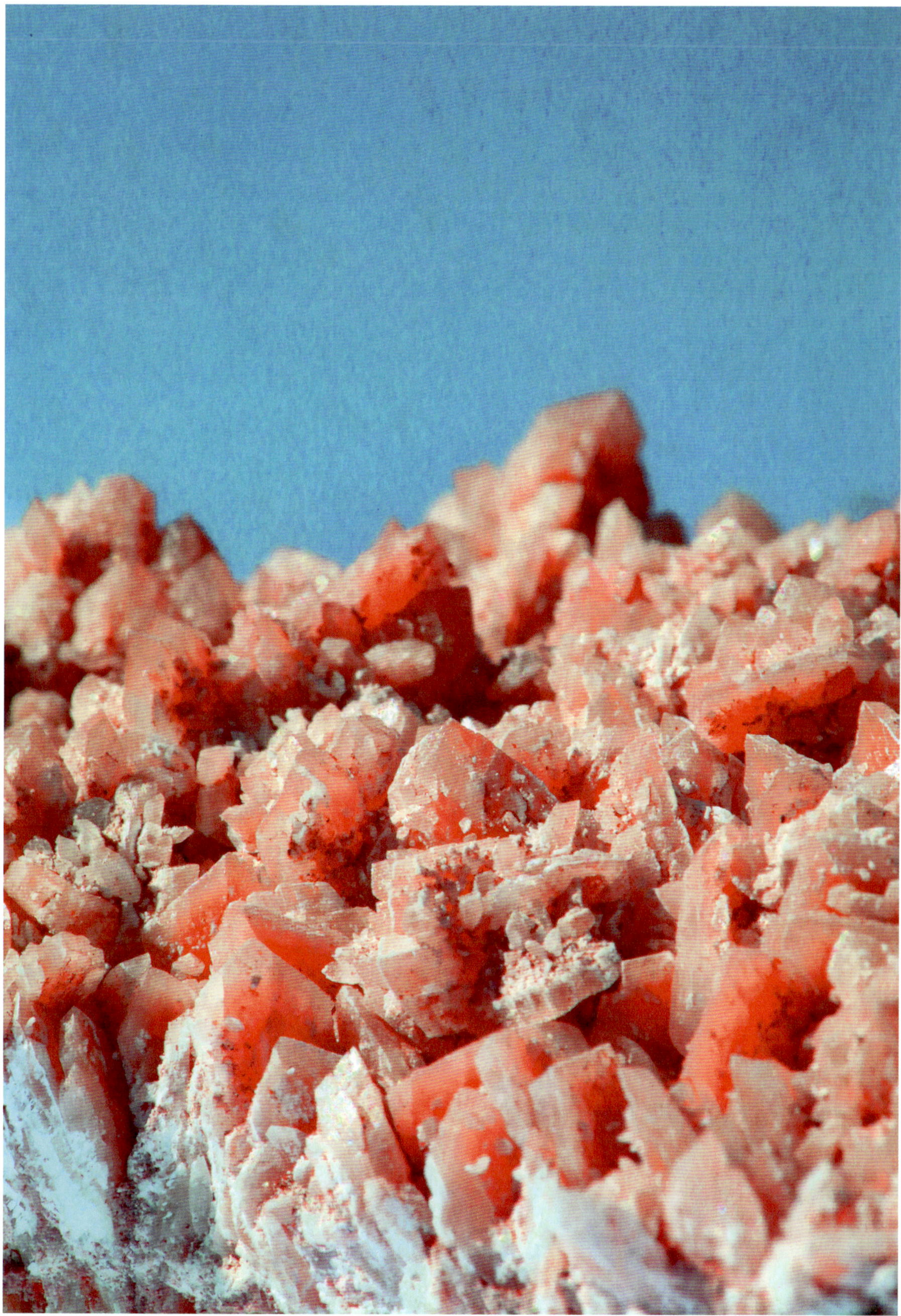

Zielplattform, Saltonsee, Kalifornien

In den Jahren 1944 bis 1945 wurde eine Folge von geheimen Übungsflügen mit neun B-29-Bombern von Utah zum Saltonsee durchgeführt. Laut dem 1977 erschienenen Buch *Ruin From The Air. The Atomic Mission to Hiroshima* von Gordon Thomas und Max Morgan-Witts standen den Besatzungen 300 sogenannte Blockbuster-Bombenhüllen zur Verfügung, die sie bei ihren Übungsflügen einsetzen konnten. »Die Crews führten Hunderte von Übungsflügen über der Mojave-Wüste und dem Saltonsee durch. Die Testbomben waren Attrappen der später eingesetzten Waffen in Originalgröße: des langen, schlanken Uran-Sprengkopfs ›Little Boy‹, der auf Hiroshima abgeworfen wurde, und des bauchigen Plutonium-Sprengsatzes ›Fat Man‹, der Nagasaki traf.« Weiter schreiben die Autoren: »Die meisten dieser Attrappen waren mit Beton gefüllt, einige enthielten jedoch sämtliche Komponenten mit Ausnahme des nuklearen Materials. Dazu zählten auch große Mengen konventionellen Sprengstoffs in den Zündmechanismen.«

Platform Target, Salton Sea, California

In 1944–5 a series of classified practice flights using nine B-29 bombers were made from Utah to the Salton Sea. According to the 1977 book *Ruin From the Air: The Atomic Mission to Hiroshima* by Gordon Thomas and Max Morgan-Witts, three hundred so-called blockbuster bomb casings were available for the crews to use on their practice missions. ‘Crews made hundreds of practice runs over the Mojave Desert and the Salton Sea. The test bombs were full-sized mock-ups of the real thing – the long and slender uranium “Little Boy” that would fall on Hiroshima and the bulbous plutonium “Fat Man” that would hit Nagasaki’. They continue, ‘Most of the mock-ups were filled with concrete, but some contained everything but the nuclear components, including large quantities of conventional explosives in the triggering mechanisms.’

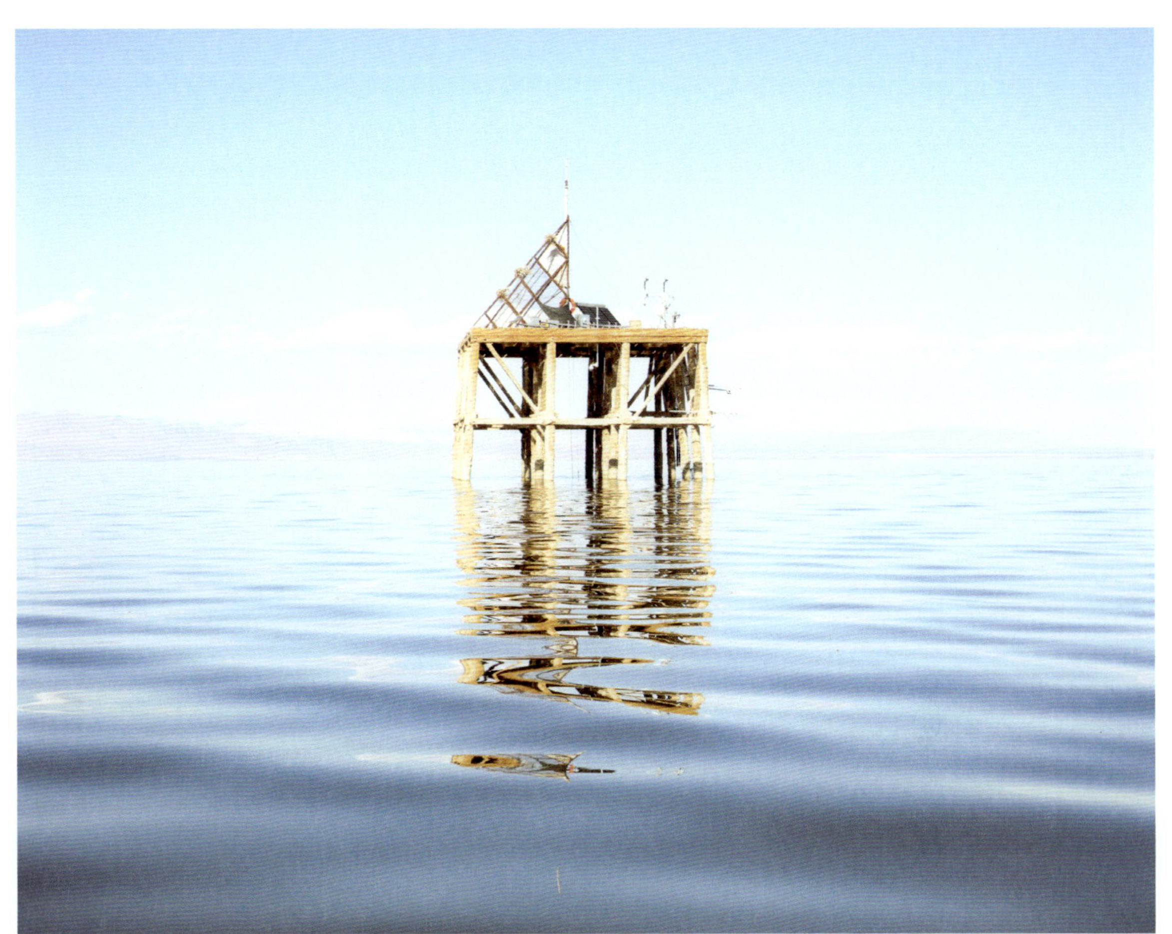

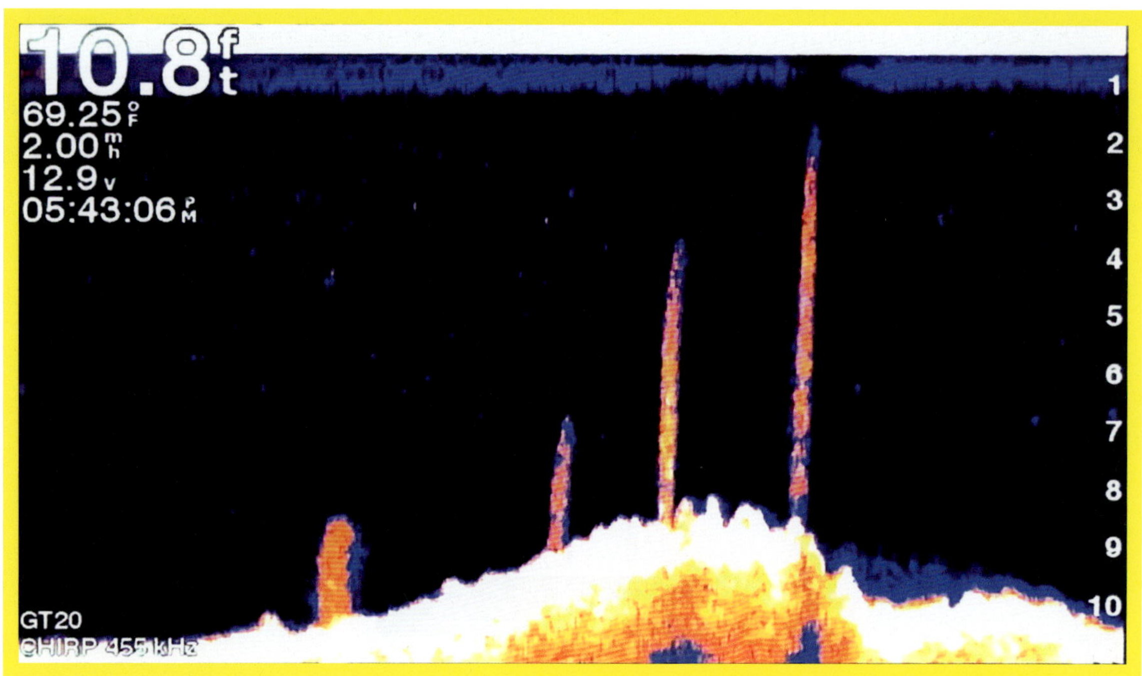
10.8 ft
69.25 °F
2.00 mh
12.9 v
05:43:06 PM
1
2
3
4
5
6
7
8
9
10
GT20
CHIRP 455 kHz

22.3 ft
69.75 °F
2.68 mh
12.9 v
05:32:20 PM
0
5
10
15
20
25
27
GT20
CHIRP 77 kHz

GARMIN-Fishfinder-Bildgebung zur Objekterkennung im Saltonsee, Kalifornien

»Fish Finding« und Sonarsysteme können Fische, aber auch andere Objekte unter Wasser aufspüren. Auf dem Grund des Saltonsees liegen mit Beton gefüllte Atombombenattrappen. Außerdem ruhen dort die Wracks von 28 Flugzeugen, die bei Tiefflugübungen über dem See abgestürzt sind. In diesem Zusammenhang spielt die Echoortung eine zentrale Rolle. Sie ist entscheidend, um mithilfe von Wellenimpulsen die Unterwassertopografie zu erfassen.

GARMIN Fish-Finder Imagery Detecting Objects Within the Salton Sea, California

'Fish-finding' and sonar systems can detect underwater fish, but also other objects. Lying at the bottom of the Salton Sea are faux nuclear bombs filled with concrete. Twenty-eight aeroplanes that crashed at the location during low flying exercises also lie in the mud of the Salton Sea. Echolocation plays a crucial role in this context and is essential for understanding underwater topography through wave pulses.

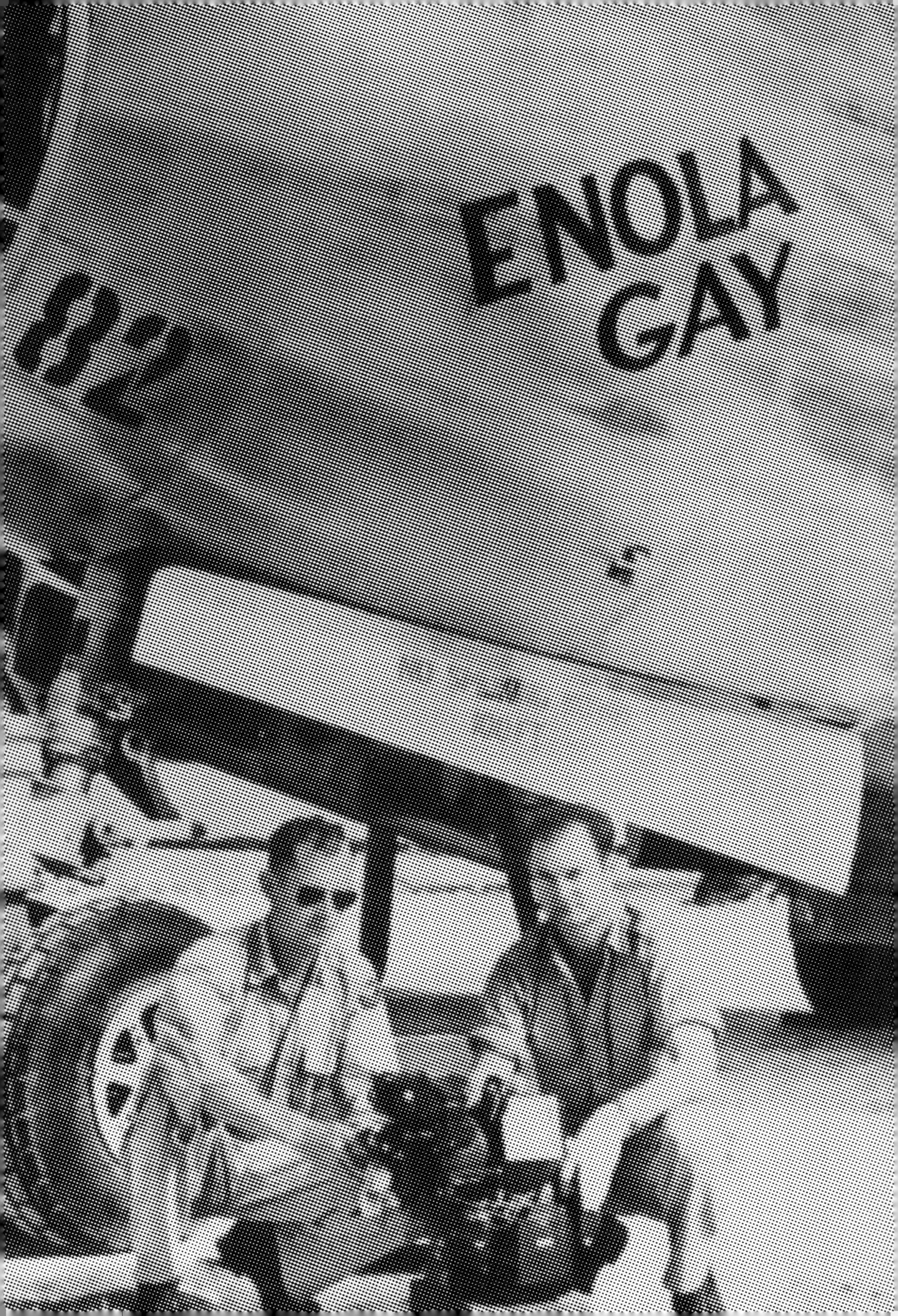
ENOLA
GAY

Bombenschütze Thomas Ferebee mit unbekanntem Kollegen und dem Norden-Bombenzielgerät vor dem B-29-Bomber Enola Gay, 1945

Das Norden-Bombenzielgerät war ein Vorläufer der Objekterkennung bei hoher Geschwindigkeit und hatte eine berüchtigte Verbindung zum B-29-Bomber Enola Gay. Es nutzte ein tachometrisches Design und konnte ein Ziel verfolgen, indem es den Abwurfpunkt der Bombe fortlaufend neu berechnete. In der Geschichte des Saltonsees spielte das Norden-Bombenzielgerät eine wichtige Rolle und gilt als erstes Sichtgerät, das den haptischen Raum erfasste. Wie das Teleskop und die unbemannten Luftfahrzeuge der jüngeren Vergangenheit war es in der Lage, unsere Wahrnehmung von Entfernungen und Dimensionen entweder aufzulösen oder zu beschleunigen. Mit seinem apokalyptischen Blick war das unter Verschluss gehaltene Bombenzielgerät ein frühes Beispiel für das, was Joanna Zylinska eine »Wahrnehmungsmaschine« nennt: ein Bestandteil eines multisensorischen Systems, das eine Aufgabe erfüllt und Funktionen im Rahmen einer Operation übernimmt. Sein oberstes Ziel war es, besser zu sehen – das heißt: schneller und effizienter als jeder Mensch.

Bombardier Thomas Ferebee with Unknown Colleague and the Norden Bombsight in Front of the *Enola Gay* B-29 Bomber, 1945

The Norden bombsight was a forerunner to object detection at speed and had an infamous connection to the *Enola Gay* B-29 bomber. It utilised a tachometric design and could track a bomb target, recalculating the release point of a bomb as it flew. It played an important role in the history of the Salton Sea and was arguably the first vision machine to understand the haptic space; much like the telescope, and more recently Unmanned Aerial Vehicle Systems, it was capable of obliterating or accelerating our experiences of distances and dimensions. With its apocalyptic gaze, the bombsight was shrouded in secrecy, and an early example of what Joanna Zylinska calls a 'perception machine', part of a multisensory system that performs a task and carries out functions as part of an operation. Its ultimate goal was to see better – that is, faster and more efficiently than humans.

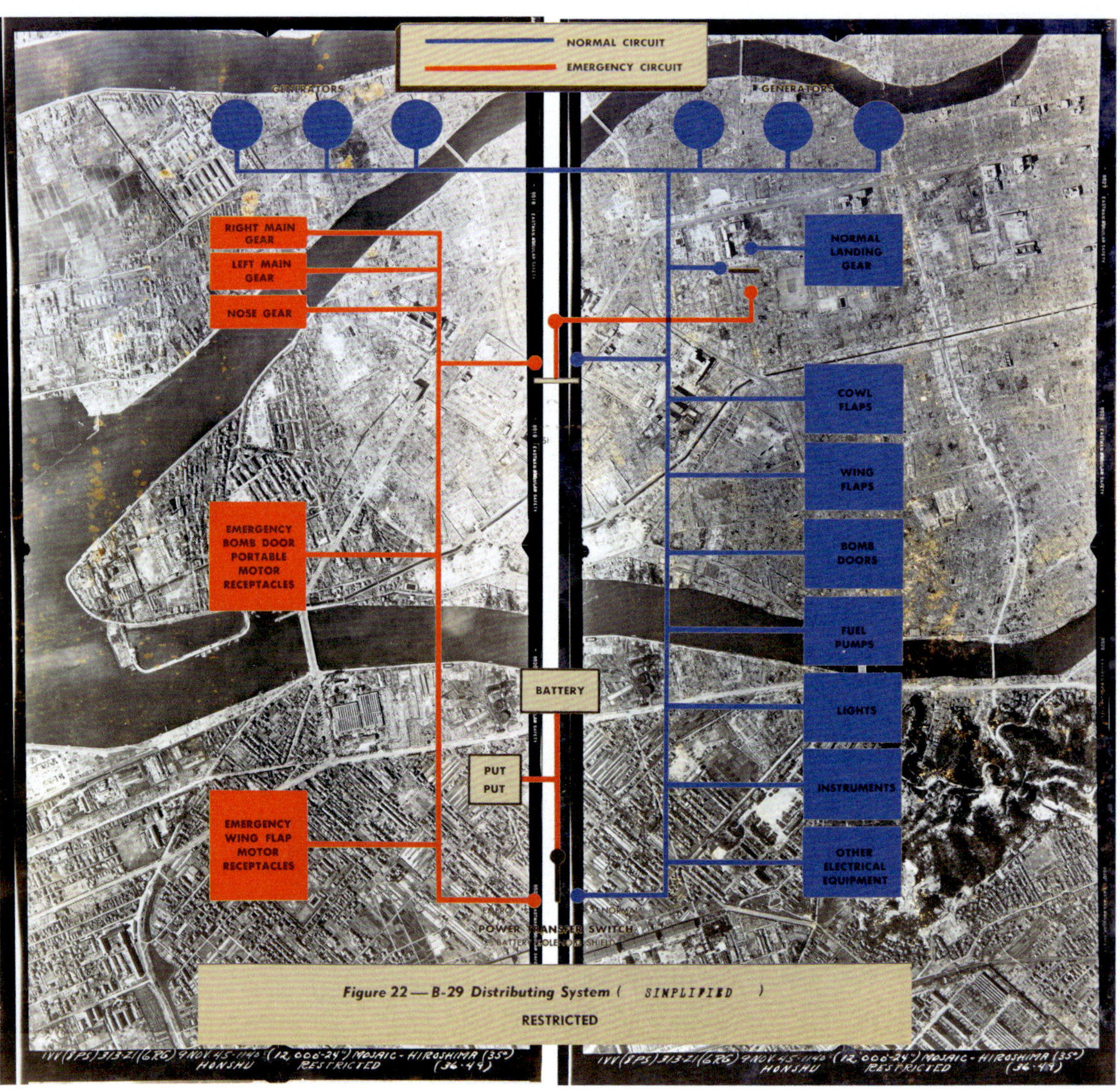

Figure 22 — B-29 Distributing System (SIMPLIFIED)

RESTRICTED

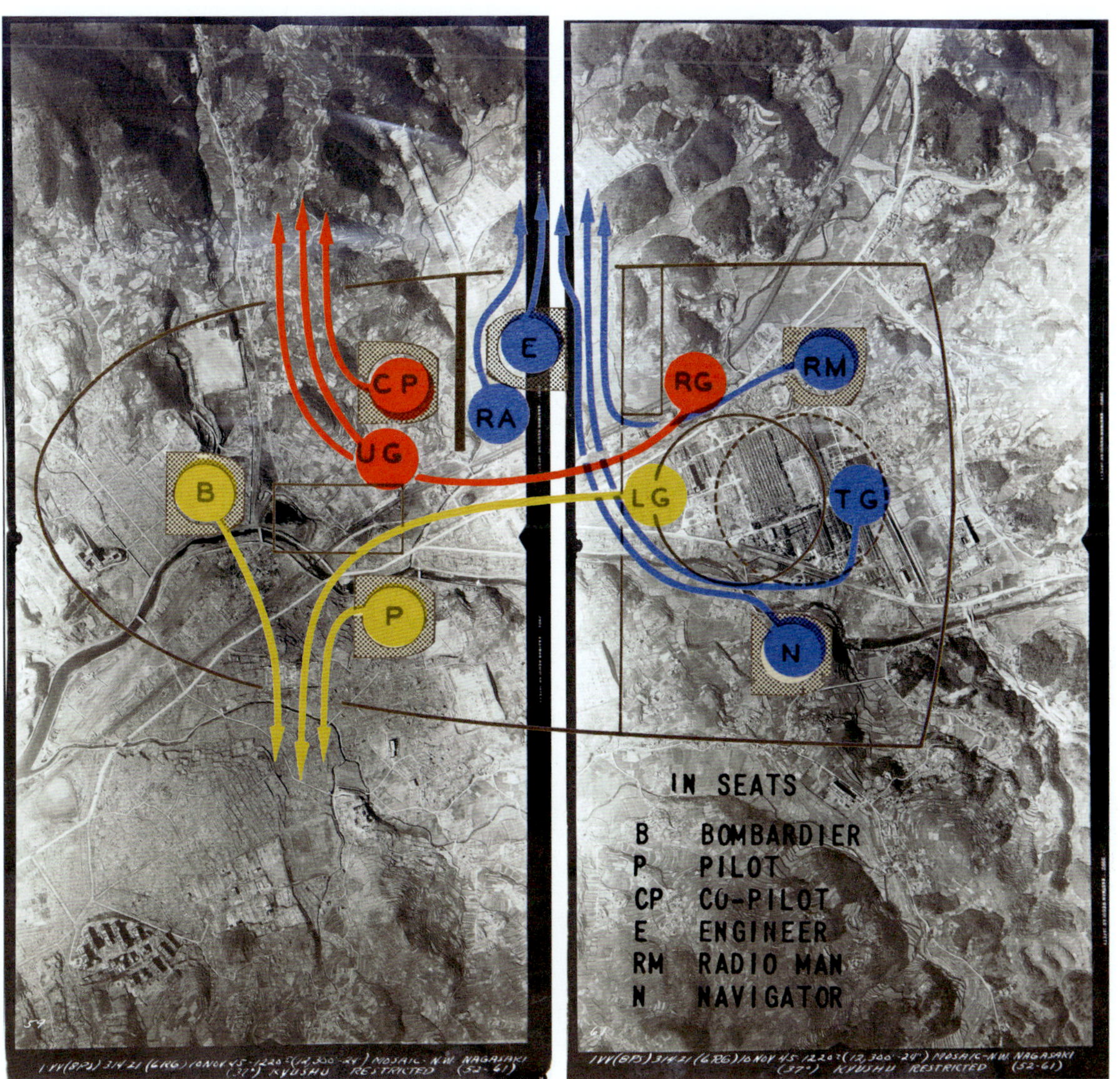
CP
E
RA
RG
RM
UG
B
LG
TG
P
N
IN SEATS
B BOMBARDIER
P PILOT
CP CO-PILOT
E ENGINEER
RM RADIO MAN
N NAVIGATOR
MOSAIC-N.W. NAGASAKI
(37°) KYUSHU RESTRICTED (52-61)
MOSAIC-N.W. NAGASAKI
(37°) KYUSHU RESTRICTED (52-61)

Originalaufnahmen der Zerstörung nach den Atombombenabwürfen auf Hiroshima und Nagasaki, kombiniert mit Grafiken aus dem Handbuch des B-29-Bombers

Am 6. August 1945 warf der Bomber Enola Gay die Atombombe »Little Boy« über Hiroshima ab. Drei Tage später, am 9. August 1945, wurde die zweite Atombombe, »Fat Man«, von einem anderen B-29-Bomber namens Bockscar über Nagasaki abgeworfen. Die hier gezeigten Luftaufnahmen entstanden in den Tagen nach den Explosionen. Sie dienten der dokumentarischen Erfassung und erfüllten somit eine rein beschreibende Funktion.

Die fotografische Luftperspektive war Teil der Weiterentwicklung militärischer Blickregime und wurde bereits im Ersten Weltkrieg zur Erstellung von Bildmosaiken der Schützengräben eingesetzt. Im Jahr 1921 präsentierten die Industrieingenieur:innen Frank und Lillian Gilbreth der American Society of Mechanical Engineers das sogenannte »Flow Process Chart« – ein Ablaufdiagramm, das bald in zahlreichen Anwendungsfeldern zur Analyse, Optimierung und klaren Darstellung komplexer Abläufe genutzt wurde. In den 1940er-Jahren fanden solche Ablaufdiagramme Verwendung bei der Entwicklung früher Computerprogramme und kommen bis heute bei der Gestaltung von Algorithmen zum Einsatz. Das Flughandbuch für Pilot:innen der B-29- und B-29A-Bomber aus dem Zweiten Weltkrieg gilt als ein frühes Beispiel für den Gebrauch grafischer Ablaufdiagramme im militärischen Kontext.

Original Images from the Aftermath of the Nagasaki and Hiroshima Atomic Bombs with Graphics from the B-29 Bomber Instruction Manual

The *Enola Gay* dropped the 'Little Boy' atomic bomb on Hiroshima on 6 August 1945. The second atomic bomb, 'Fat Man', was dropped on Nagasaki three days later, on 9 August 1945, by a different B-29 bomber named *Bockscar*. These aerial images were taken to document the area in the days after the bombings and carry a purely denotative function.

The photographic aerial perspective is part of the advancement of military vision, first used to create mosaics of the World War I trenches. In 1921, industrial engineers Frank and Lillian Gilbreth introduced the 'Flow Process Chart' to the American Society of Mechanical Engineers – a tool that was soon applied across various fields to analyse, optimise, and clearly represent complex processes. By the 1940s, flow charts were being used to develop early computer programmes, and are still used for that function in the development of algorithms. The *B-29/B-29A Pilot's Flight Operating Instructions World War II Book Flight Manual* is an early example of the use of graphic flow charts.

Nachtsichtaufnahmen von Geothermiekraftwerken am Saltonsee, Niland, Kalifornien

Die Bilder wurden mit einem militärischen Nachtsichtgerät des Typs PVS14-3 aufgenommen. Diese Technologie ist Teil eines umfassenden Überwachungssystems, das von der US-Zoll- und Grenzschutzbehörde (Customs and Border Protection, kurz: CBP) eingesetzt wird, um auch bei schwachem Licht und in der Nacht eine effektive Überwachung zu gewährleisten. Das Gerät verfügt über einen integrierten Infrarotstrahler, der zusätzliches Licht liefert, wenn das Umgebungslicht besonders gering ist.

Das Nachtsichtgerät wurde auf einem iPhone 14 Pro montiert. Die Aufnahmen entstanden mit Unterstützung von Carolyn Drake, da es für eine britische Staatsbürgerin rechtlich problematisch ist, eine solche Kamera in den USA eigenständig zu bedienen.

→

Night Vision Geothermal Plants at the Salton Sea, Niland, California

Images created using a PVS14-3 military night vision camera. Part of the broader surveillance technology employed by Customs and Border Protection (CBP) for enhanced surveillance in low-light and night-time conditions. It also has a built-in infrared illuminator, providing additional illumination when ambient light is extremely low.

The camera was attached to an iPhone 14 Pro. Photographed with support from Carolyn Drake, due to the legality of a UK citizen operating the camera in the US.

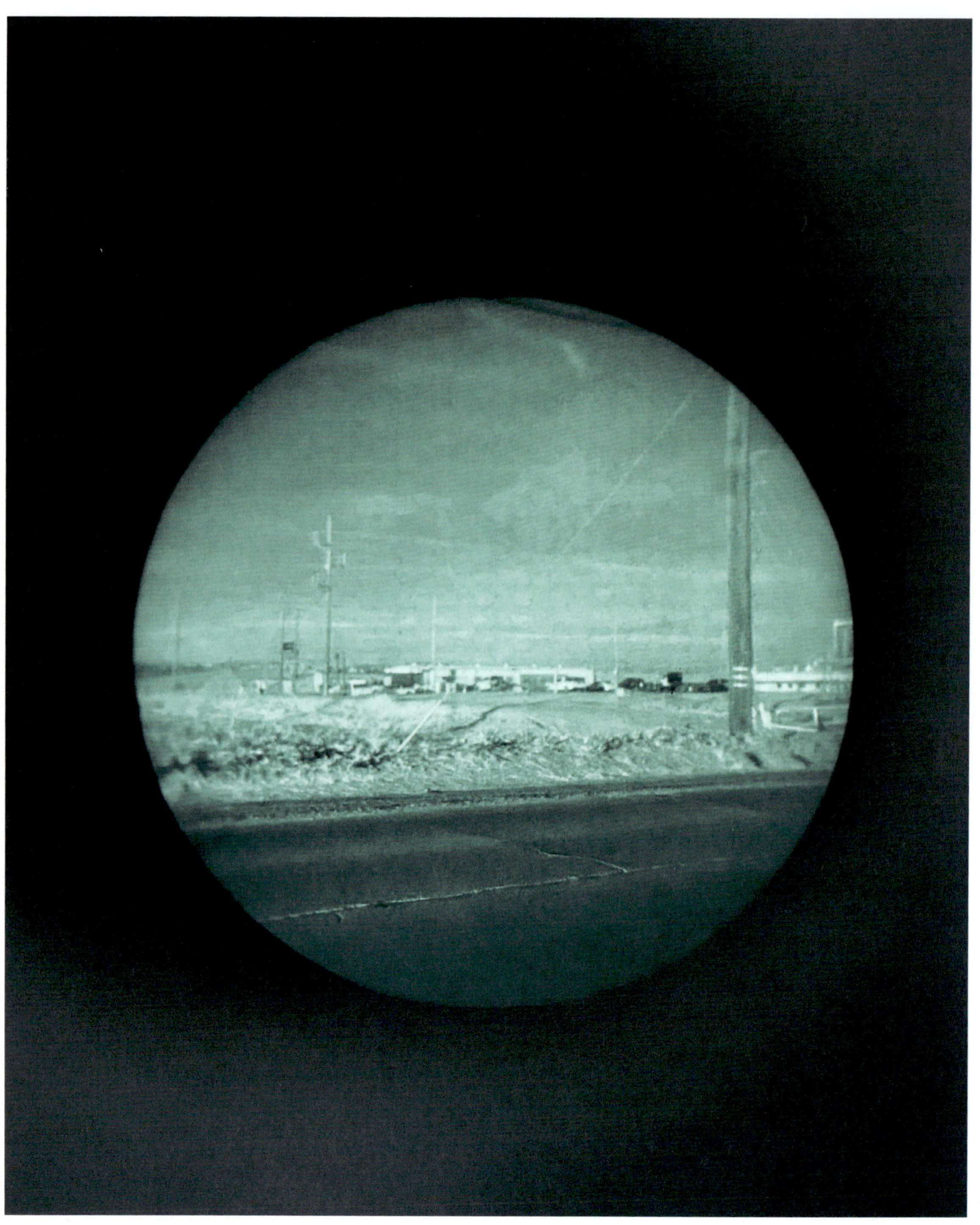

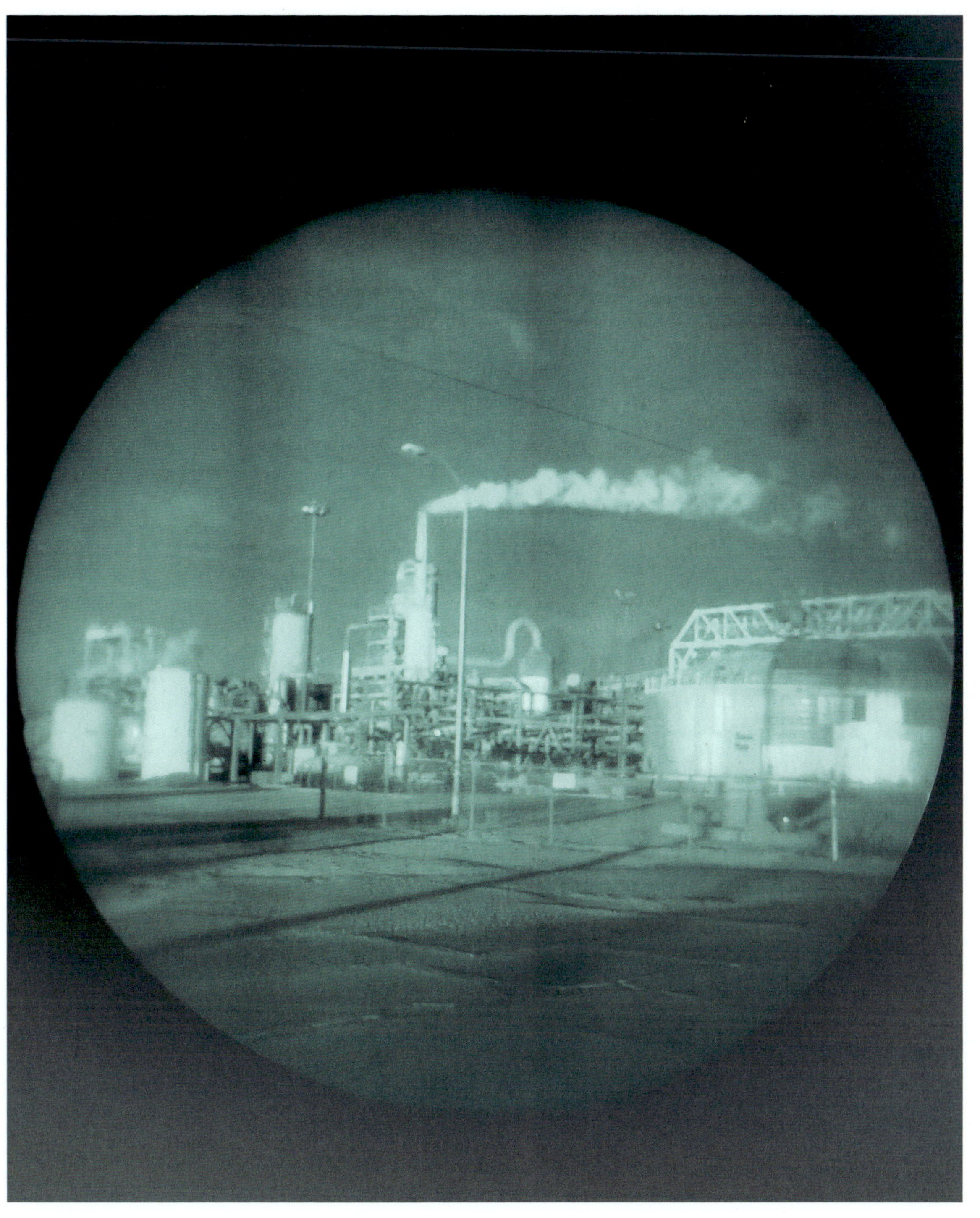

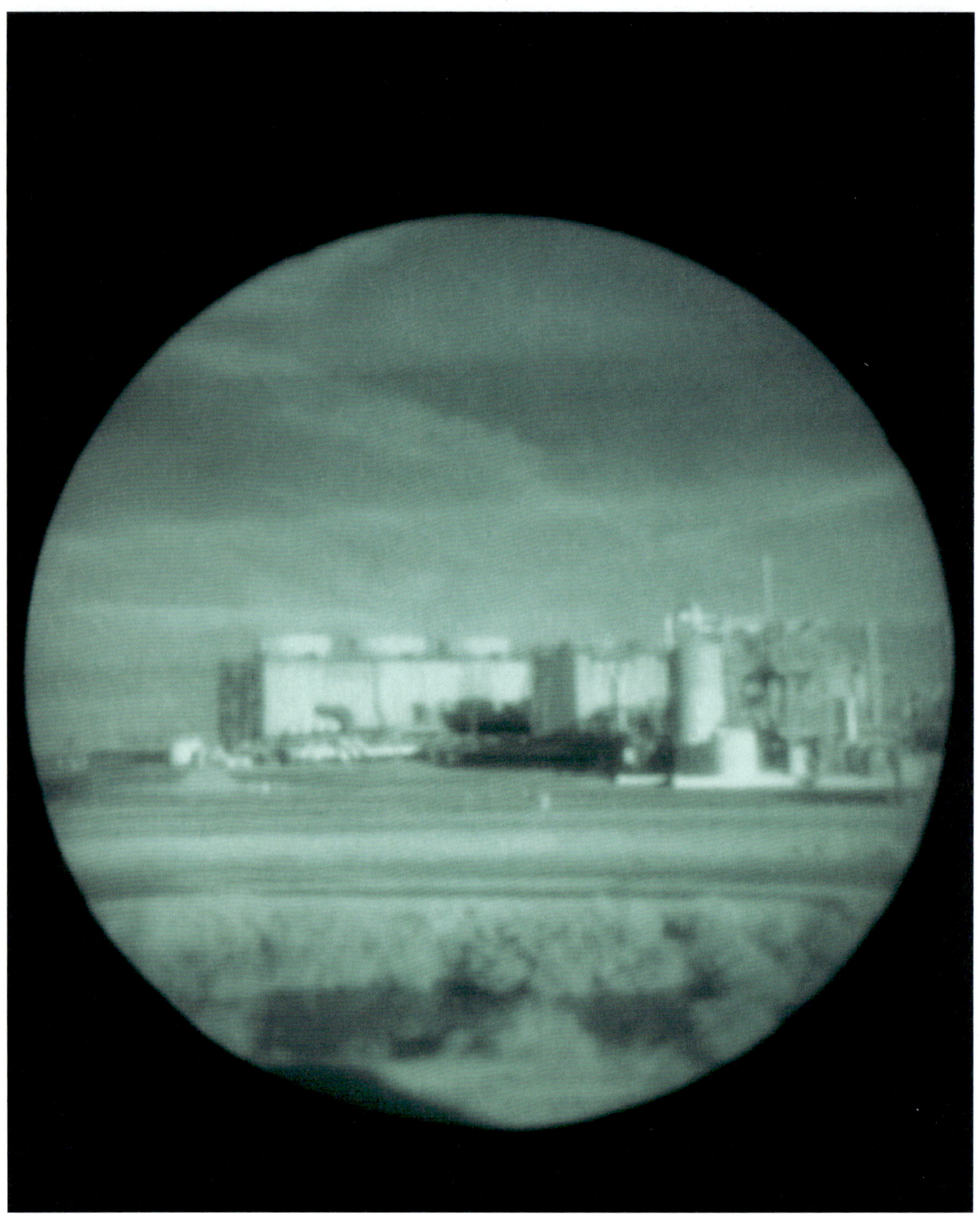

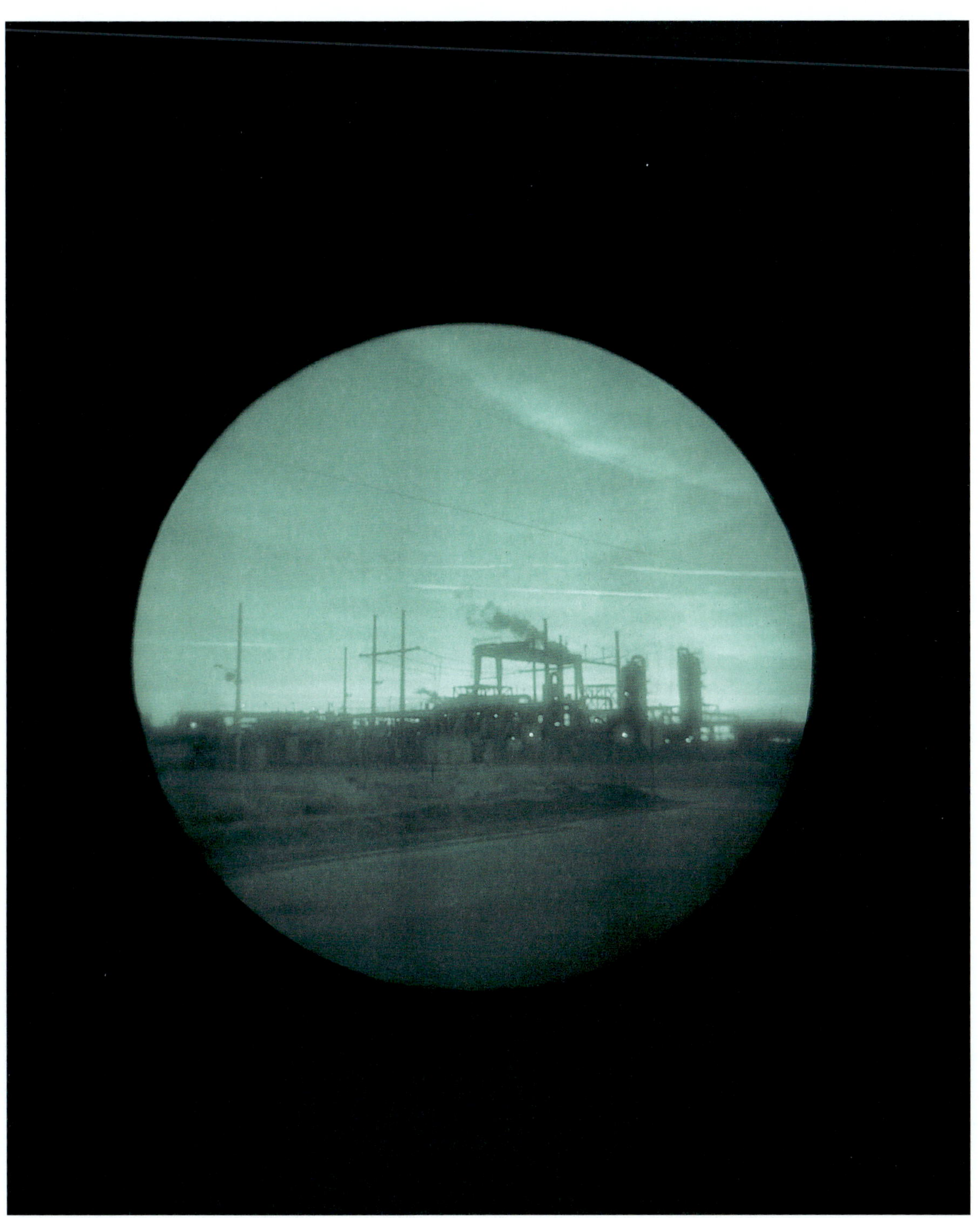

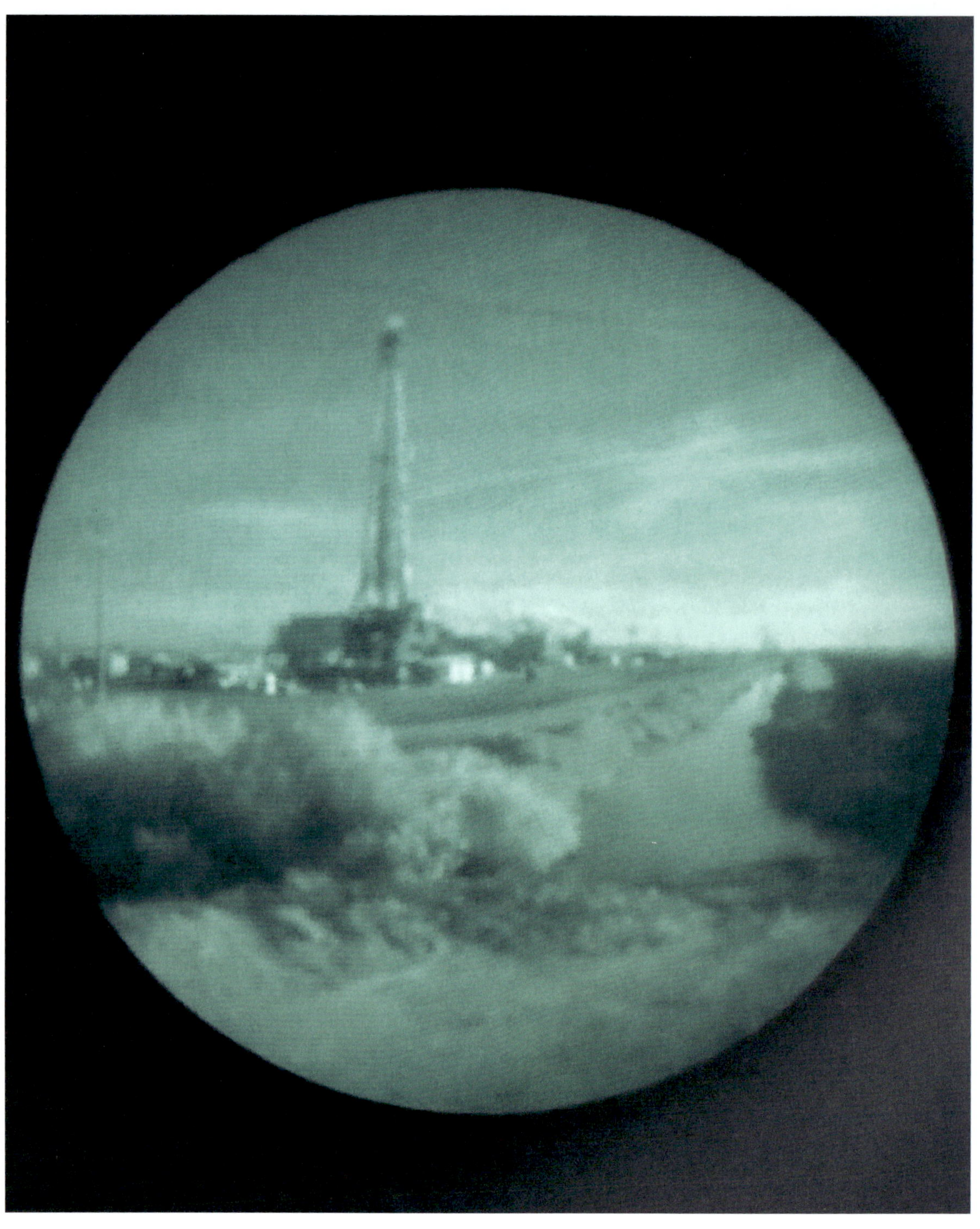

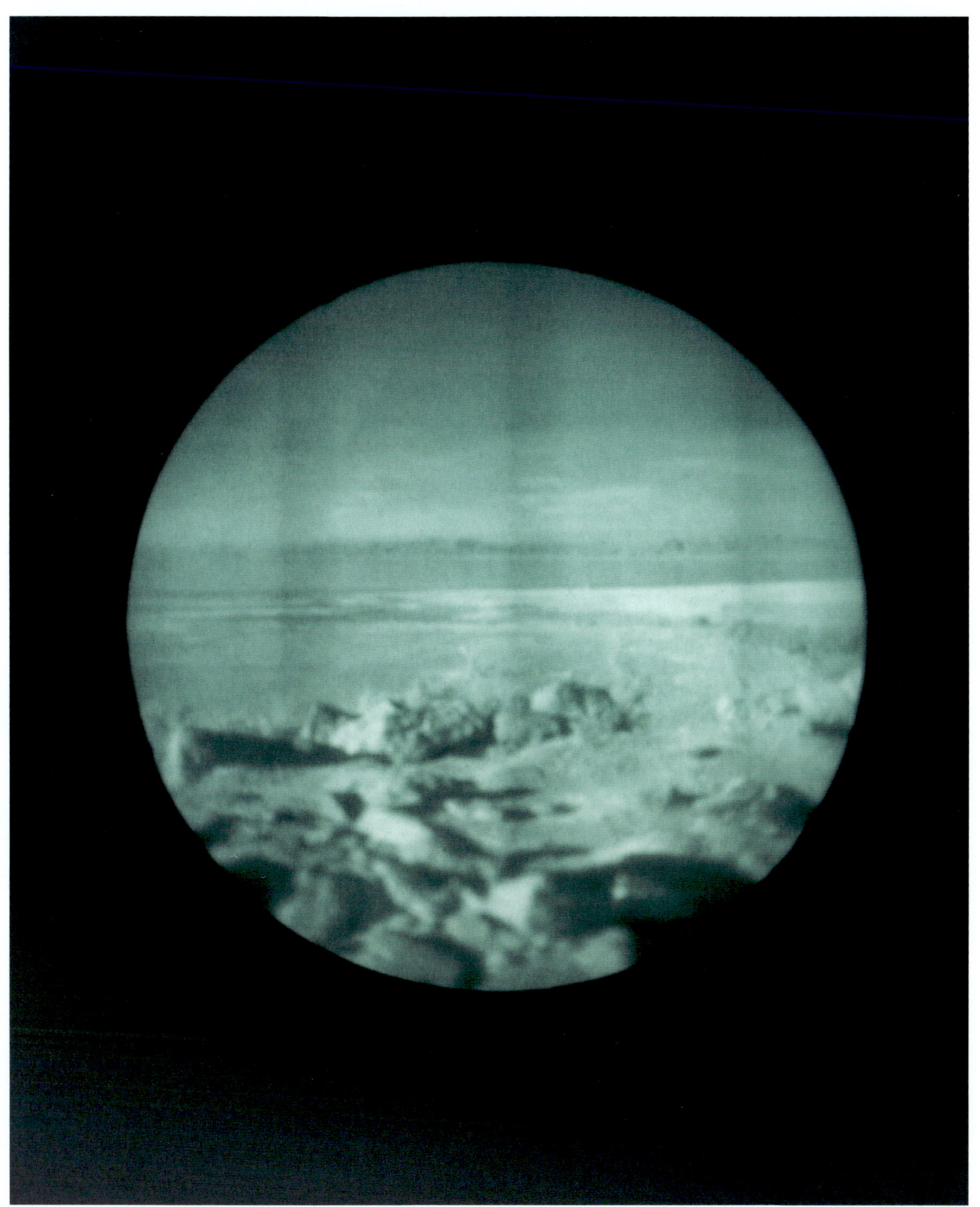

Sehmaschinen existierten einst an den Rändern unseres Lebens, in der Peripherie, wo Schatten von Lichtschimmern durchzuckt wurden. Die Sorge um das Klima und technologische Heilsversprechen haben sich in einem Meer aus Widersprüchen verfangen, während unser Bewusstsein zunehmend von den Technologien und Maschinen geprägt wird, die wir verwenden. Die Wahrnehmung der Realität ist ins Wanken geraten: Sehen und Hören sind nicht länger verlässlich, Erfahrungen zersplittern in Vertrautes und Fremdes, verwoben in ein Netz aus Halluzinationen. Wenn Wahrnehmung das Fundament des Bewusstseins bildet, wie gliedern sich dann KI-Systeme in dieses Gefüge ein? Systeme, die zwar Daten verarbeiten, aber keine eigenen Erfahrungen machen können? Letztendlich hat unser Vertrauen in wahrnehmende und sich ausdrückende Technologien die menschliche Kognition tiefgreifend verändert und die Grenze zwischen organischen und künstlichen Wissensformen verwischt.

Vision machines once existed on the fringes of our lives, in the peripheries, where shadows flickered with glimmers of light. Climate concerns and solutionist technologies have become blurred in a sea of contradiction as human consciousness is increasingly mediated by the technologies and machines we use. Perception of reality has become confused; seeing and hearing are no longer reliable, fragmented into both familiar and unfamiliar experiences, and woven into a web of hallucinations. If perception is foundational to consciousness, how do AI systems – which process data but may lack genuine experience – fit into this framework? Ultimately our reliance on perceptive and expressive technologies has reshaped human cognition, blurring the boundaries between organic and artificial ways of knowing.

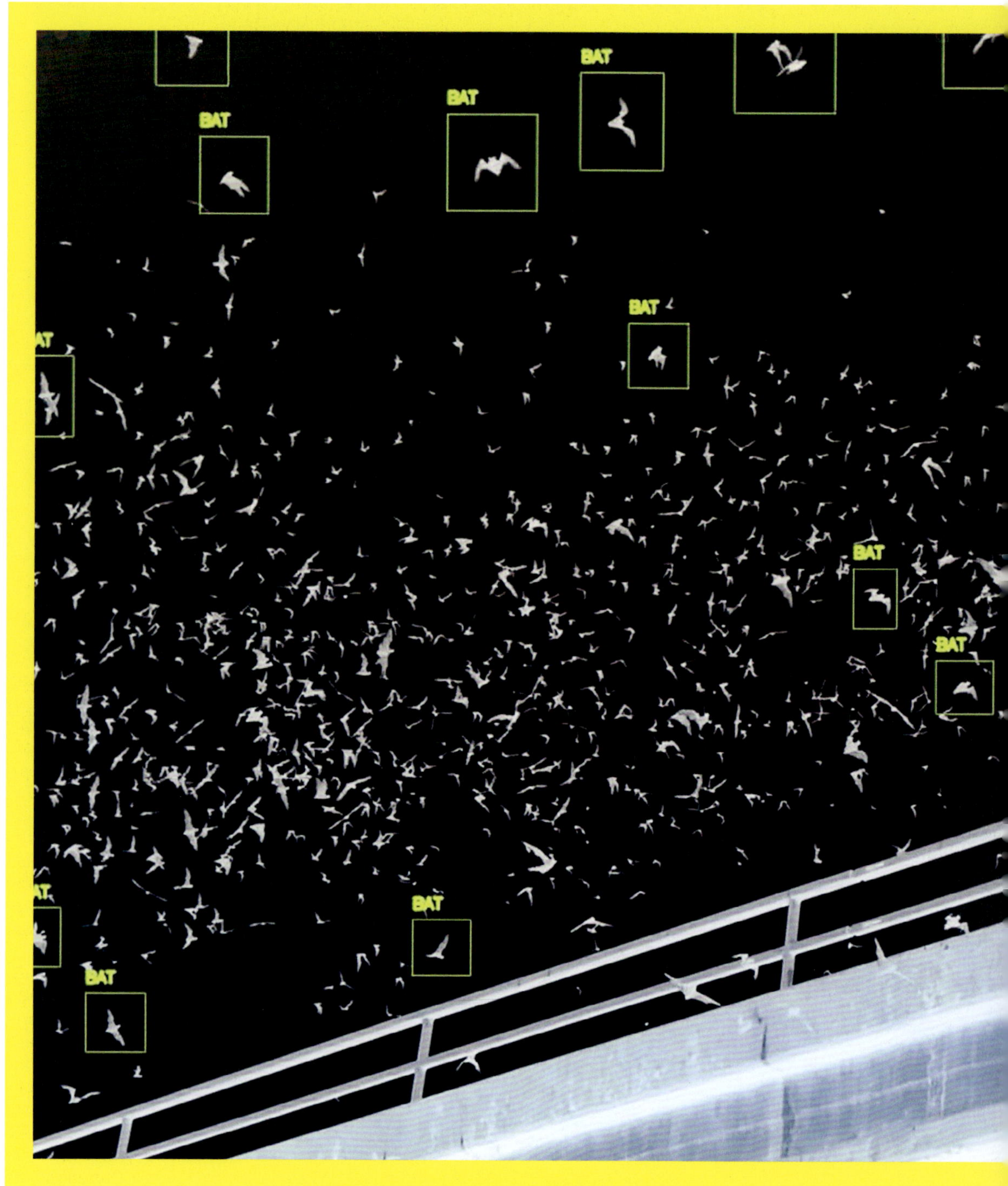
BAT
BAT
BAT
BAT
BAT
BAT
BAT
BAT
BAT

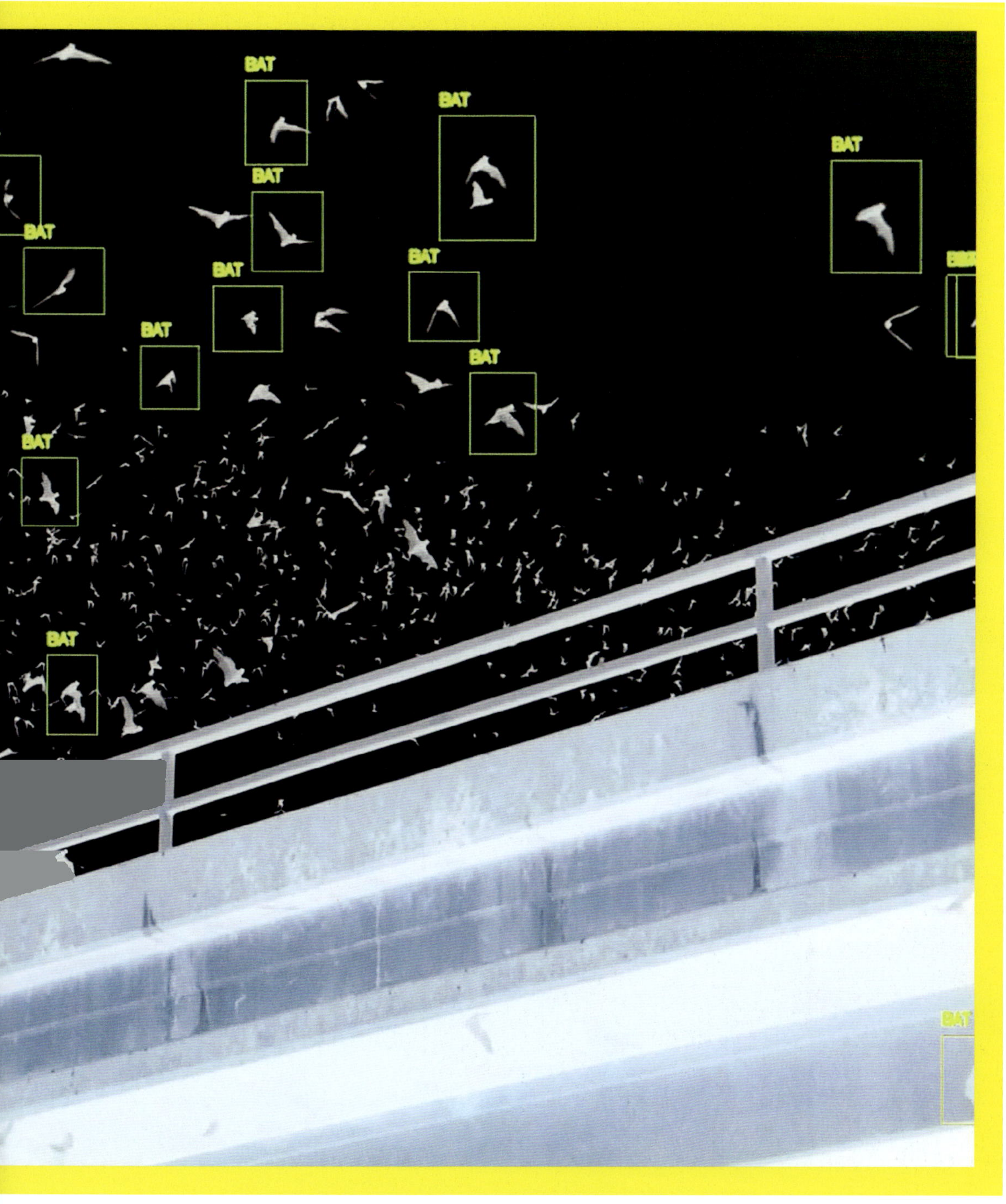
BAT
BAT
BAT
BAT
BAT
BAT
BAT
BAT
BAT
BAT
BAT

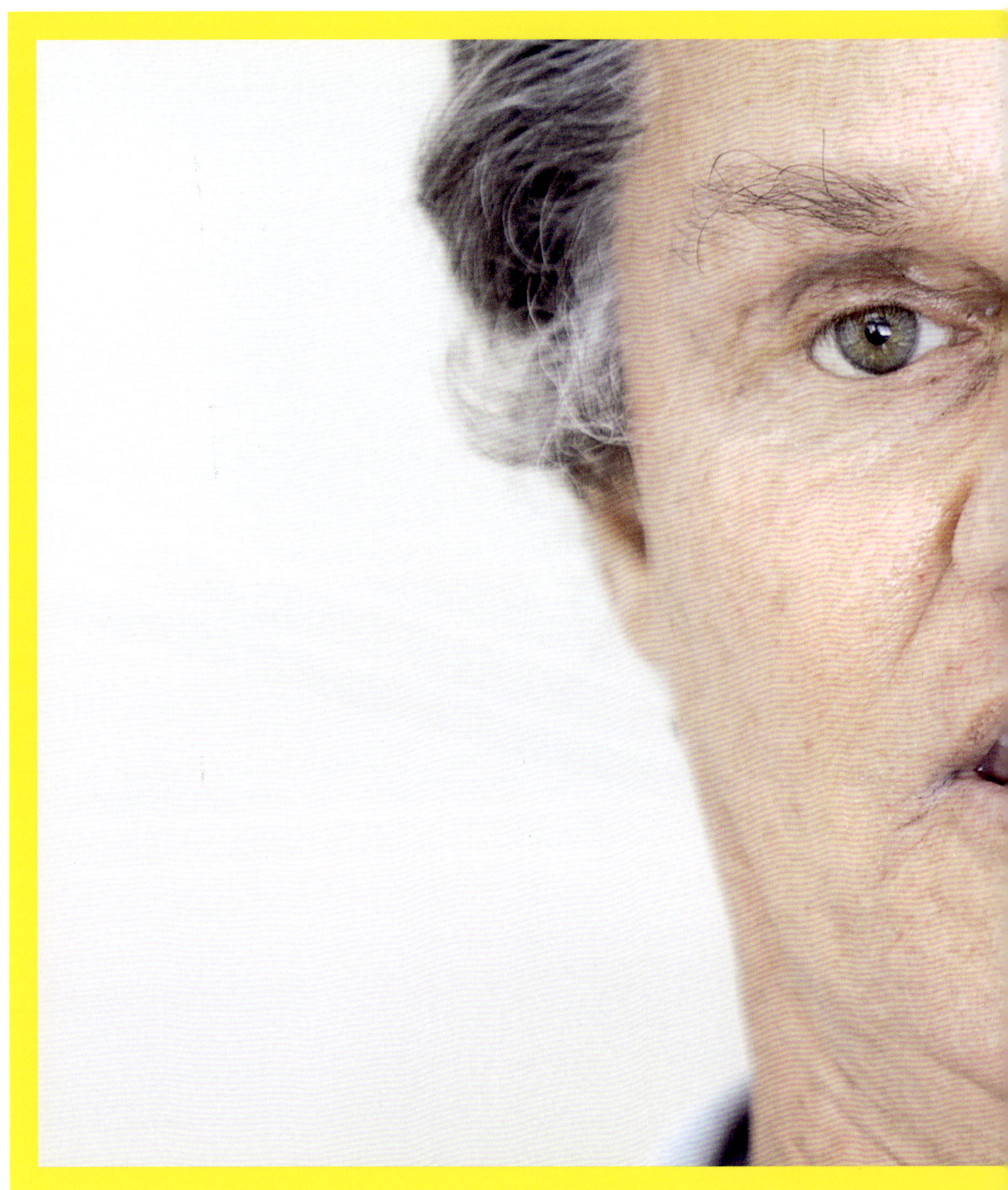

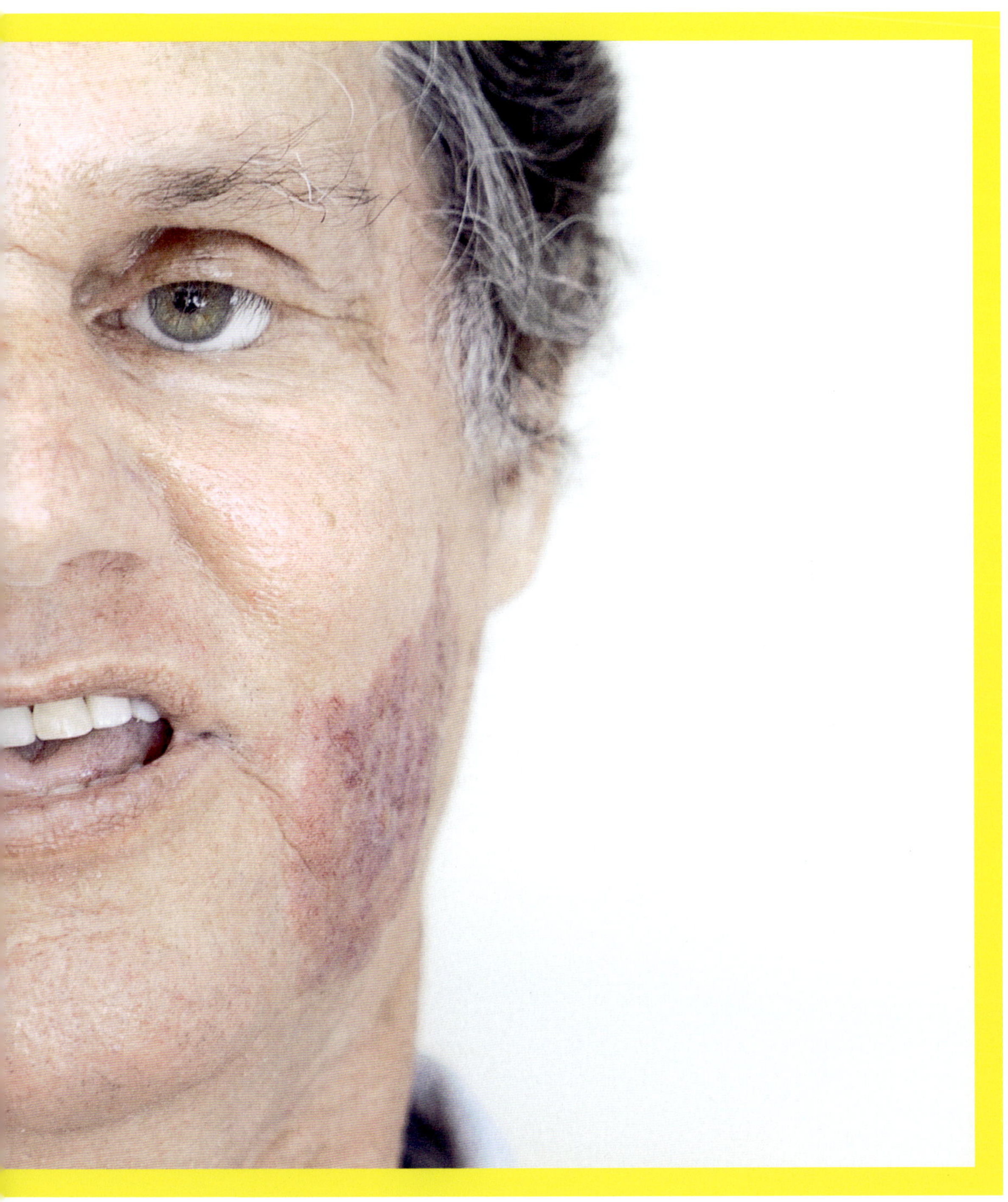

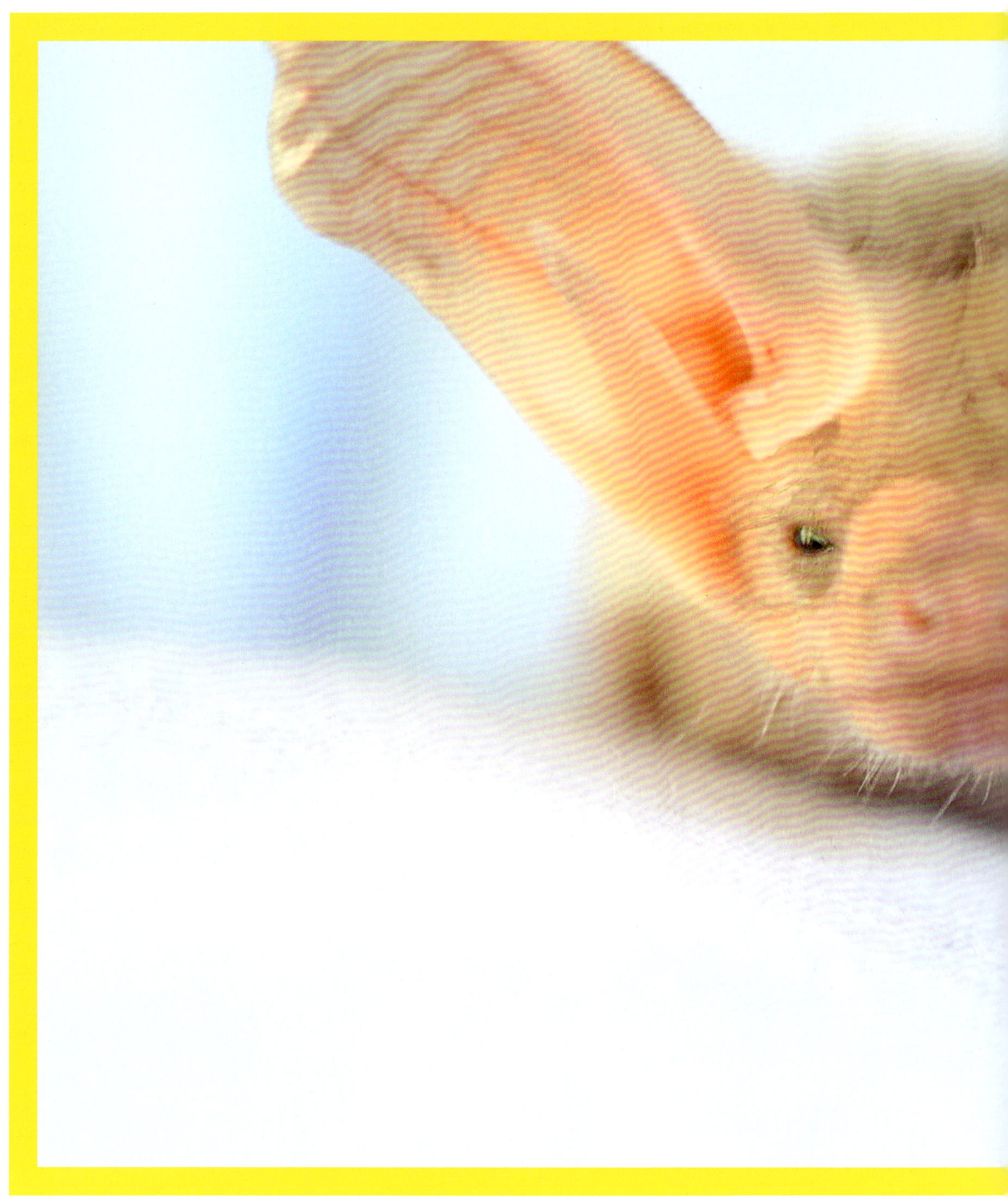

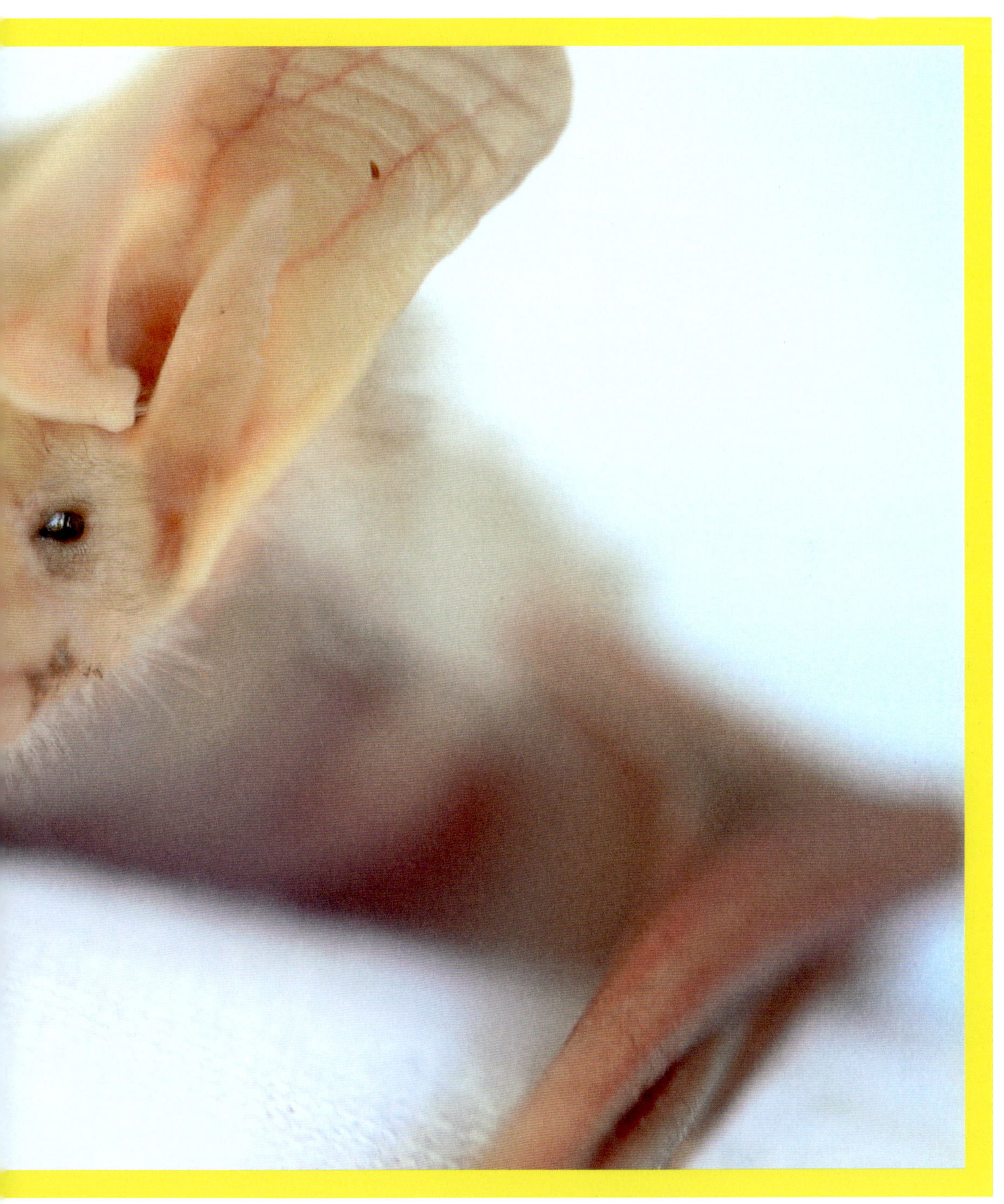

»You Only Look Once«-Algorithmus zur Objekterkennung in Echtzeit, angewendet auf 4K-Filmmaterial einer »Fledermauswolke«, Yolo Basin, Sacramento, Kalifornien

Fledermäuse nutzen Echoortung, um zu »sehen«: Sie senden hochfrequente Schallwellen aus und interpretieren deren Echos, wodurch eine mentale Karte ihrer Umgebung entsteht. Anders als das Sehen, das auf Licht angewiesen ist, basiert die Echoortung auf Schallreflexionen und ermöglicht so eine ganz eigene Form der Raumwahrnehmung. In ähnlicher Weise verwenden autonome Fahrzeuge Techniken wie LiDAR und Radar zur Navigation, unterstützt von Algorithmen wie YOLO zur Objekterkennung in Echtzeit. Ziel des maschinellen Lernens ist es, Informationen aus Bildmaterial zu extrahieren, damit Maschinen visuelle Aufgaben schneller und effizienter ausführen können als der Mensch. In einer kreativen Anwendung wurde der YOLO-Algorithmus eingesetzt, um Fledermausschwärme am Yolo Causeway zu kartieren – ein Beispiel dafür, wie Maschinen »sehen« und komplexe Szenen interpretieren können. Ein speziell entwickeltes Modell, das gemeinsam mit Jack Lander entstand, wurde mit über 1.000 Einzelbildern aus Fledermausaufnahmen trainiert. Nach dem Deep Learning war das Modell in der Lage, Fledermäuse in neuen Bildern oder Live-Videomaterial zu identifizieren. Was ihm jedoch fehlt, ist jedes Verständnis oder Interesse – es erweckt lediglich den Anschein von Wahrnehmung, ohne über ein Bewusstsein zu verfügen. Genau hierin zeigt sich der Unterschied zwischen sensorischer Nachbildung und echtem Verstehen.

←

'You Only Look Once' Real-Time Object Detection Machine Learning Algorithm Used in Conjunction with 4K Footage of a 'Bat Cloud', Yolo Basin, Sacramento, California

Bats use echolocation to 'see' by emitting high-frequency sound waves and interpreting the echoes, creating a mental map of their surroundings. Unlike vision, which relies on light, echolocation depends on sound wave reflections, offering a unique way to perceive space. Similarly, autonomous vehicles use LiDAR and radar to navigate, alongside machine learning algorithms such as YOLO for real-time object detection. Machine learning aims to extract information from images, enabling machines to perform visual tasks faster and more efficiently than humans. In a creative application, the YOLO algorithm was used to map bat swarms at the Yolo Causeway, showcasing its ability to 'see' and interpret complex scenes. A custom model, developed with Jack Lander, was trained on over one thousand stills from bat footage. After deep learning, the model could identify bats in new images or live video. However, it lacks comprehension or curiosity about bats, merely mimicking perception without consciousness. This highlights the distinction between sensory replication and true understanding.

Daniel Kish demonstriert seine Echoortungstechnik und Wüstenfledermaus (Antrozous Pallidus), Bewegtbild, 4K

Daniel Kish (* 1966 in Montebello, Kalifornien) ist Experte für menschliche Echoortung und Präsident von World Access for the Blind, einer in Kalifornien registrierten gemeinnützigen Organisation, die er im Jahr 2000 gründete, um die »selbstbestimmte Entfaltung von Menschen mit allen Formen von Blindheit« zu fördern. Er entwickelte eine eigene Methode, bei der er Klicklaute mit dem Mund erzeugt und deren Echos nutzt, um seine Umgebung zu erkennen und sich darin zu bewegen. Er kann auf Grundlage von Schallwellen, die in seinem Gehirn eine »eiförmige« Form annehmen, ein dreidimensionales Bild seiner Umgebung entwerfen. Anders als unsere auf den Sehsinn angewiesene Lebensweise erlaubt ihm diese Fähigkeit – ähnlich wie bei einer Fledermaus –, Größe, Form und Oberflächenstruktur von Objekten sowohl in der Nähe als auch auf Distanz zu bestimmen.

Die Wüstenfledermaus wurde 2024 zum offiziellen Symbol des Bundesstaats Kalifornien ernannt. Gefilmt in Zusammenarbeit mit der Organisation Los Angeles Bat Rescue und mit wiederholter Unterstützung von Chumi Paul, einer ehrenamtlichen Fledermausschützerin in Altadena.

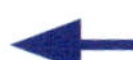

Daniel Kish Demonstrating His Echolocation Technique and Pallid Bat (*Antrozous pallidus*), Moving Image, 4K

Daniel Kish (b. 1966 in Montebello, California) is an expert in human echolocation and the president of World Access for the Blind, a California-registered non-profit organisation founded by Kish in 2000 to facilitate 'the self-directed achievement of people with all forms of blindness'. He developed his own method of generating vocal clicks and using their echoes to identify his surroundings and move about. Daniel can sketch a 3D image from sound waves that form an 'egg shape' wrap in his brain. Unlike our ocularcentric existence, Daniel, much like a bat can determine the size, shape, and surface construct of objects both nearby and at a distance.

The pallid bat was officially designated as the California state bat in 2024. Filmed with the Los Angeles Bat Rescue organisation and the repeated support of Chumi Paul, one of the bat volunteers in Altadena.

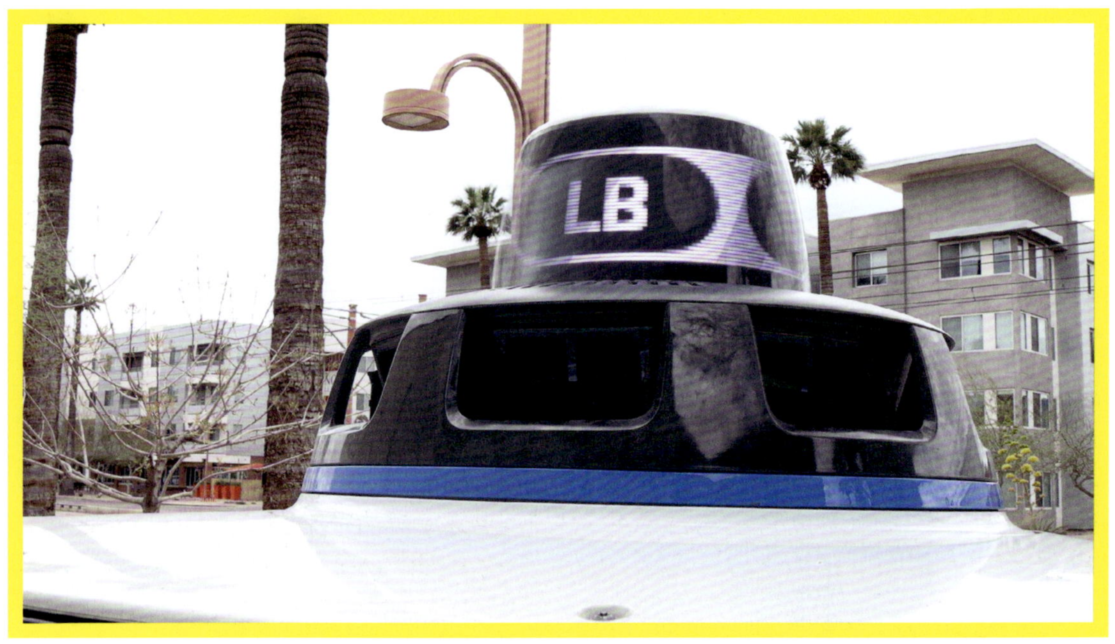

LiDAR-Sensor mit Fahrgastinformationen von Lisa Barnard (LB), Bewegtbild, 4K /
LiDAR Sensor with Lisa Barnard (LB) Passenger Information, Moving Image, 4K

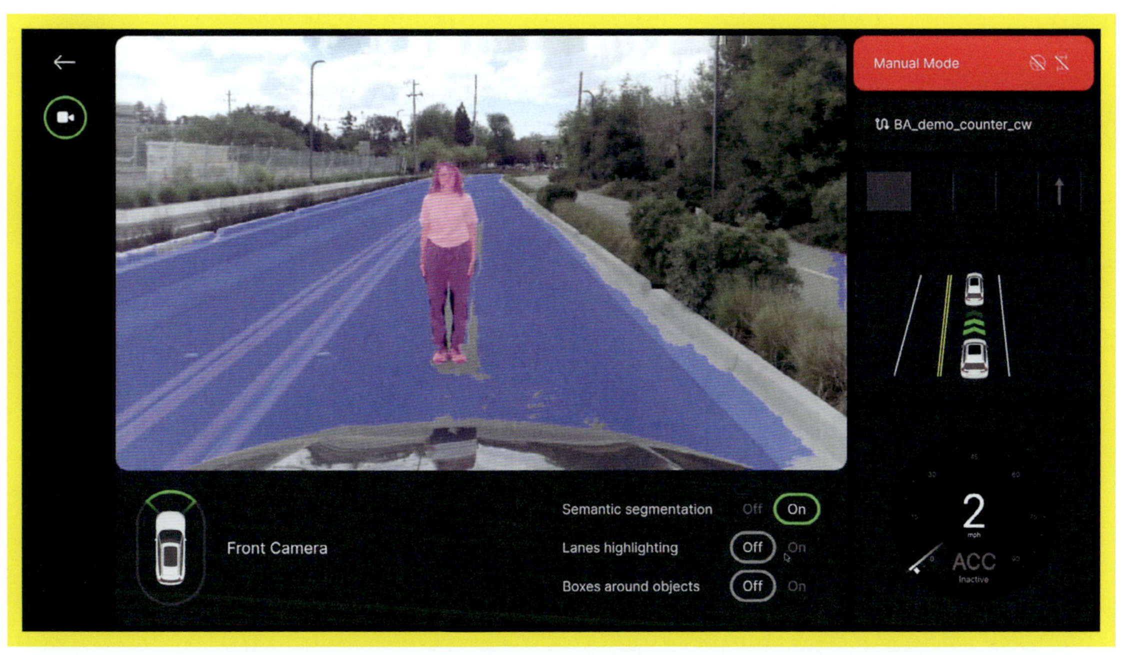

Selbstporträt, aufgenommen mit einem Helm.ai-System vor dem Facebook-Hauptsitz mithilfe eines semantischen Vollbild-Segmentierungssystems, Menlo Park, Kalifornien / Self-Portrait Recording Made with a Helm.ai System in Front of Facebook Headquarters, Using a Full Scene Semantic Segmentation System, Menlo Park, California

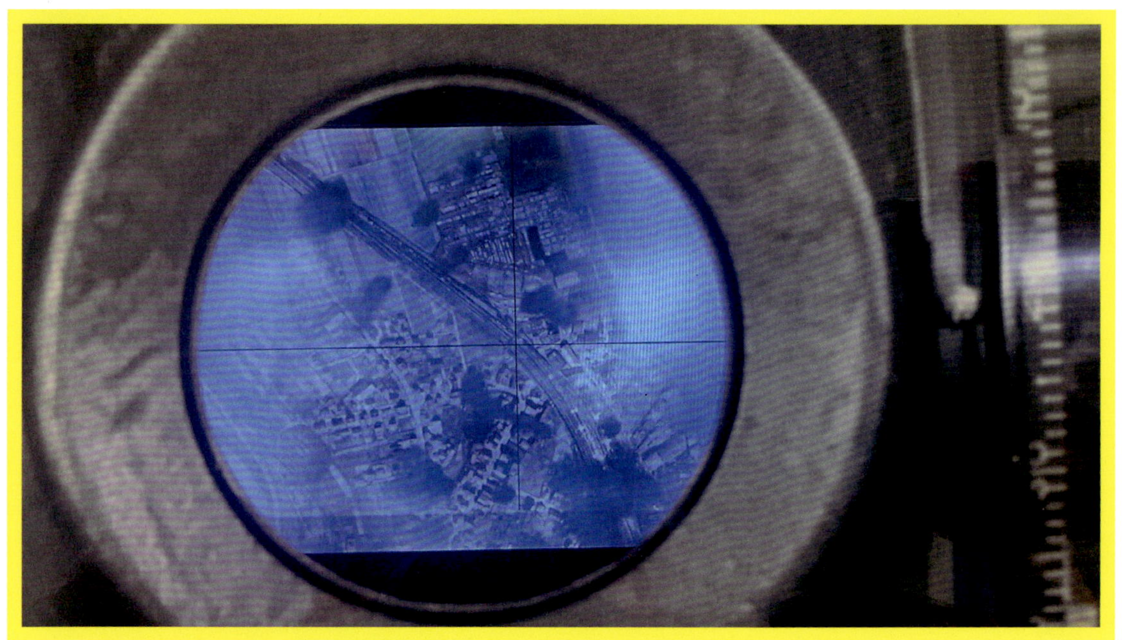

Norden-Bombenzielgerät, Palm Springs Air Museum, Bewegtbild, 4K /
Norden Bombsight Installation, Palm Springs Air Museum, Moving Image, 4K

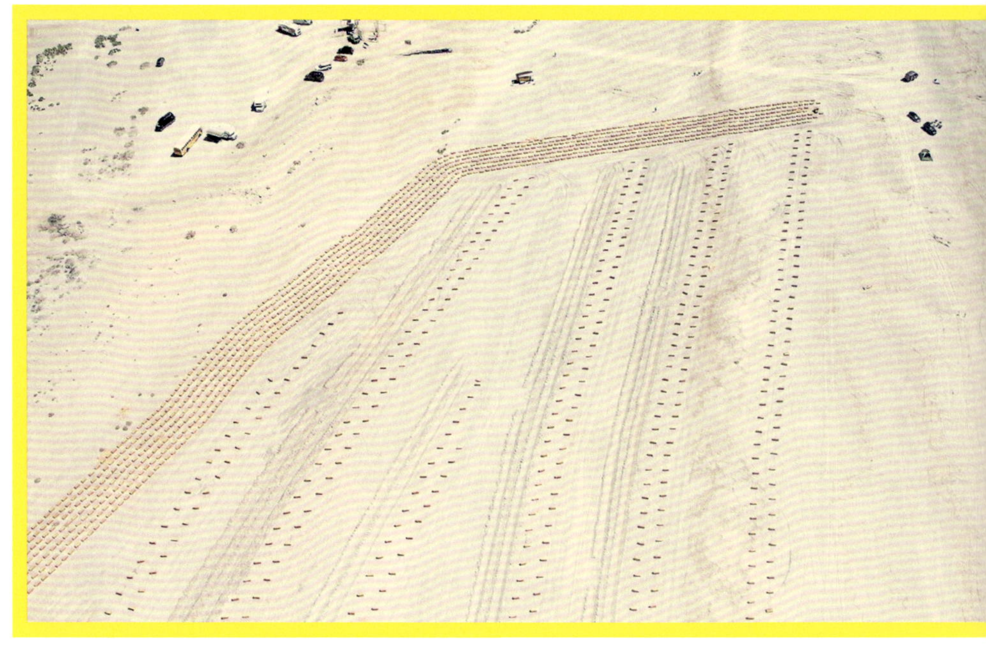

Staubprävention, Saltonsee, Kalifornien, Bewegtbild, Mavic Air2s, 4K /
Dust Prevention, Salton Sea, California, Moving Image, Mavic Air2s, 4K

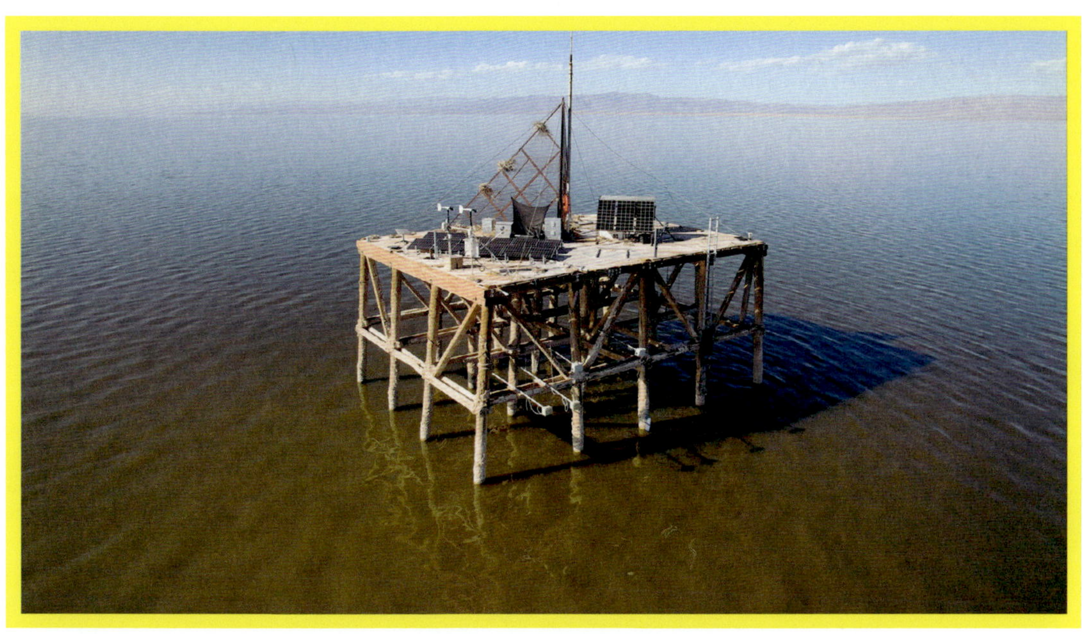

Zielmarkierung für B-29-Bomber, Saltonsee, Kalifornien, Bewegtbild, Mavic Air2s, 4K / B-29 Bomber Target, Salton Sea, California, Moving Image, Mavic Air2s, 4K

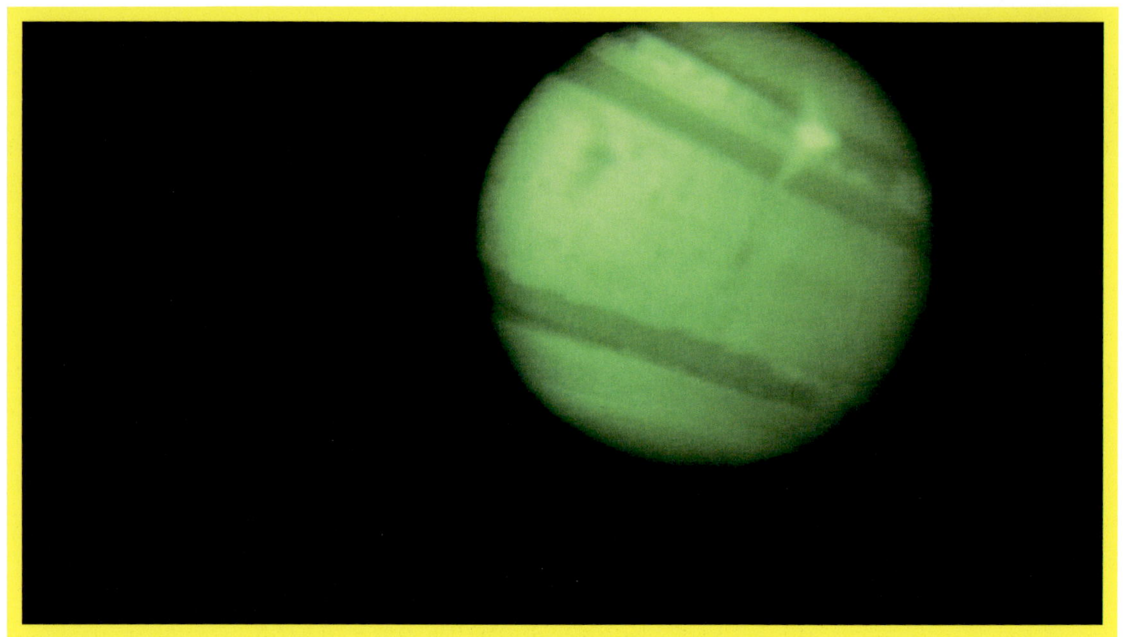

Nachtsichtkamera-Aufnahme an der Fresno-Canyon-Brücke, Kalifornien /
Night-Time Vision Camera Recording Made at Fresno Canyon Bridge, California

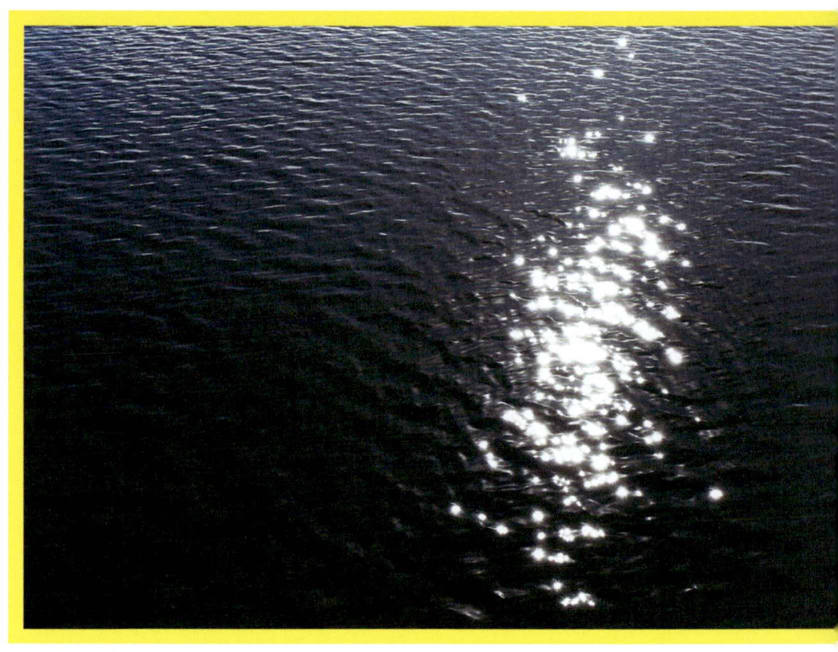

Saltonsee, Kalifornien, Bewegtbild, Mavic Air2s, 4K /
Salton Sea, California, Moving Image, Mavic Air2s, 4K

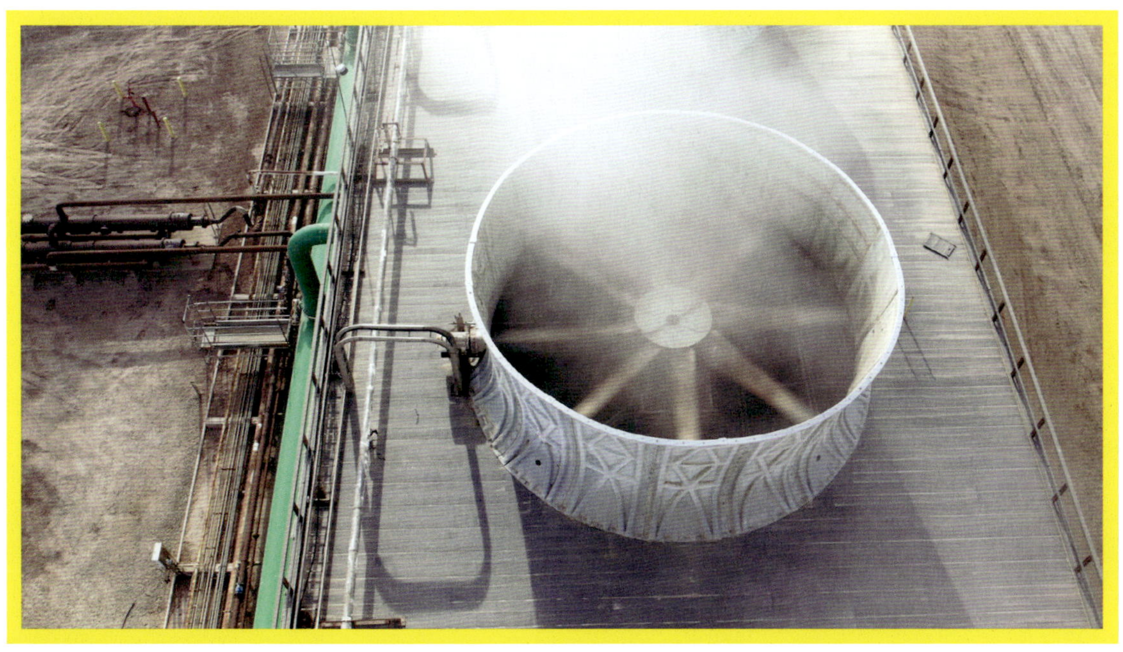

Geothermiekraftwerk, Niland, Kalifornien, Bewegtbild, Mavic Air2s, 4K /
Geothermal Plant, Niland, California, Moving Image, Mavic Air2s, 4K

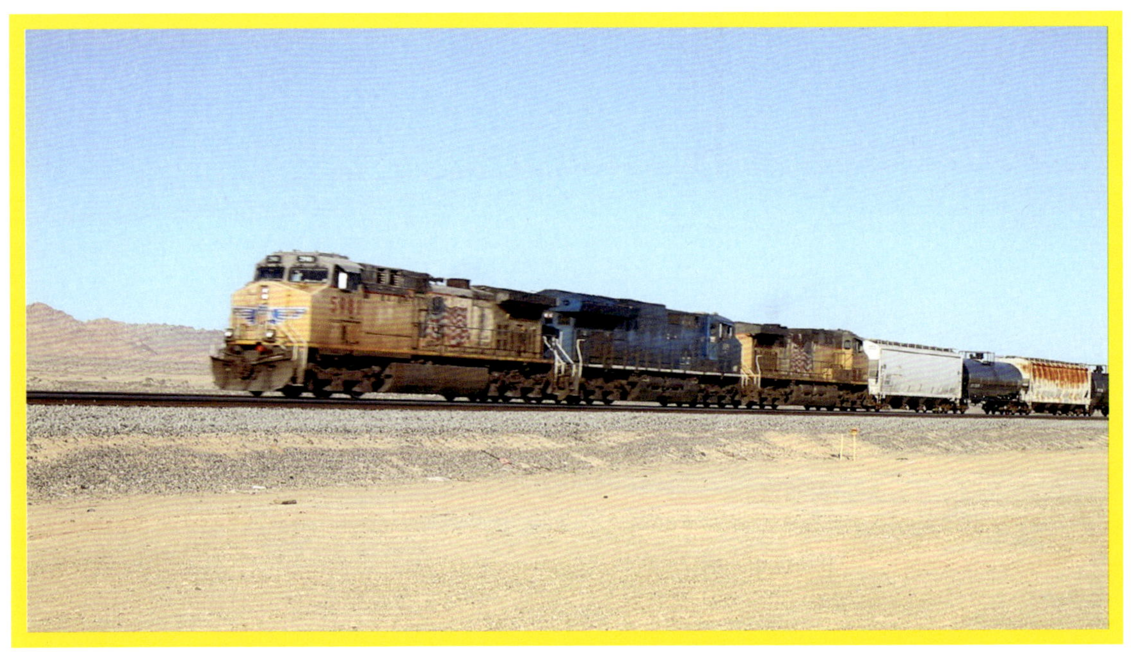

Der unter dem Meeresspiegel liegende Abschnitt (zwischen Indio und Niland) der Bahnstrecke entlang der Union Pacific Sunset Route, Bewegtbild, 4K / The 'Below Sea Level' Part (Between Indio and Niland) of the Train Track Along the Union Pacific Sunset Route, Moving Image, 4K

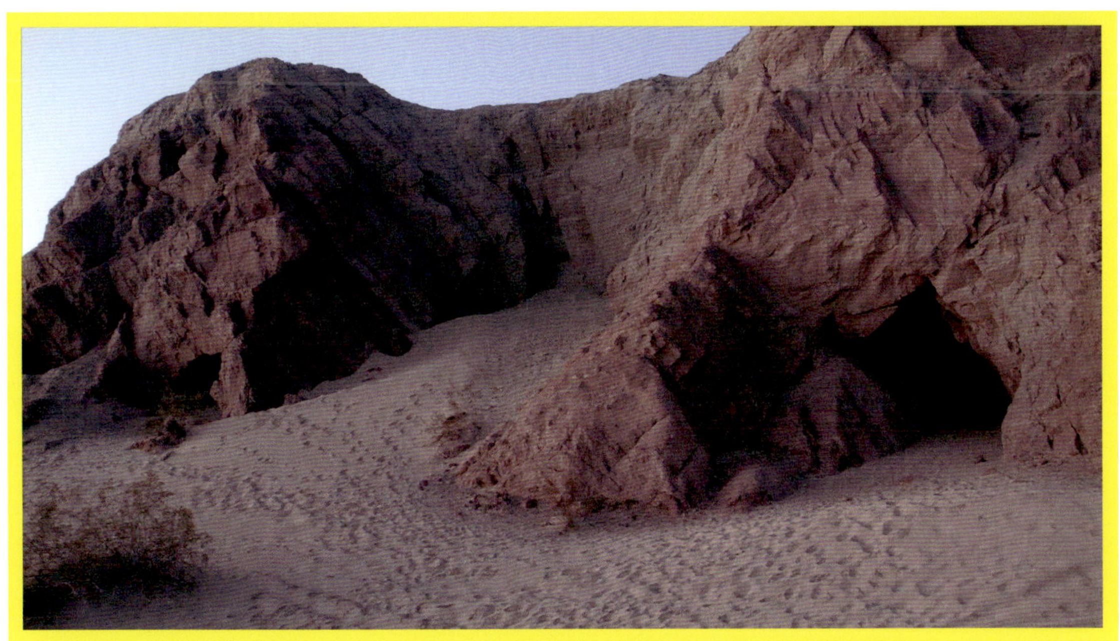

Fledermaushöhlen, Highway 111, Saltonsee, Kalifornien, Bewegtbild, Mavic Air2s, 4K /
Bat Caves, Highway 111, Salton Sea, California , Moving Image, Mavic Air2s, 4K

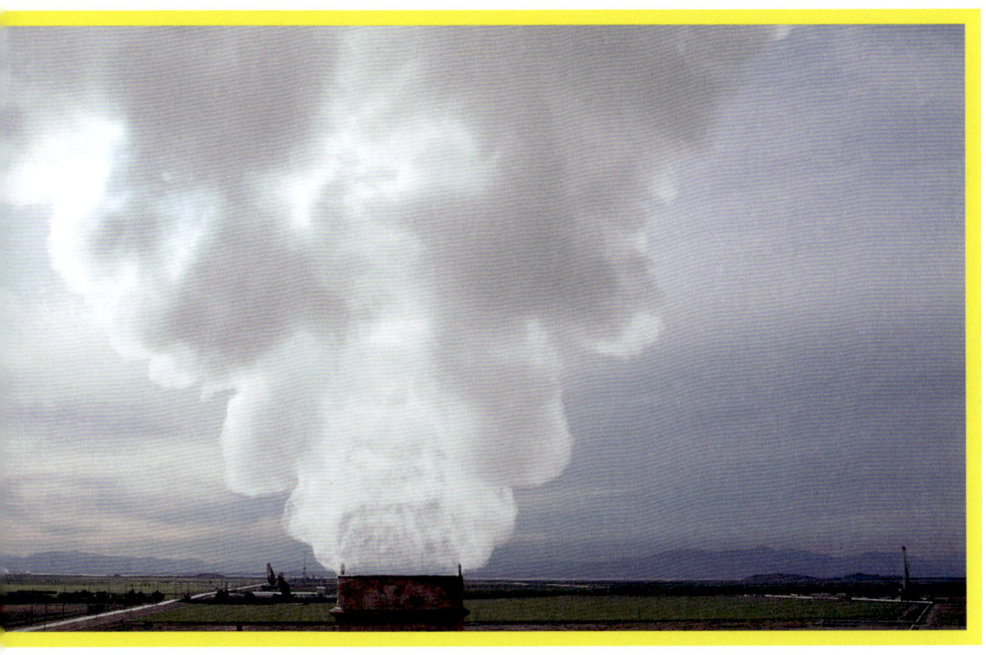

Geothermiekraftwerk, Niland, Kalifornien, Bewegtbild, Mavic Air2s, 4K /
Geothermal Plant, Niland, California, Moving Image, Mavic Air2s, 4K

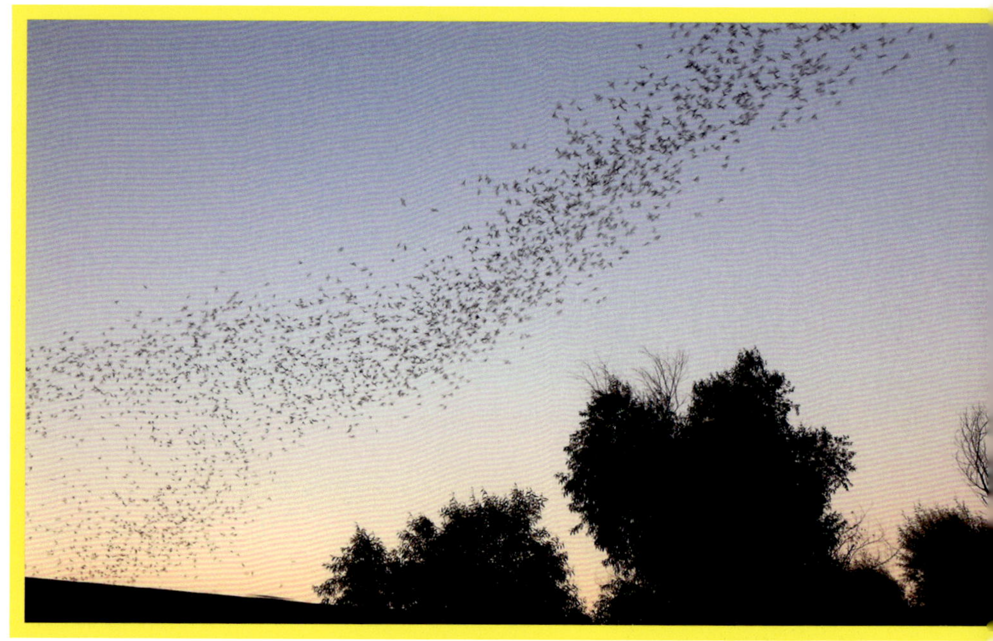

Fledermäuse am Yolo Causeway, Sacramento, Kalifornien, Bewegtbild, 4K /
/ Ribbon of Bats, Yolo Causeway, Sacramento, California, Moving Image, 4K

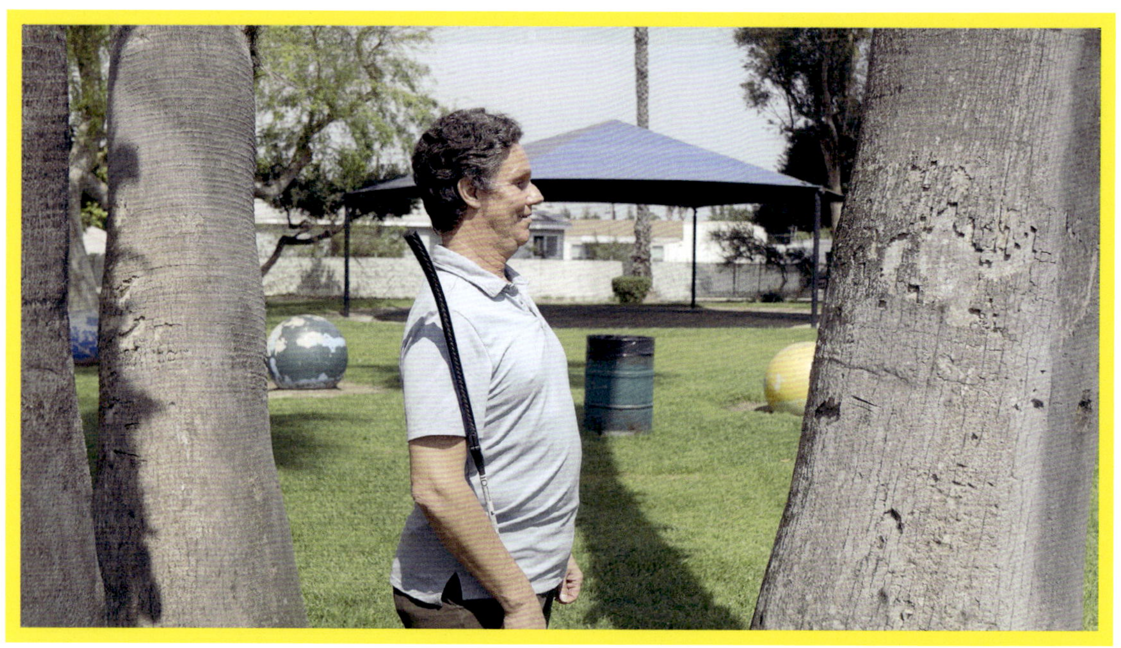

Daniel Kish umgeht Hindernisse, Los Angeles, Kalifornien, Bewegtbild, 4K /
Daniel Kish Navigating Obstacles, Los Angeles, California, Moving Image, 4K

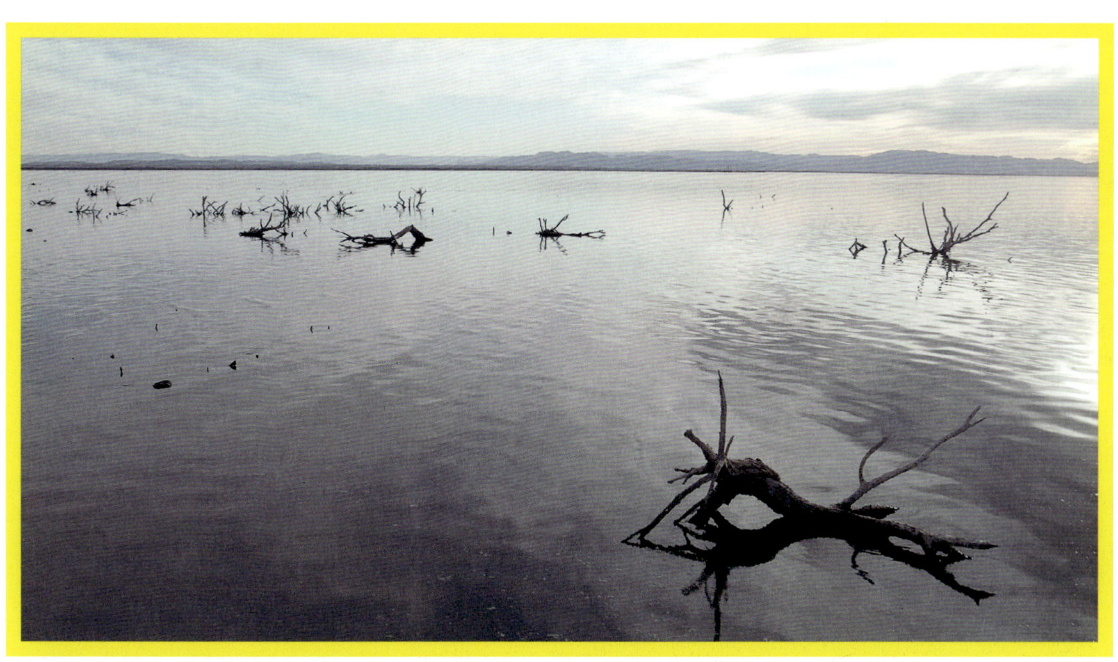

Abgestorbene Bäume, Saltonsee, Kalifornien, Bewegtbild, Mavic Air2s, 4K /
Dead Trees, Salton Sea, California, Moving Image, Mavic Air2s, 4K

Die Kluft zwischen menschlicher Wahrnehmung und technischem Sehen wächst – eine Verschiebung zwischen legitimem und illegitimem Wissen und damit auch dessen, was als unmittelbare Bedrohung gilt. Die Entwicklung einer »mehr-als-menschlichen« Wahrnehmung hat neue Risiken und Ungleichheiten hervorgebracht und eröffnet Möglichkeiten für Ausbeutung und Manipulation. Die 360-Grad-Perspektive, mit der Maschinen – etwa autonome Fahrzeuge – die Welt erfassen, hat unser Erleben von Zeit, Raum und Realität grundlegend verändert. Diese Form der Wahrnehmung wirkt zugleich als Schwelle und Grenze: Sie verwischt die Trennung zwischen objektiver Wahrheit und einer subjektiven, bewussten Begegnung mit der Welt. Das Infragestellen unserer Existenz – der politische Akt, einen automatisierten Apparat gegen seine eigene Bestimmung zu richten – hat eine lange Geschichte in der Kunst, in der die Wahrnehmung und das Bild grundlegend für unser Bewusstsein sind.

The gap is widening between human perception and technological vision, a slippage between legitimate and illegitimate knowledge and subsequently what constitutes an imminent threat. Developments in 'more-than-human' perception have created new forms of risk and inequality and are open to exploitation and manipulation. The elliptical or 360-degree perspective through which machines, such as autonomous vehicles, engage with the world has reshaped our experience of time, space, and reality. This mode of perception acts as both a gateway and a boundary, blurring the line between objective truth and a more subjective, conscious encounter with the world. Challenging how we exist, the political act of turning an automatic apparatus against its own condition has a long history in art, where perception and the image are fundamental to our own consciousness.

Yolo Causeway, Sacramento, Kalifornien, Bewegtbild, Mavic Air2s, 4K

Das Yolo Basin ist eine Überflutungsebene im kalifornischen Central Valley, westlich von Sacramento. Es spielt eine zentrale Rolle im Wassermanagement, in der Landwirtschaft und beim Schutz von Wildtieren. Mit seiner Fertigstellung im Jahr 1916 wurde der Yolo Causeway zu einem wichtigen Bestandteil des kalifornischen Fernstraßennetzes – als erste ganzjährig und bei jedem Wetter befahrbare Autobrücke über das Yolo Basin zwischen Sacramento und Davis. Mit einer Länge von 5 Kilometern, einer Höhe von rund 6 Metern und einer Breite von etwa 6,5 Metern galt sie damals als die längste Betonstraße der Welt. Unterhalb der Brücke nisten Schätzungen zufolge jedes Jahr rund 250.000 Mexikanische Bulldoggfledermäuse (Tadarida brasiliensis). Fledermäuse gehören zu den effektivsten Insektenjägern der Natur. Die Betonbrücke spendet ihnen Wärme, während Dehnungsfugen und Spalten Schutz vor Fressfeinden bieten.

Yolo Causeway, Sacramento, California, Moving Image, Mavic Air2s, 4K

The Yolo Basin is a vast floodplain in California's Central Valley, primarily west of Sacramento. It is crucial in water management, agriculture, and wildlife conservation. When it was completed in 1916, the Yolo Causeway became a vital link in the California state highway system because it was the first all-year, all-weather automobile bridge across the Yolo Basin between Sacramento and Davis. At 3.1 miles long, twenty feet high and twenty-one feet wide, it was considered the longest concrete highway in the world at that time. It is said that under the causeway there are approximately 250,000 Mexican free-tailed bats (*Tadarida brasiliensis*) nesting each year. Bats are one of nature's most effective insect predators. The concrete bridge provides them with warmth, and the expansion joints and crevices protect them from predators.

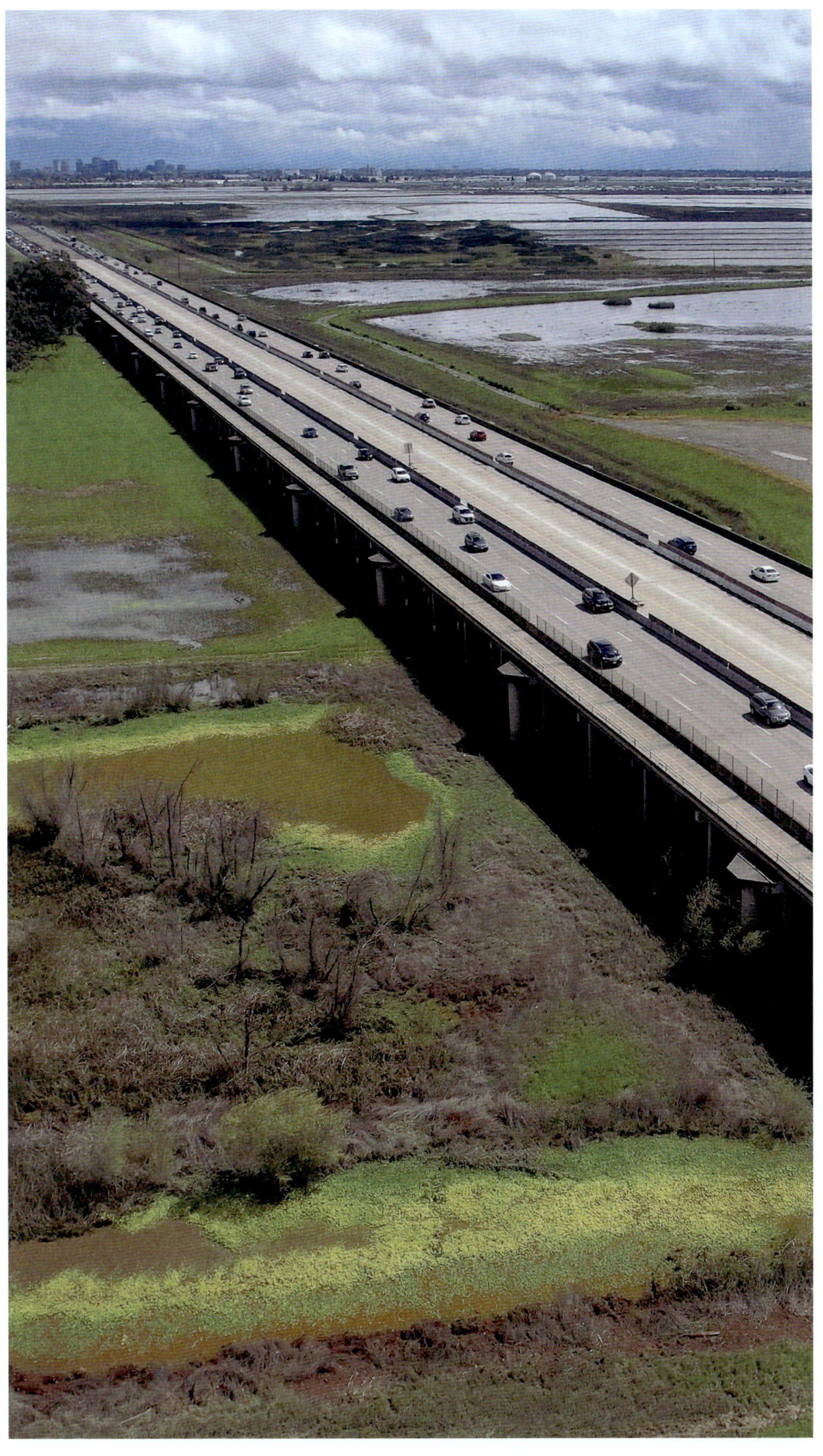

Unter dem Yolo Causeway, Sacramento, Kalifornien

In ihrem Essay »In Free Fall. A Thought Experiment on Vertical Perspective« untersucht Hito Steyerl, inwiefern der perspektivische Blick mit sozialen, politischen und technologischen Dynamiken verknüpft ist. Sie verfolgt die historischen Ursprünge der perspektivischen Darstellung bis zum europäischen Kolonialismus und Kapitalismus zurück und zeigt auf, wie diese Techniken die Kartierung der Welt und die Visualisierung von Macht beeinflusst haben.

Beneath the Yolo Causeway, Sacramento, California

In her essay 'In Free Fall: A Thought Experiment on Vertical Perspective', Hito Steyerl explores how perspective is tied to social, political, and technological dynamics. She traces the historical roots of perspective drawing to European colonialism and capitalism, showing how these techniques shaped world mapping and power visualisation.

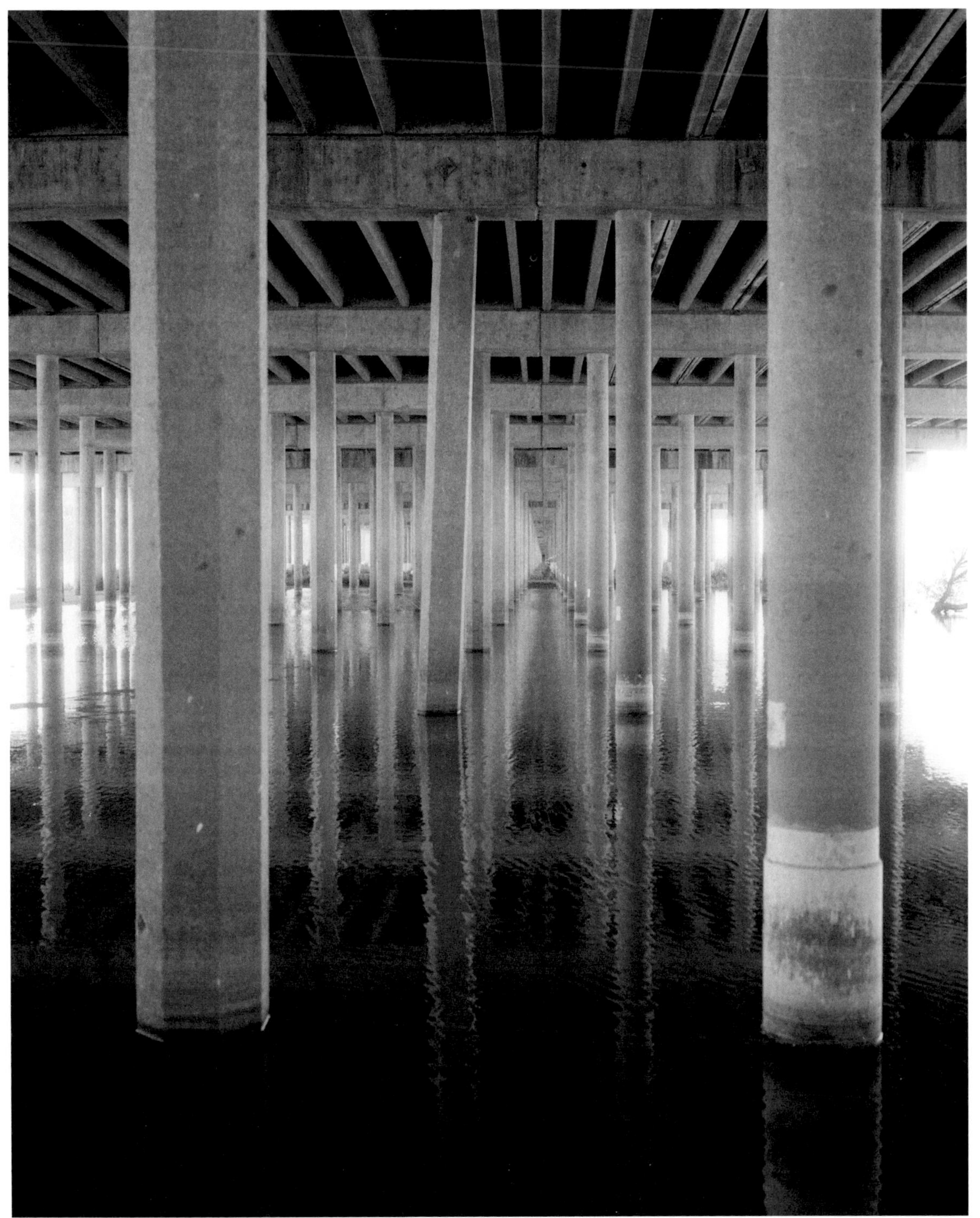

Testgelände des Transportation Research Center (TRC), Atwater, Kalifornien

Das Transportation Research Center in Kalifornien testet moderne Fahrassistenzsysteme sowie automatisiertes Fahren und Kollisionsvermeidung mithilfe simulierter Stadtlandschaften. Der Standort ist ein ehemaliger Militärflughafen, auf dem ab 1946 auch B-29-Bomber und das Strategische Luftkommando (Strategic Air Command) stationiert waren. Die Bilder zeigen die simulierte Umgebung der Trainingsareale, in denen autonome Fahrzeuge das Navigieren auf unebenem Terrain erlernen.

Assets at the Transportation Research Center (TRC), Atwater, California

The Transportation Research Center in California tests advanced driving systems and automated driving and collision avoidance using cityscape simulation assets. The location is a historical military airport where B-29 bombers and the Strategic Air Command were based from 1946. These images examine the simulated landscape of the test centre's training areas where autonomous vehicles learn to navigate uneven terrain.

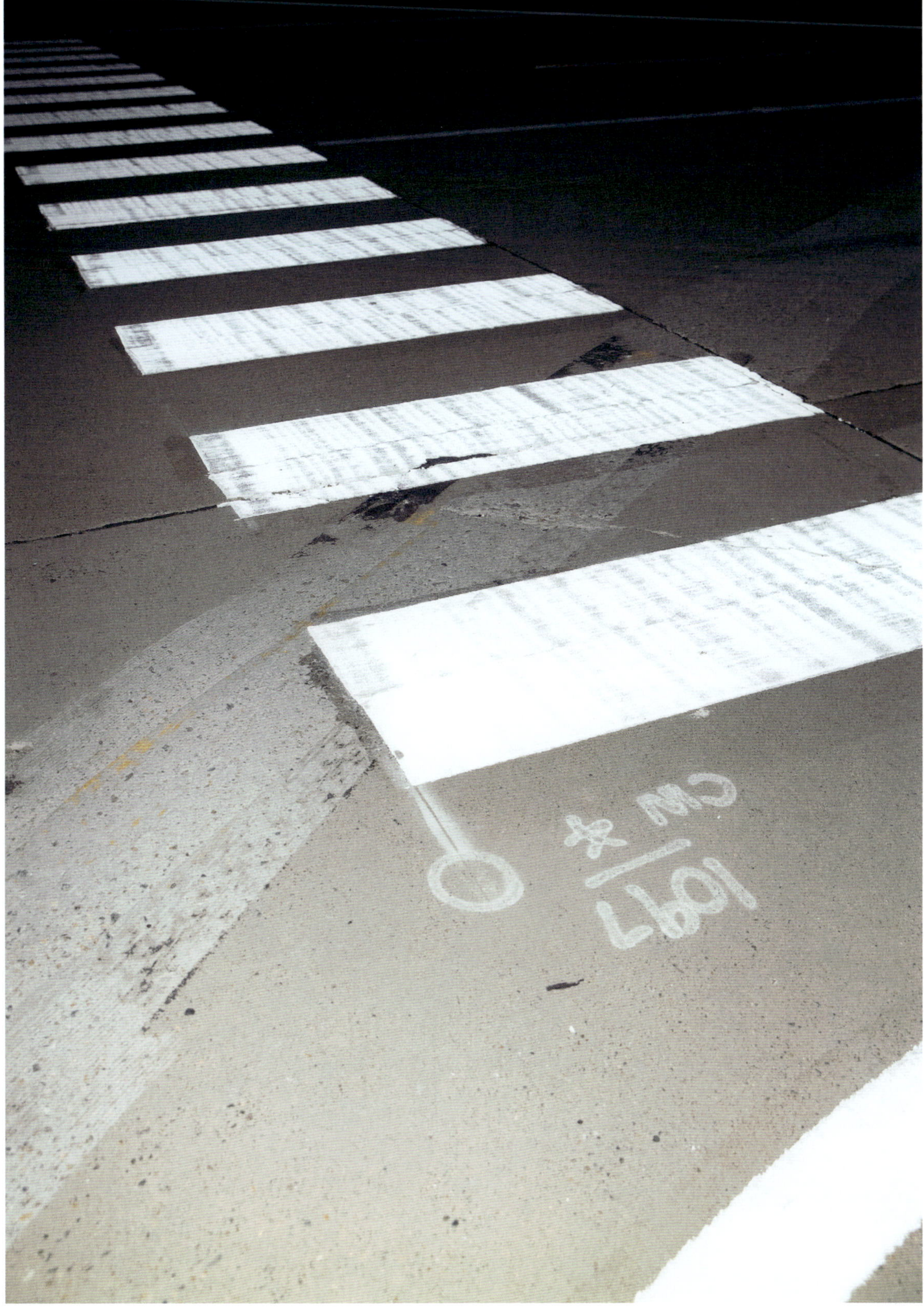
CW
1097

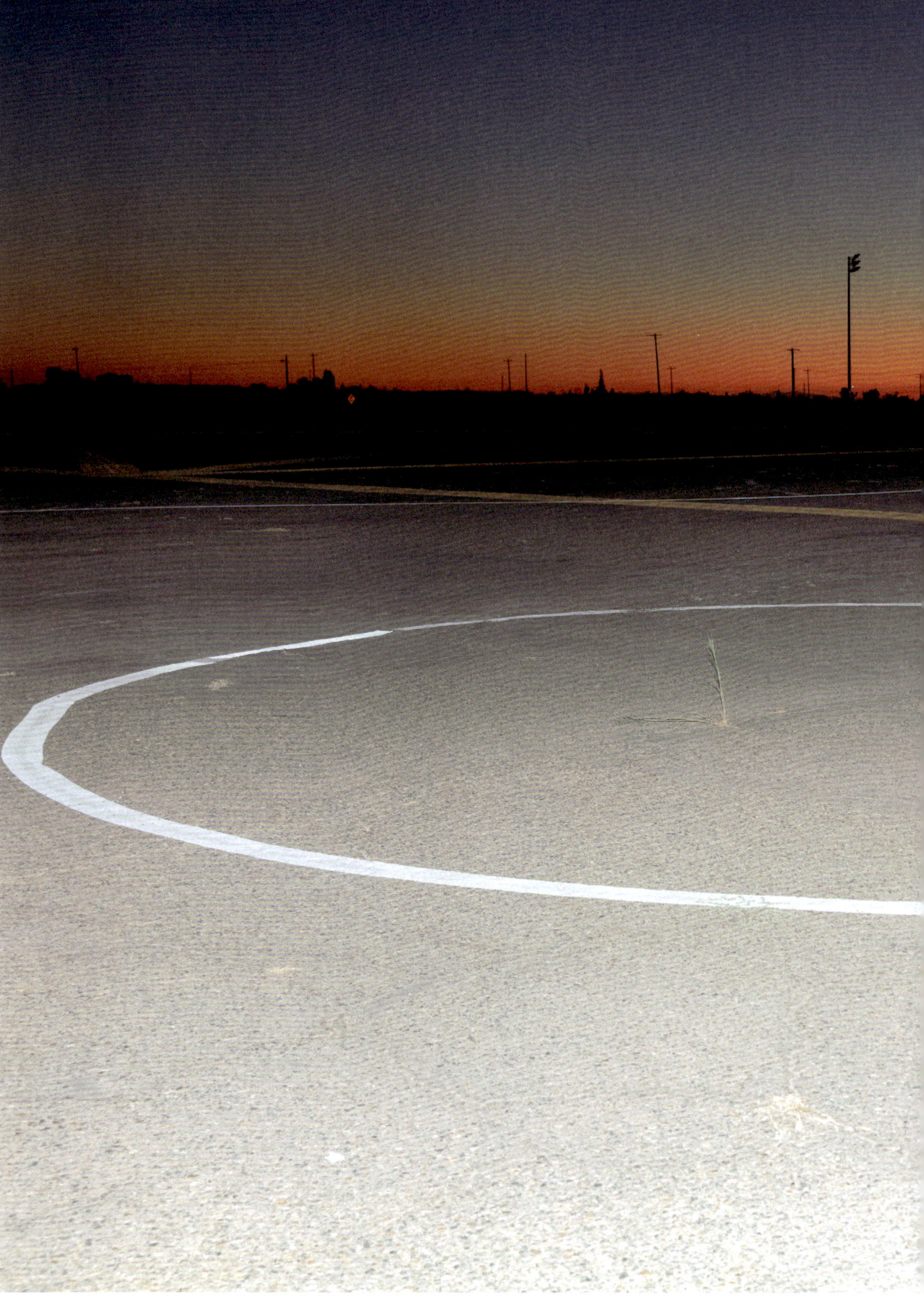

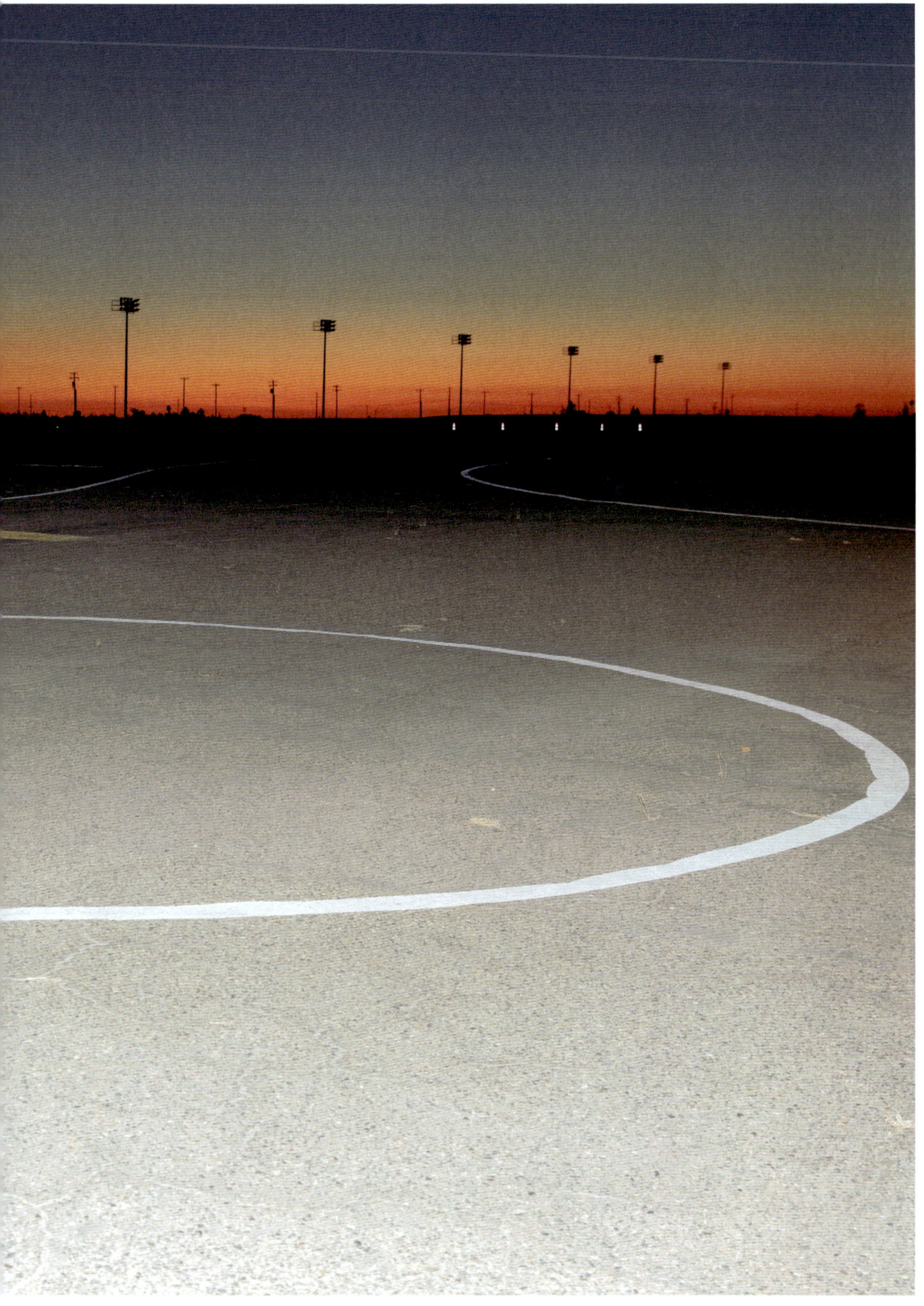

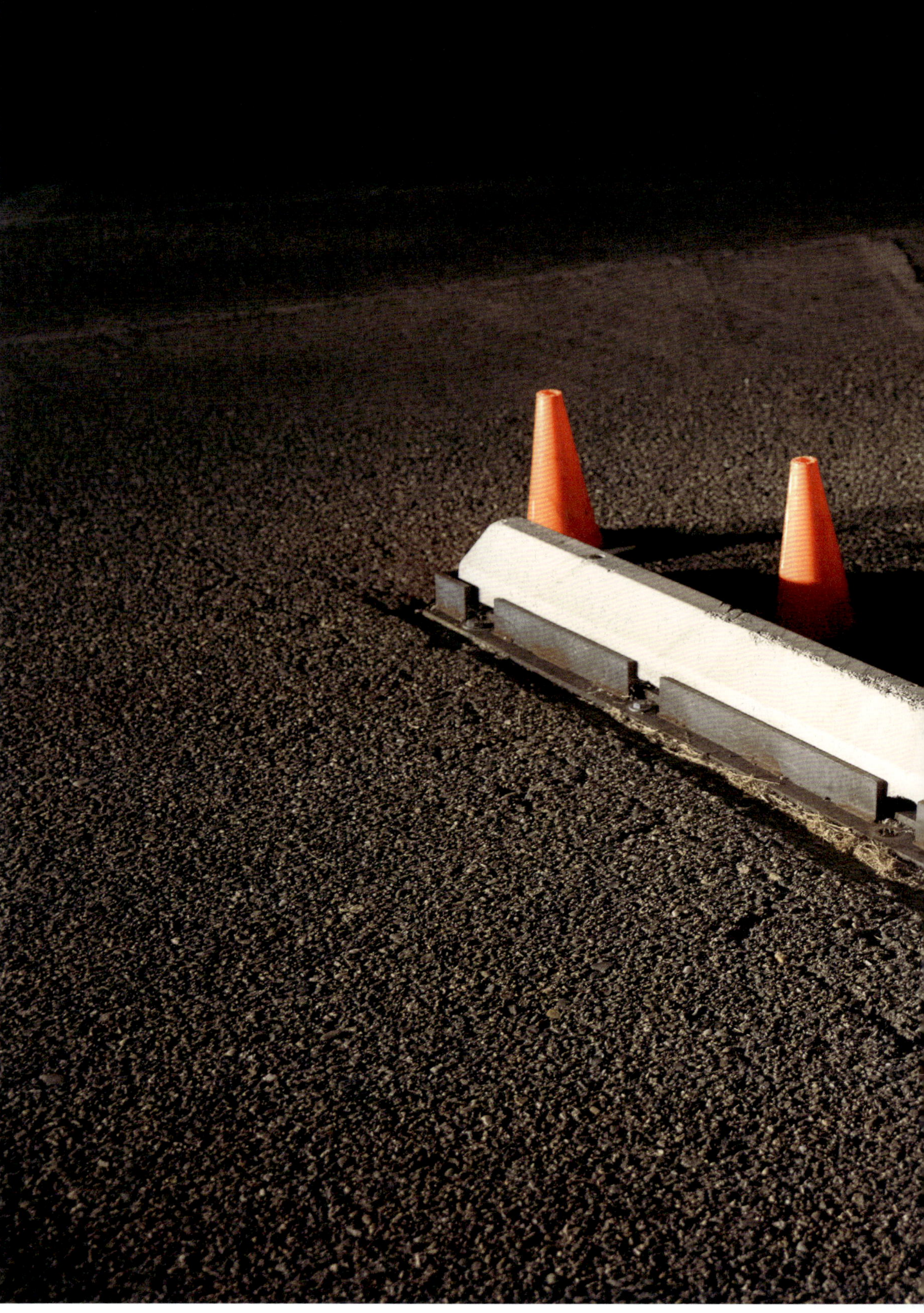

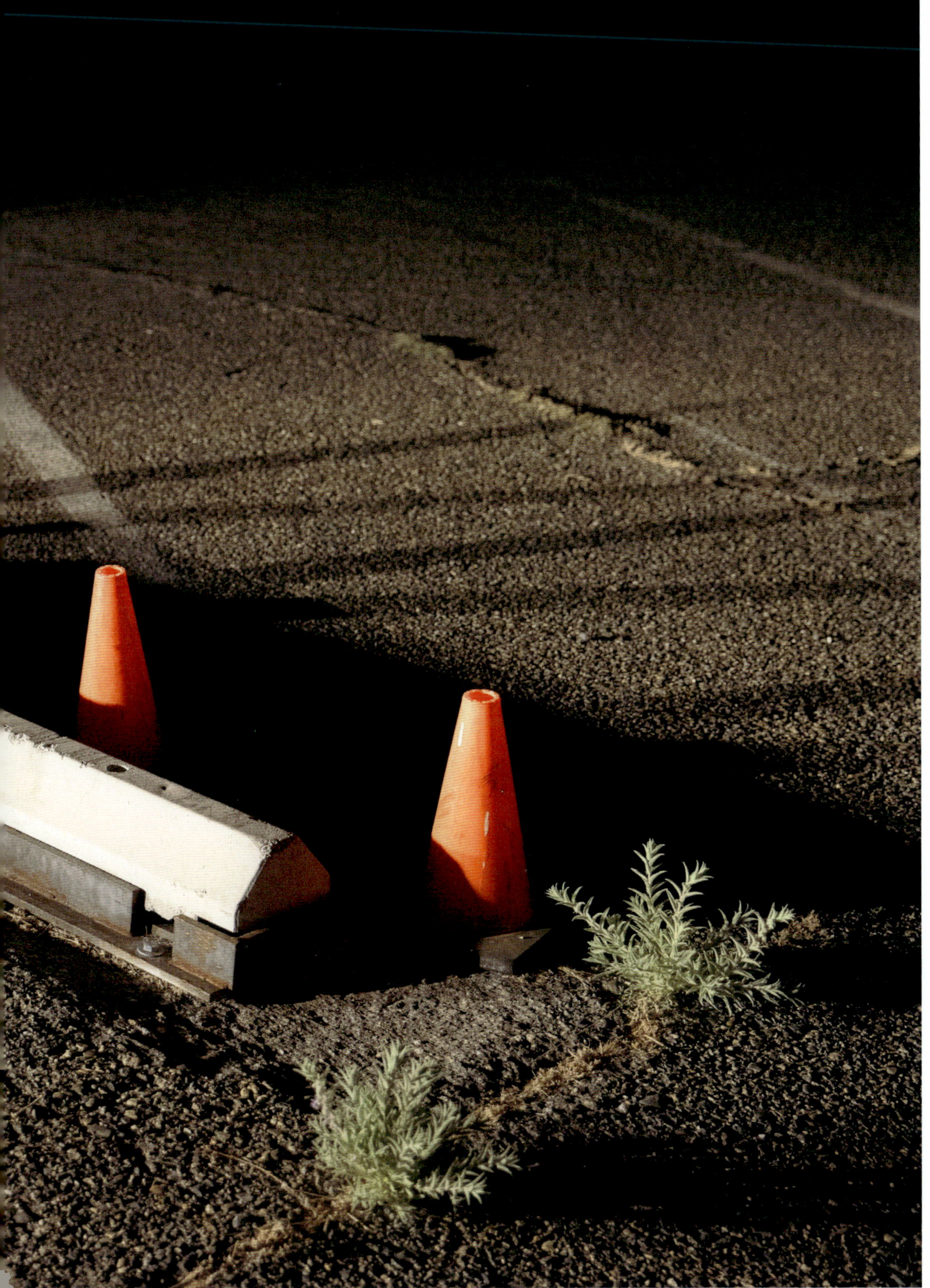

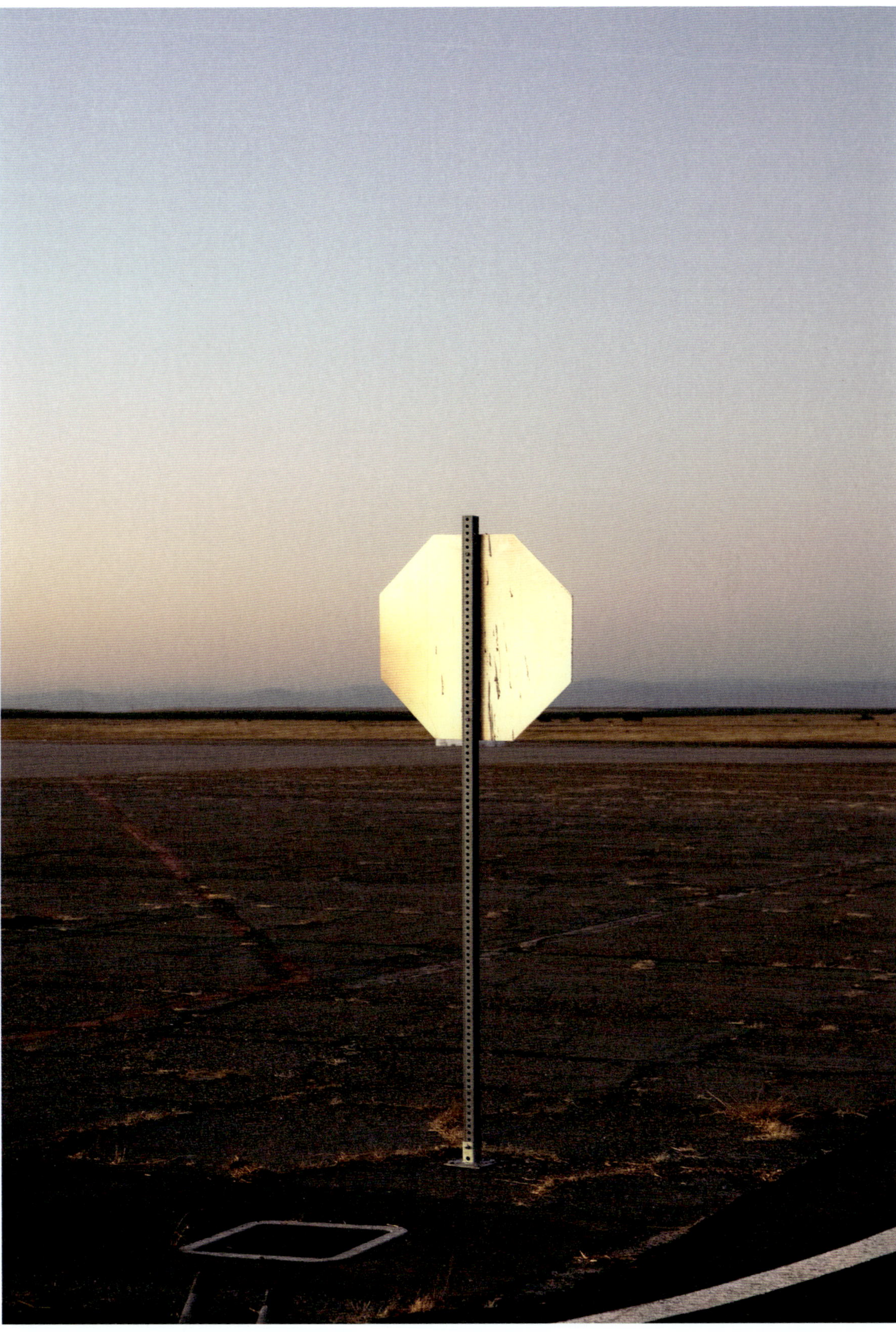

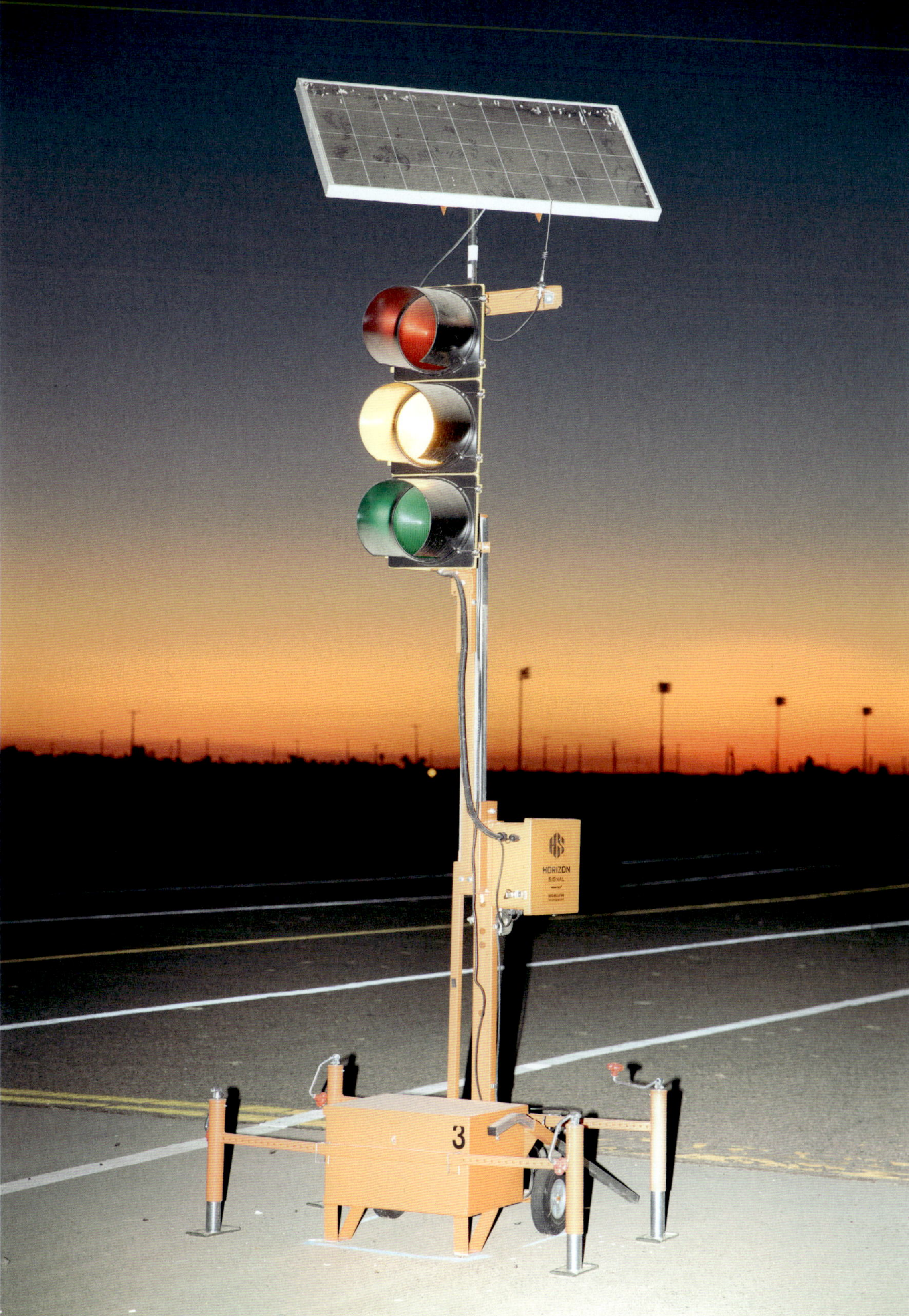
HORIZON
SIGNAL
3

Selbstporträt, aufgenommen mit einem Helm.ai-System vor dem Facebook-Hauptsitz mithilfe eines semantischen Vollbild-Segmentierungssystems, Menlo Park, Kalifornien

Deep Teaching™ ist eine firmeneigene unbegleitete Lerntechnologie von Helm.ai. Sie kombiniert Praxisdaten, Deep Learning und angewandte Mathematik, um anpassungsfähige, leistungsstarke Basismodelle in großem Maßstab zu trainieren. Diese Modelle werden auf umfangreichen Datensätzen trainiert und mit generativer KI weiterentwickelt. Im Unterschied zum Stufe-4-System von Waymo passt sich dieses System automatisch an neue geografische Gegebenheiten und unbekannte Fahrbedingungen an; durch Feinabstimmung kann zugleich ein effizienter Umgang mit seltenen und komplexen Randfällen ermöglicht werden.

Es gibt verschiedene Szenarien, in denen autonome Fahrzeuge auf Betriebsprobleme stoßen können. Dazu gehören etwa das Platzieren lebensgroßer Puppen auf der Fahrbahn, das Verändern von Verkehrsschildern, das gezielte Ausrichten von Lichtquellen auf LiDAR-Sensoren (wodurch reflektiertes Licht fehlgedeutet und ein Hindernis nicht erkannt werden könnte) oder das Projizieren dreidimensionaler Bilder auf die Straßenoberfläche. Zwar zeichnen autonome Fahrzeuge unter normalen Bedingungen kontinuierlich Alltagsdaten auf, doch die Erfassung seltener Vorfälle, die potenziell zu Unfällen führen könnten, bleibt eine Herausforderung.

Self-Portrait Recording Made with a Helm.ai System in Front of Facebook Headquarters, Using a Full Scene Semantic Segmentation System, Menlo Park, California

Deep Teaching™ is Helm.ai's proprietary unsupervised learning method. It combines real-world data, deep learning, and applied mathematics to train adaptable, high-performance foundation models at scale. Their models are trained on large-scale datasets and enhanced using generative AI. Unlike the Level 4 system employed by Waymo, this system adapts automatically to new geographies and unfamiliar driving conditions, while fine-tuning allows for efficient handling of rare and complex edge cases.

There are a number of scenarios in which an autonomous vehicle might encounter operational difficulties. These include placing life-sized mannequins on the road, modifying road signs, directing light sources at LiDAR sensors (potentially causing the system to misinterpret the reflected light and fail to detect an obstacle ahead), or projecting three-dimensional images onto the road surface. While autonomous vehicles continuously record routine driving data under normal conditions, collecting data on rare incidents that could potentially result in accidents remains challenging.

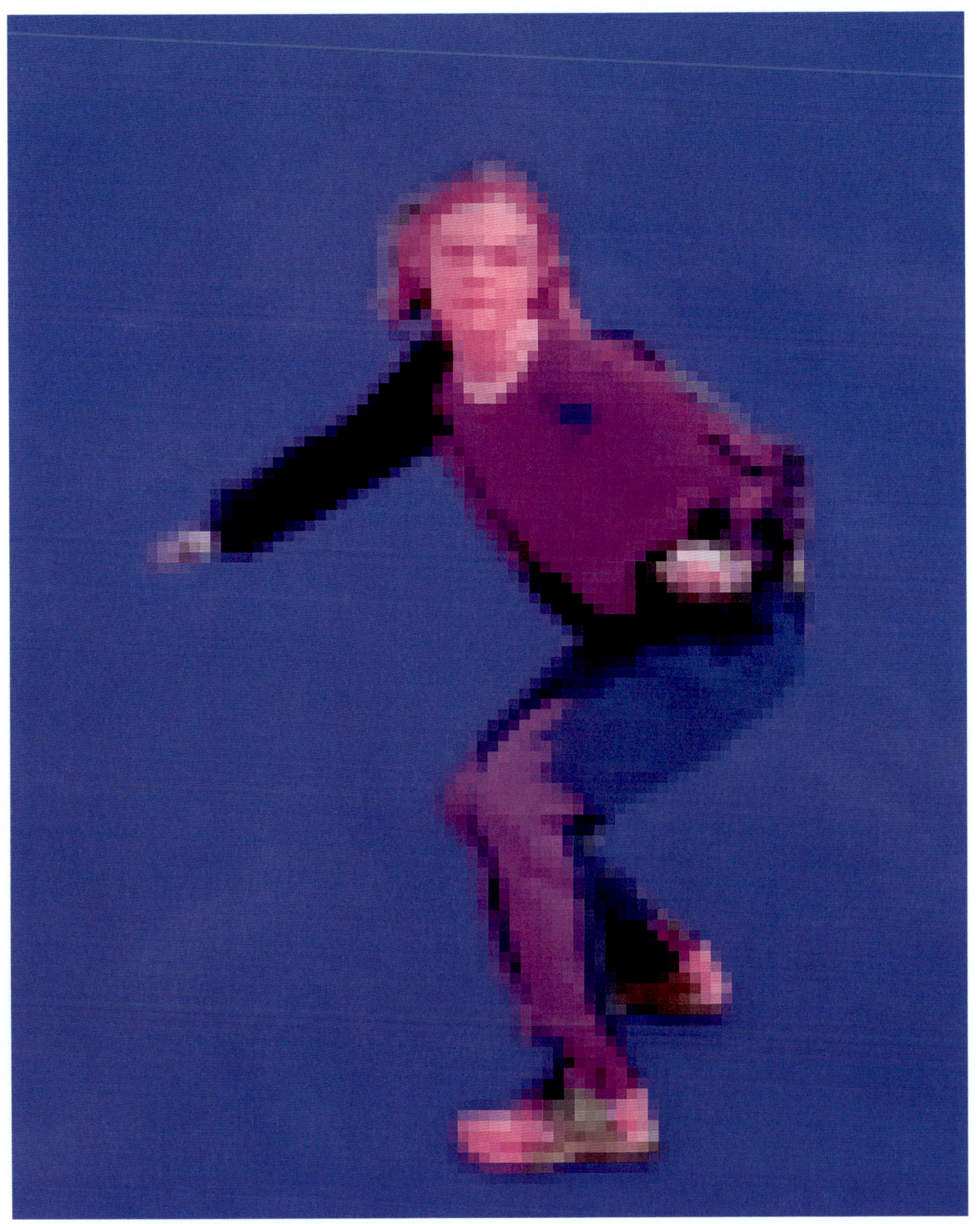

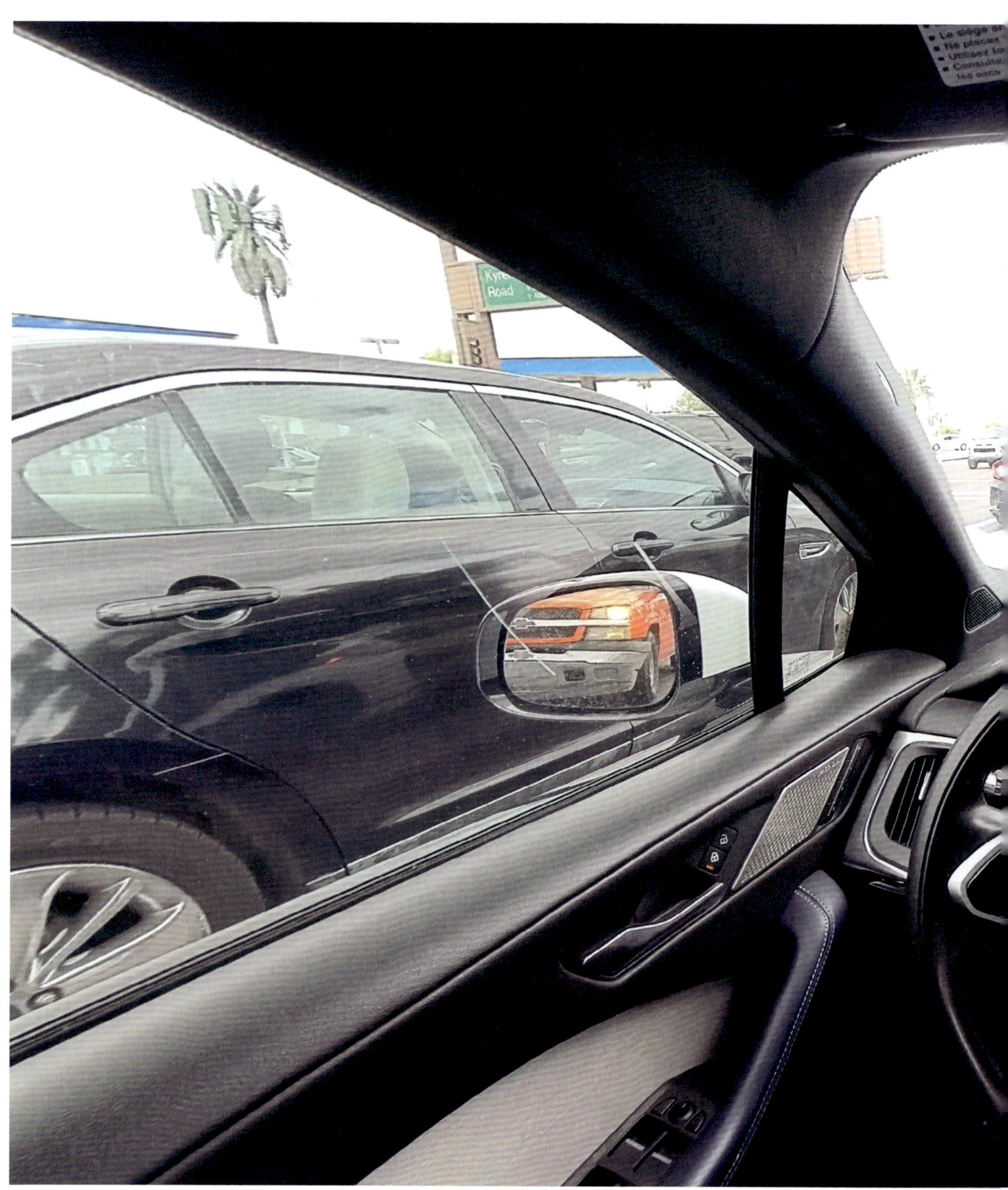
Road

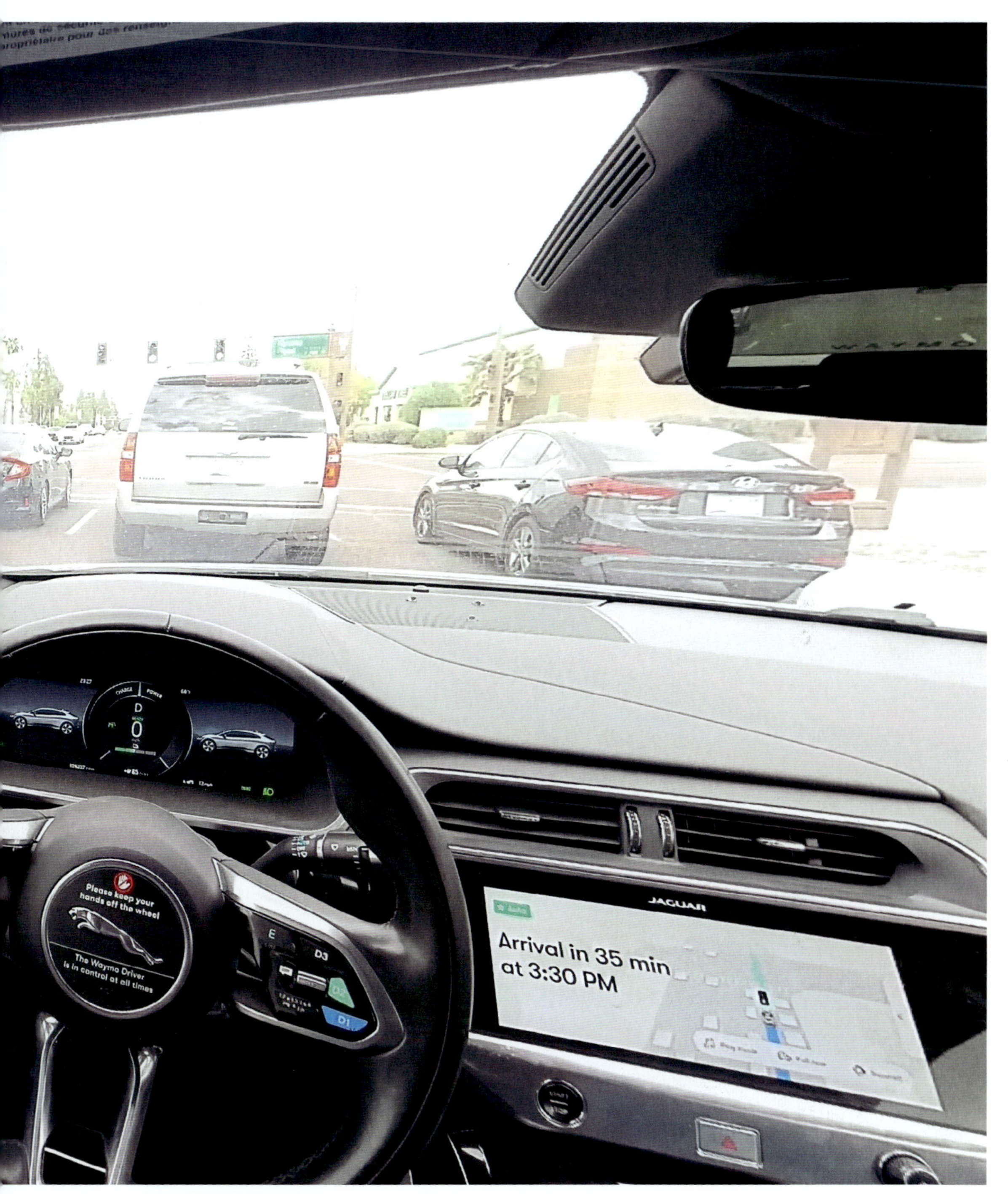
Please keep your hands off the wheel
The Waymo Driver is in control at all times
JAGUAR
Arrival in 35 min
at 3:30 PM

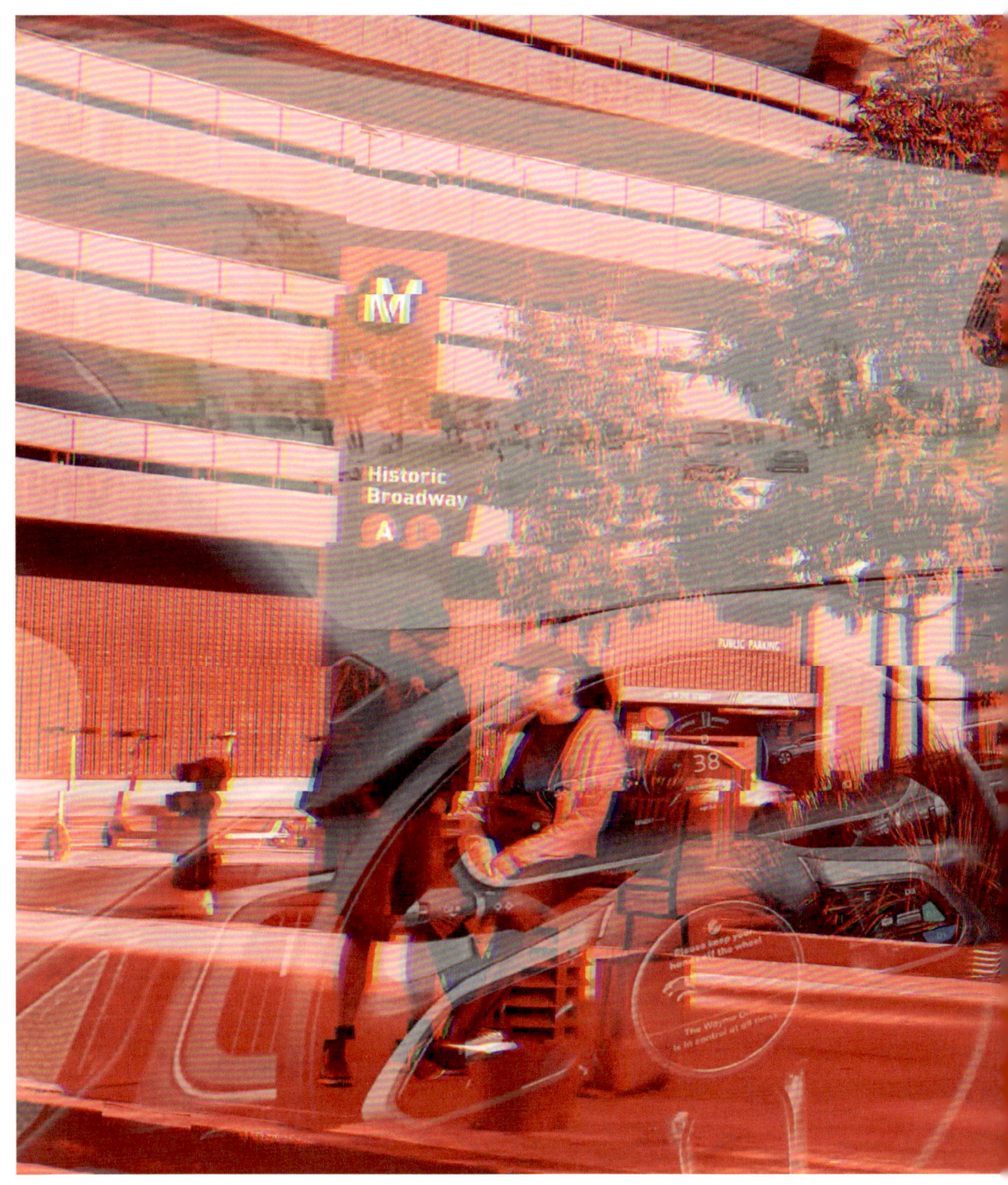
Historic
Broadway
A
PUBLIC PARKING
38

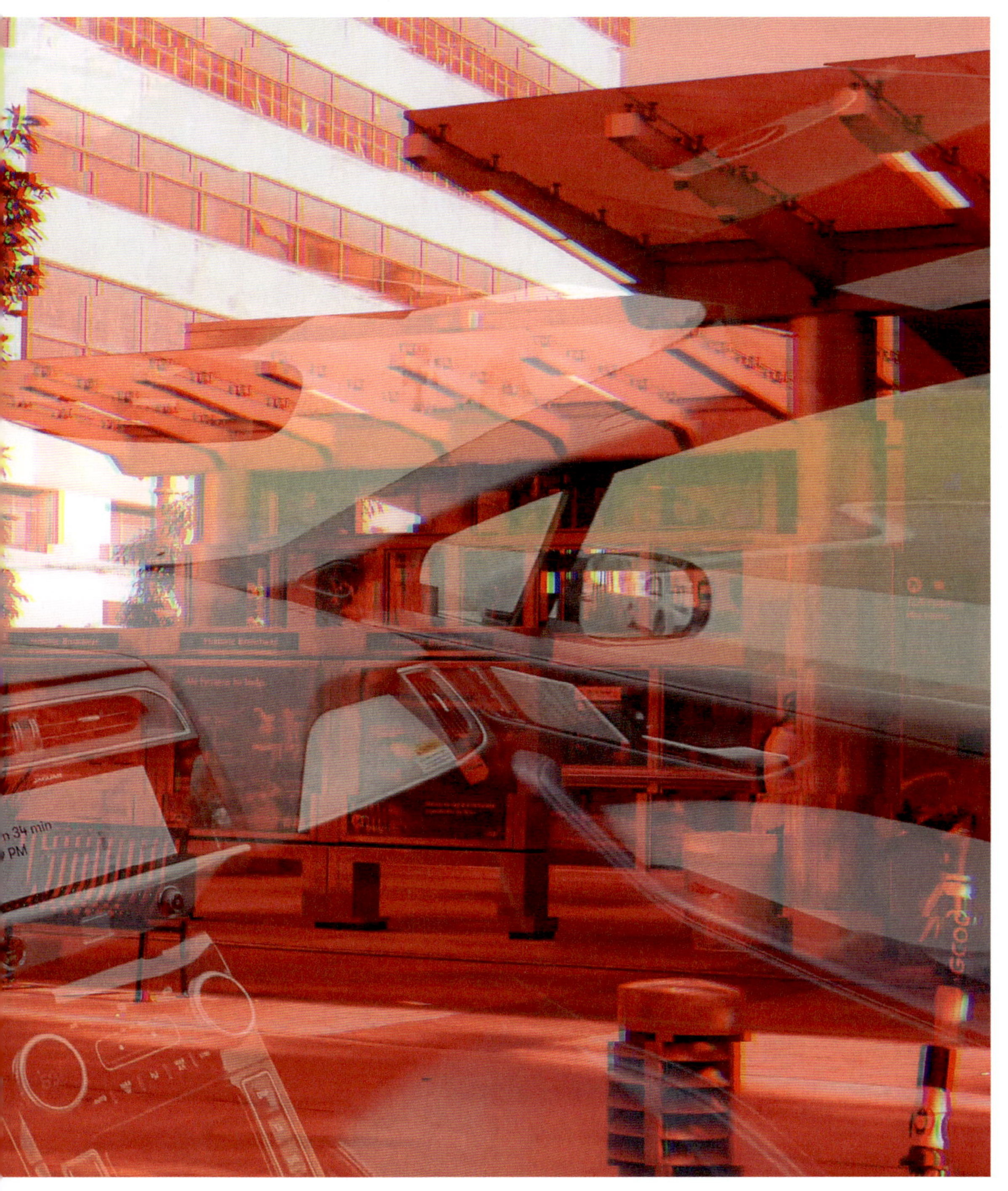
n 34 min
PM

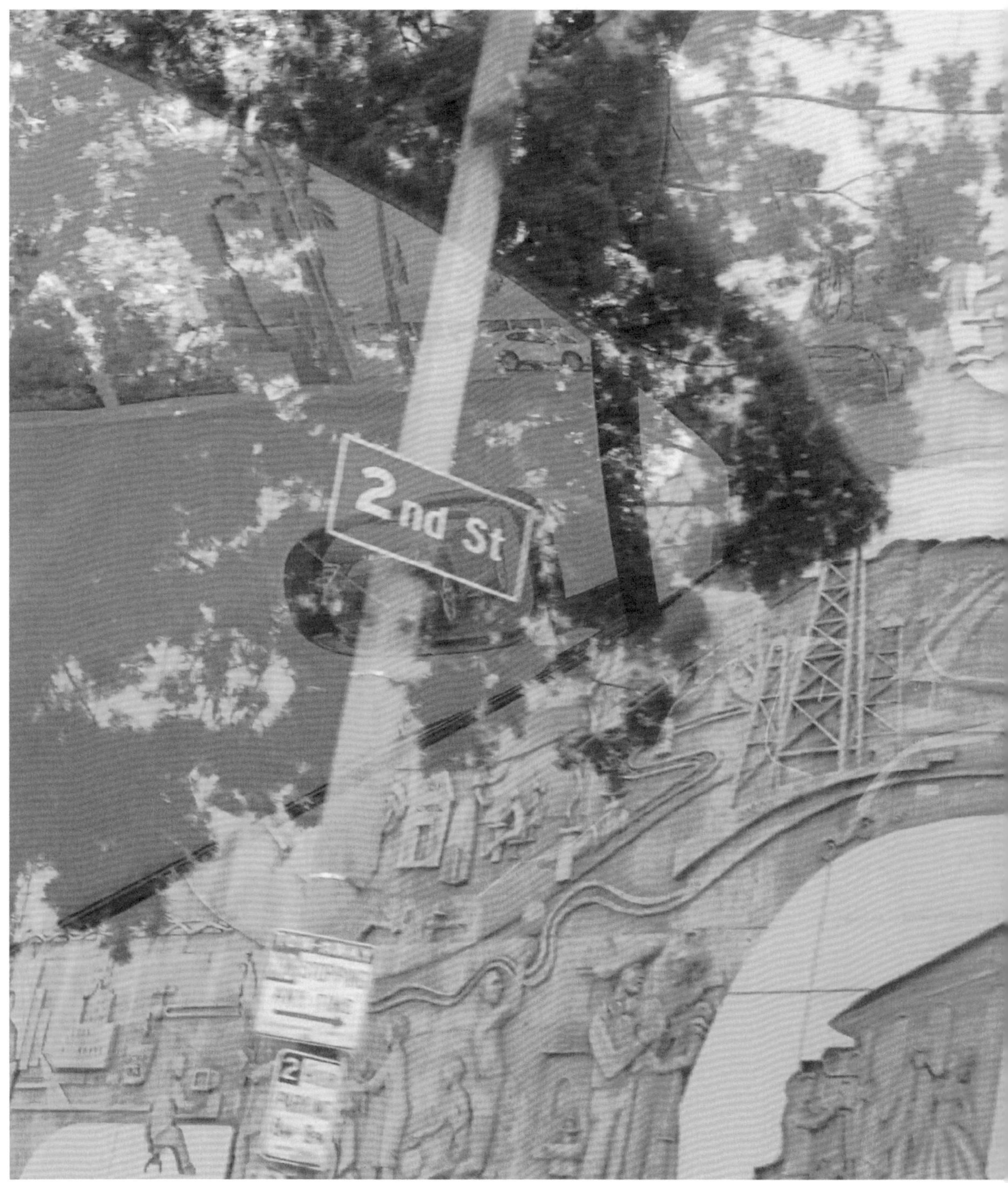
2nd St

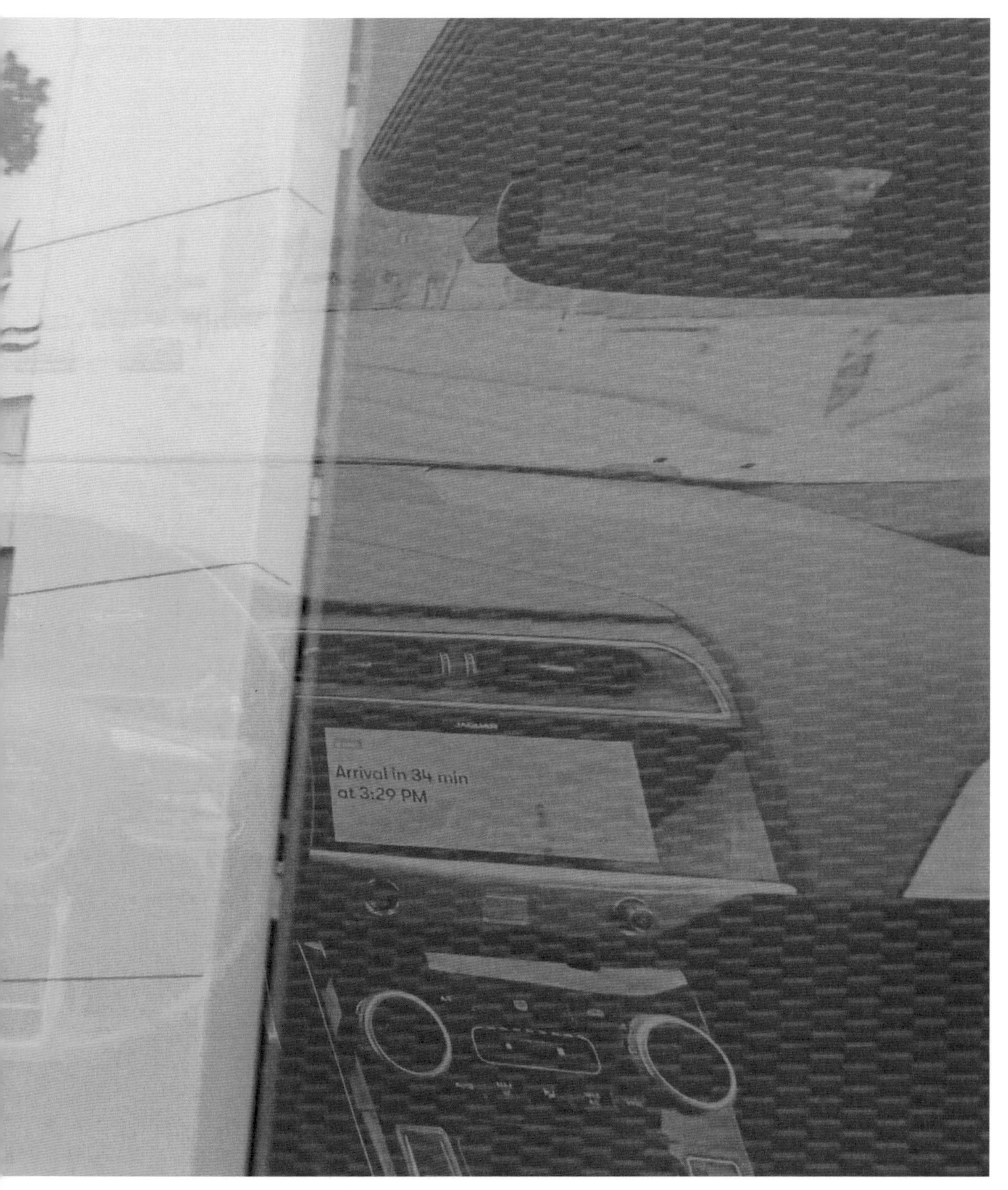
Arrival in 34 min
at 3:29 PM

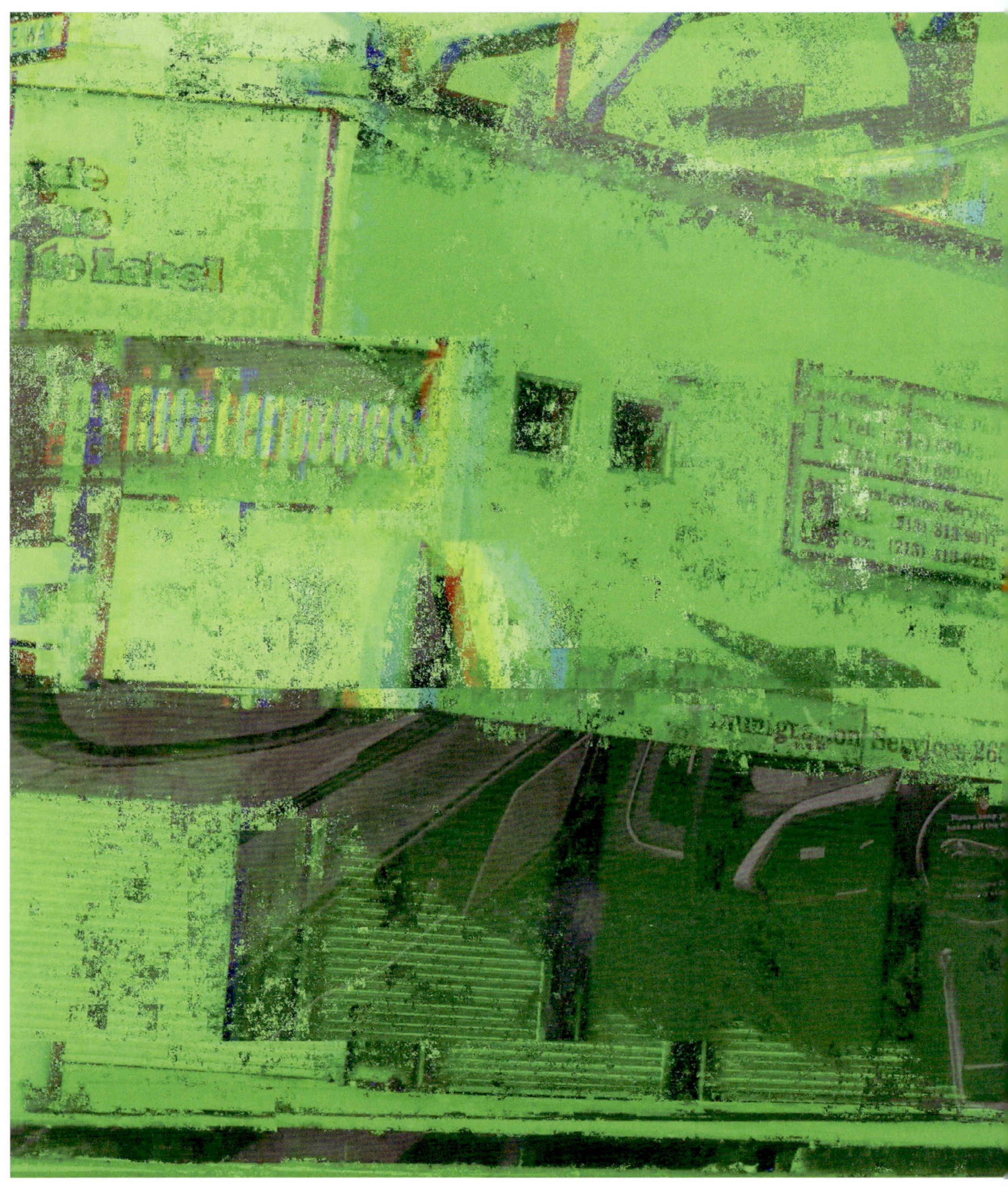

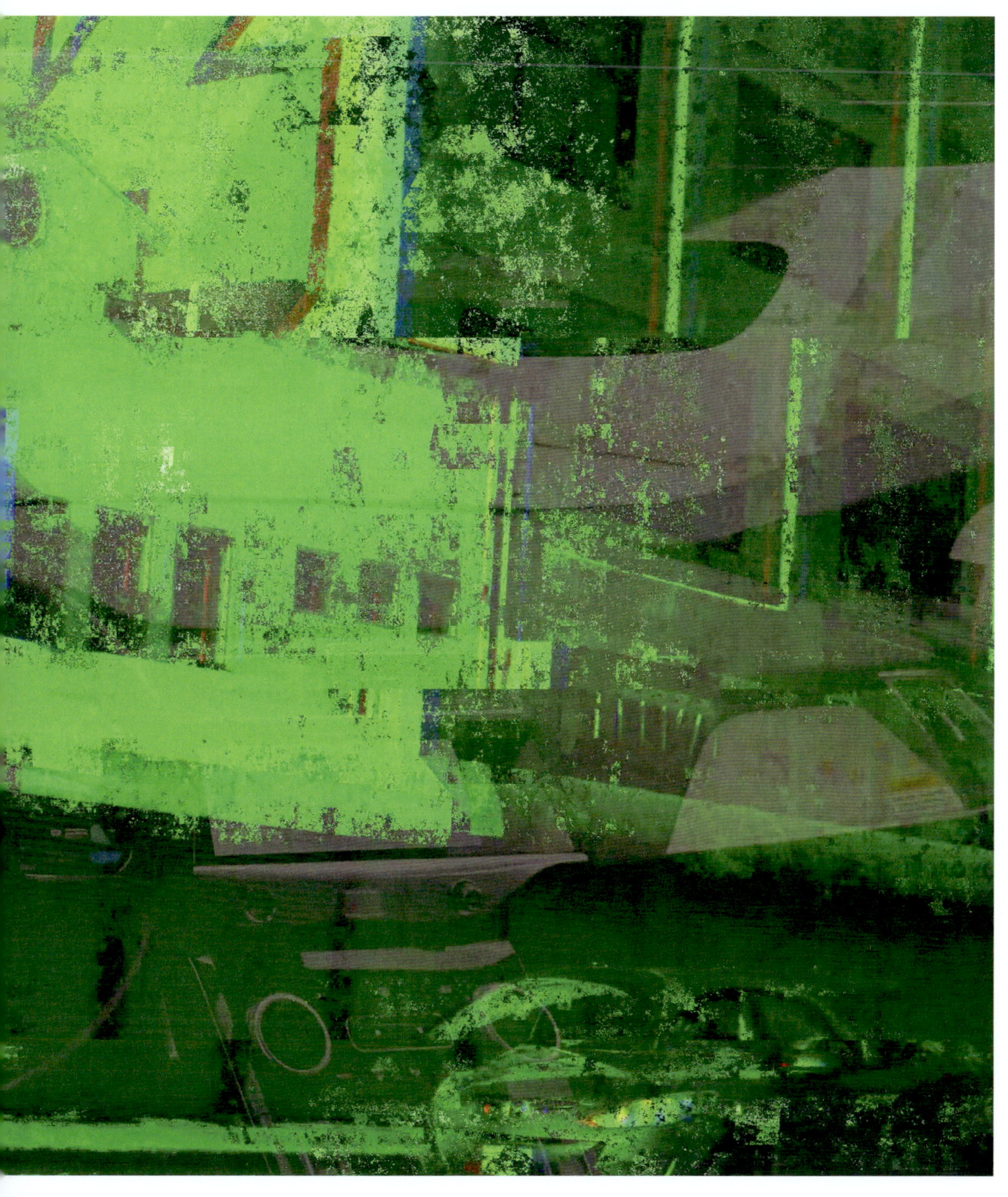

360-Grad-Videoaufzeichnung aus einem Waymo-Robotaxi während Fahrten in Phoenix, San Francisco und Los Angeles

Waymo-Fahrzeuge operieren auf Autonomiestufe 4. Das bedeutet, sie können innerhalb festgelegter, klar definierter Umgebungen vollständig autonom fahren – jedoch nicht unter allen Bedingungen, wie es erst bei Stufe 5 der Fall wäre. Zum Zeitpunkt der Arbeit an diesem Projekt verfügte ein Waymo-Fahrzeug über dreizehn Kameras. Diese ermöglichen eine 360-Grad-Rundumsicht und erlauben es dem System, seine Umgebung unter verschiedensten Licht- und Wetterverhältnissen zu erfassen. Die Aufnahmen mit der Insta360-Kamera vergrößern die Kluft zwischen menschlicher und technischer Wahrnehmung, da sie einem allumfassenden Blick auf die Welt gleichkommen. Ähnlich wie bei der Rundumsicht eines autonomen Fahrzeugs verdichtet die Insta360 zeitliche Abläufe und erleichtert es, die Umgebung aus einer einzigen Perspektive zu erfassen.

Selbstfahrende Autos verlassen sich auf ein komplexes System aus Sensoren und fortgeschrittener Software, um zu navigieren und Entscheidungen zu treffen. In diesem Fall kommen zusätzlich zu den Kameras vier LiDAR- und sechs Radarsensoren zum Einsatz, die Umgebungsdaten in Echtzeit erfassen. Die verarbeiteten Informationen werden von den Steuerungssystemen analysiert und bilden die Grundlage für Entscheidungen zu Lenkung, Beschleunigung, Bremsen und weiteren Fahrmanövern.

←

Recording of 360-Degree Moving Image Footage Taken Inside a Waymo Robotaxi Vehicle During Journeys in Phoenix, San Francisco, and Los Angeles

Waymo operates at Level 4 autonomy. 'Level 4' means their vehicles can operate fully autonomously in specific, defined environments, but they are not capable of operating everywhere under all conditions, which would be Level 5. At the time of creating this project there were thirteen cameras on a Waymo vehicle. Waymo's cameras provide a 360-degree view around the vehicle, enabling it to perceive its surroundings in various conditions. The Insta360 imagery widens the gap between human and technological vision, with its all-encompassing view of the world. Similarly to the 360-view from an automated vehicle, the Insta360 condenses time, making it easier to see the surrounding scene from one perspective.

Self-driving cars rely on a complex system of sensors, and advanced software to navigate and make driving decisions. In this instance, it operates four LiDAR units and six radar units as additional sensors to gather real-time environmental data. The processed data from the sensors and image processing algorithms is used by the vehicle's control systems to make decisions about steering, acceleration, braking, and other actions.

Siebdrucke des Tesla-Cybertruck-Prototyps mit 1,8 Millimeter dicken Türpanelen aus rostfreier Superlegierung nach Beschusstests, Petersen Automotive Museum, Los Angeles, Kalifornien

Elon Musk erklärte zu den Beschusstests des Cybertruck-Prototyps, Tesla habe »das gesamte Trommelmagazin einer Maschinenpistole in die Fahrertür geleert, ganz im Stil von Al Capone«. Als Musk 2023 in der *Joe Rogan Experience* zu Gast war, inszenierten die beiden einen PR-Stunt. »Darf ich es mit einem Pfeil versuchen?«, fragte Rogan. »Ich wette, ich komme da durch.« Musk nahm die Wette über einen Dollar an. »Wir können es sofort ausprobieren, wenn du willst«, entgegnete er. Rogan ließ daraufhin seinen Compoundbogen mit einem Zuggewicht von etwa 45 Kilogramm kommen, um den improvisierten Test durchzuführen. Der Bogen schießt Pfeile mit einem Gewicht von rund 34 Gramm und einer Geschwindigkeit von etwa 330 Kilo-metern pro Stunde. Der Pfeil hinterließ nur eine kleine Delle.

In die Kunst hat der Pfeil hat schon lange Einzug gehalten, vor allem bei Paul Klee. Während seines Militärdienstes auf Flugplätzen hatte Klee die Aufgabe, Flugzeugabstürze von Pilotenanwärtern zu dokumentieren und zu fotografieren. Klee war fasziniert vom Fliegen und Gleiten, und basierend auf seinen Erfahrungen an der Flugschule schuf er eine Reihe halbabstrakter Werke mit abstürzenden Flugzeugen. In diesen Bildern tauchen häufig Pfeile auf – teils als Anspielung auf die sogenannten »Flechettes« (Fliegerpfeile), die im Ersten Weltkrieg als Waffe abgeworfen wurden. Im Laufe der Zeit wurden sie zu einem Symbol für Bewegung, Energie und Kraft.

Screen Prints of the Tesla Cybertruck Prototype With Its 1.8mm Thick Stainless Super Alloy Door Panels After Bulletproof Testing, Petersen Automotive Museum, Los Angeles, California

Elon Musk later provided context regarding the bulletproof testing of the Cybertruck prototype, stating that Tesla had 'emptied the entire drum magazine of a Tommy gun into the driver's door, Al Capone style.' When Musk appeared on *The Joe Rogan Experience* in 2023, the two engaged in a joint PR stunt. 'Can I try with an arrow?' Rogan asked. 'I bet I can get in there.' Musk accepted the one-dollar wager. 'We can try right now if you want', he replied. Rogan then sent for his ninety-pound compound bow, capable of shooting 525-grain arrows at 300 feet per second (205 miles per hour), to conduct the impromptu test. The arrow only left a small dent.

The arrow has long been represented in art, most notably by Paul Klee. During his military deployment at airfields, Klee was tasked with recording and photographing plane crashes caused by trainee pilots. Klee was fascinated by flying and gliding, and from his experiences at the flying school, he went on to produce a series of semi-abstract works featuring plunging aeroplanes. Arrows frequently appear in these works – partly as references to the 'flechettes' (aeroplane darts) dropped from flights as weapons during the World War I. Over time, they became a symbol of movement, power, and energy.

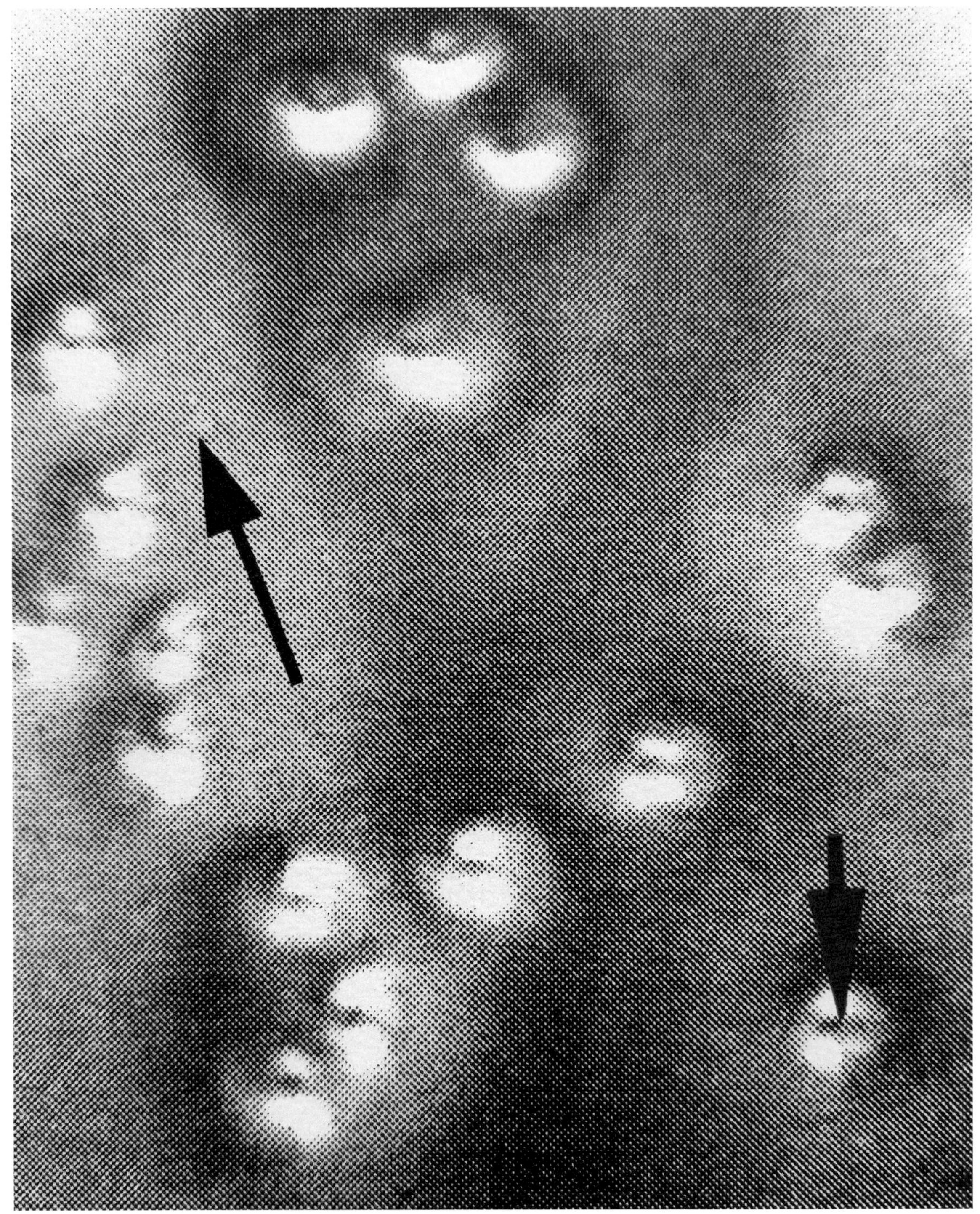

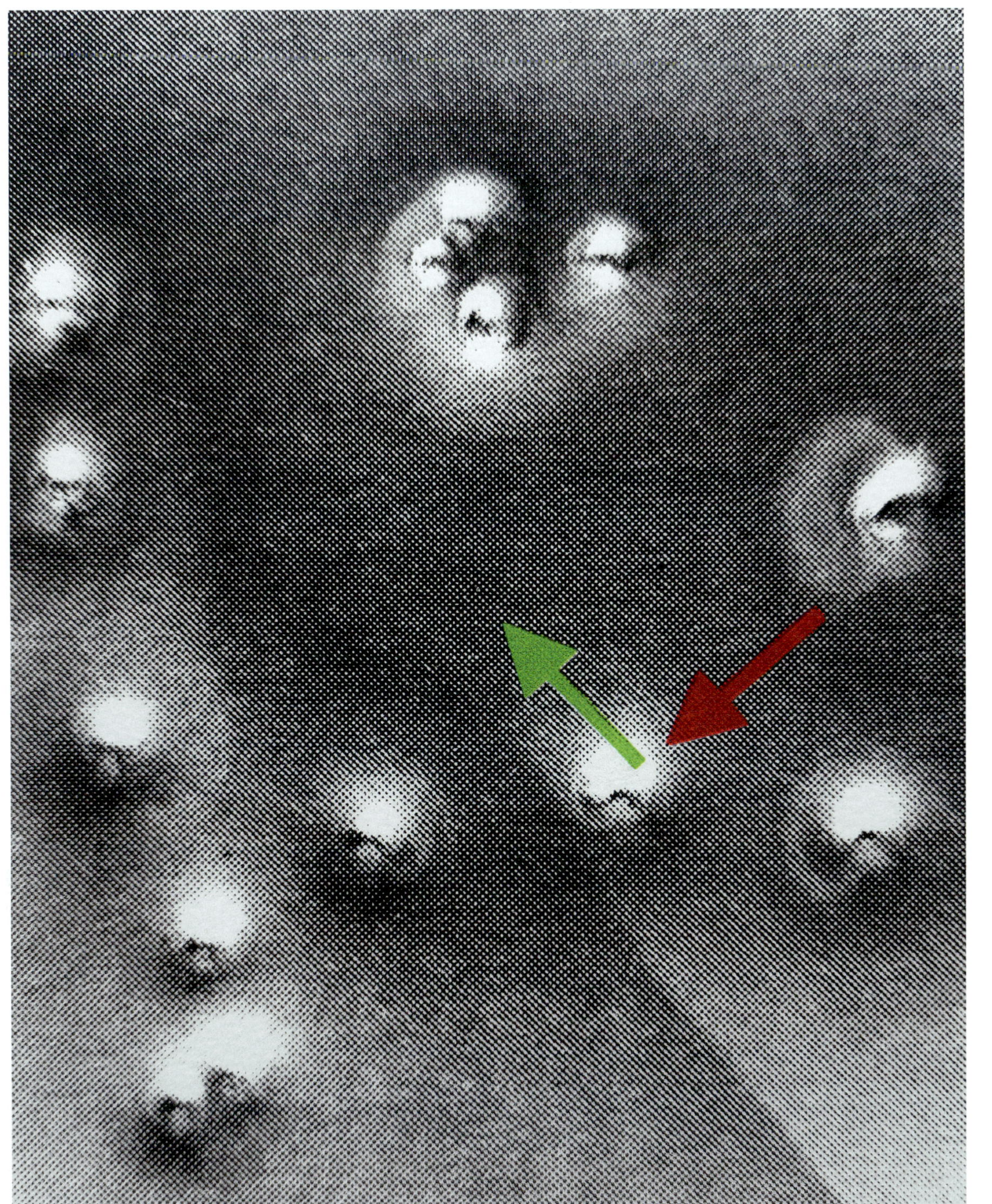

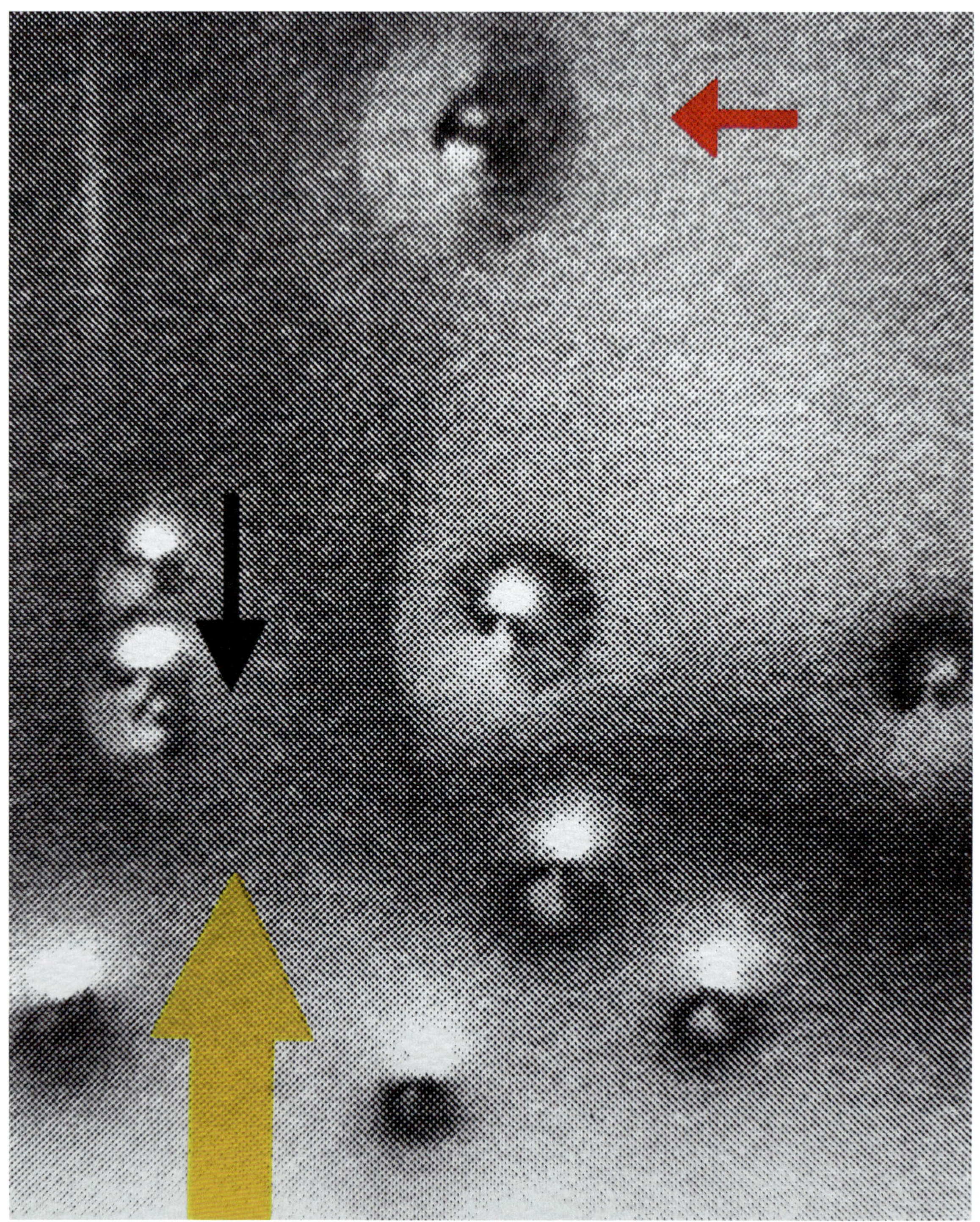

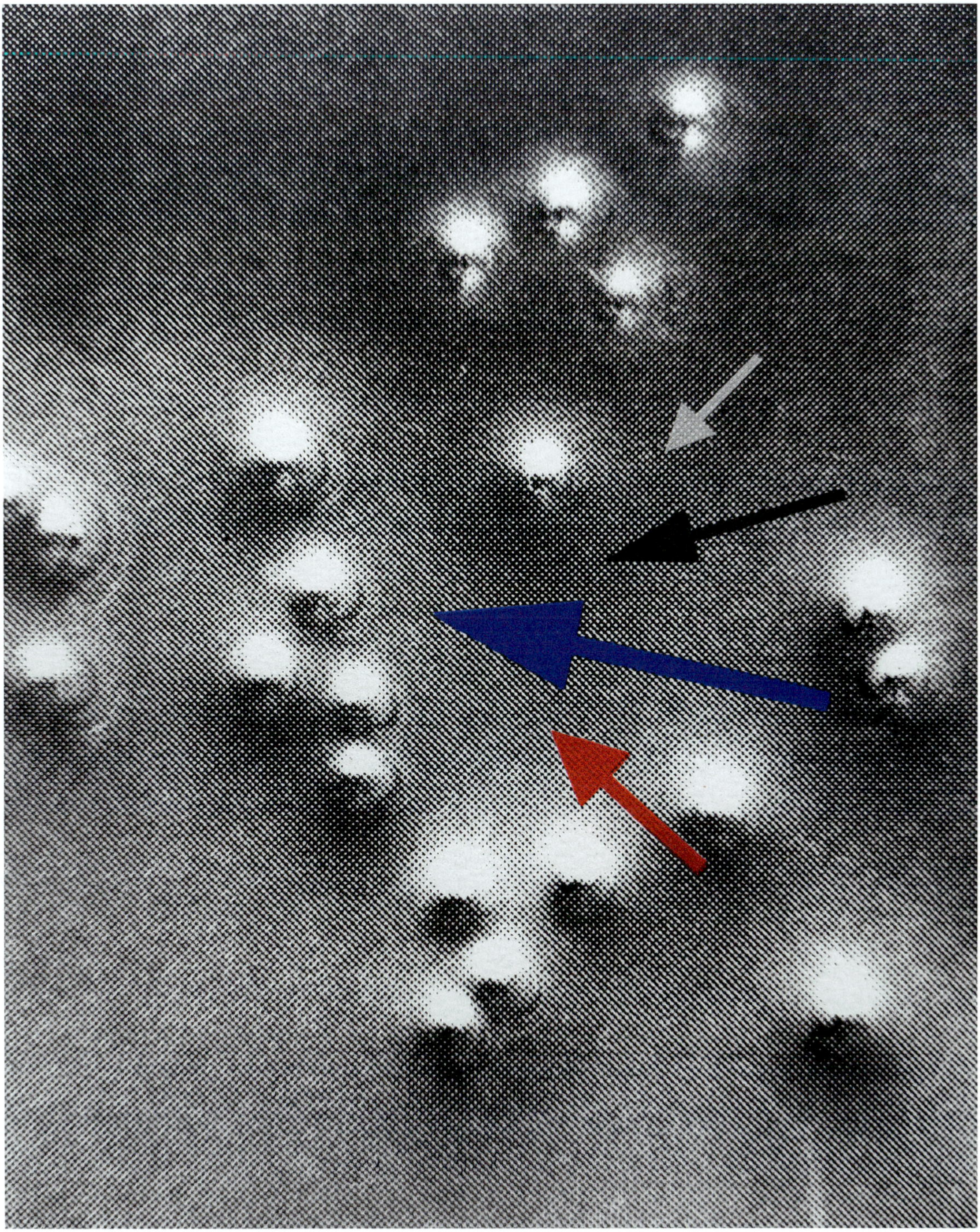

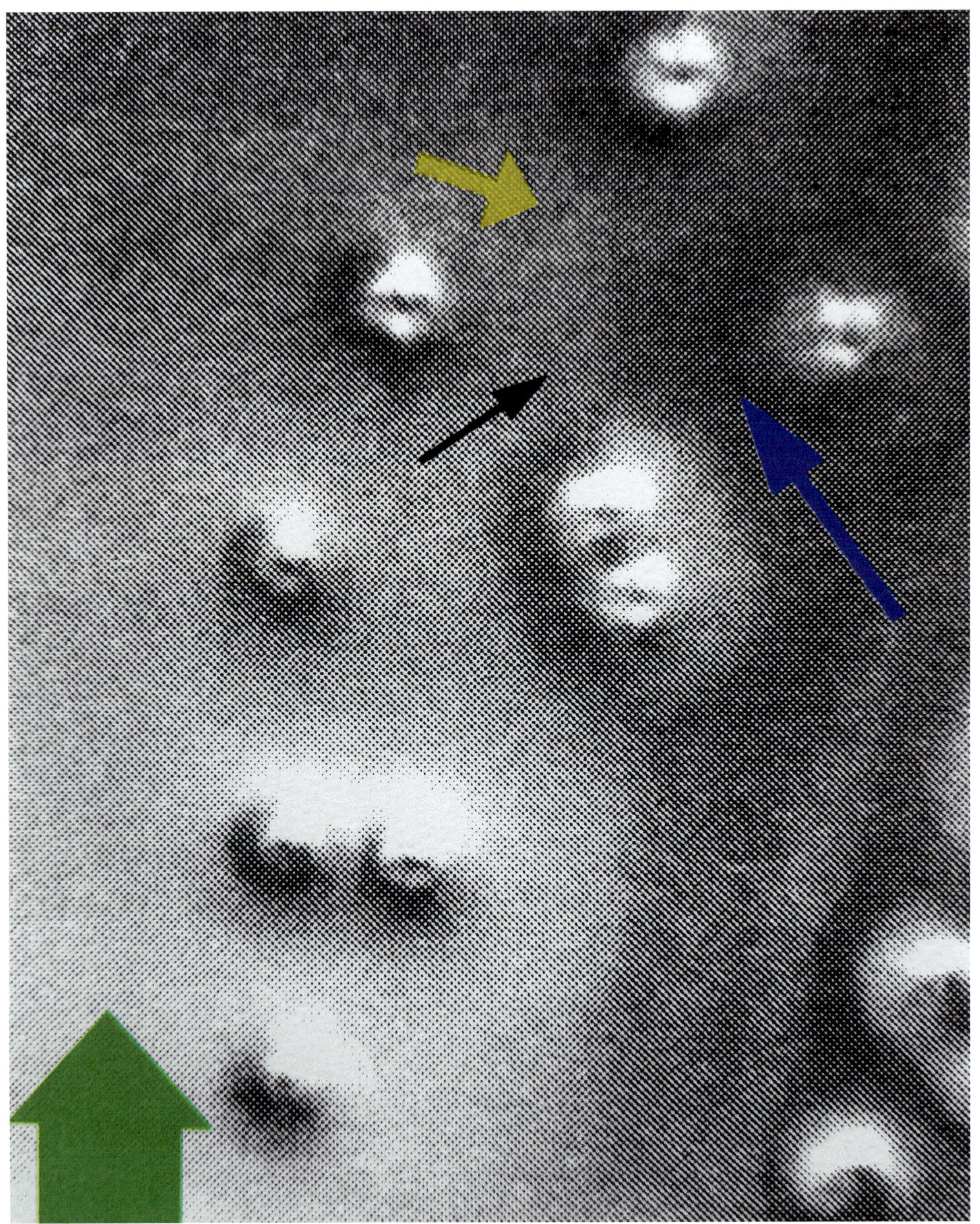

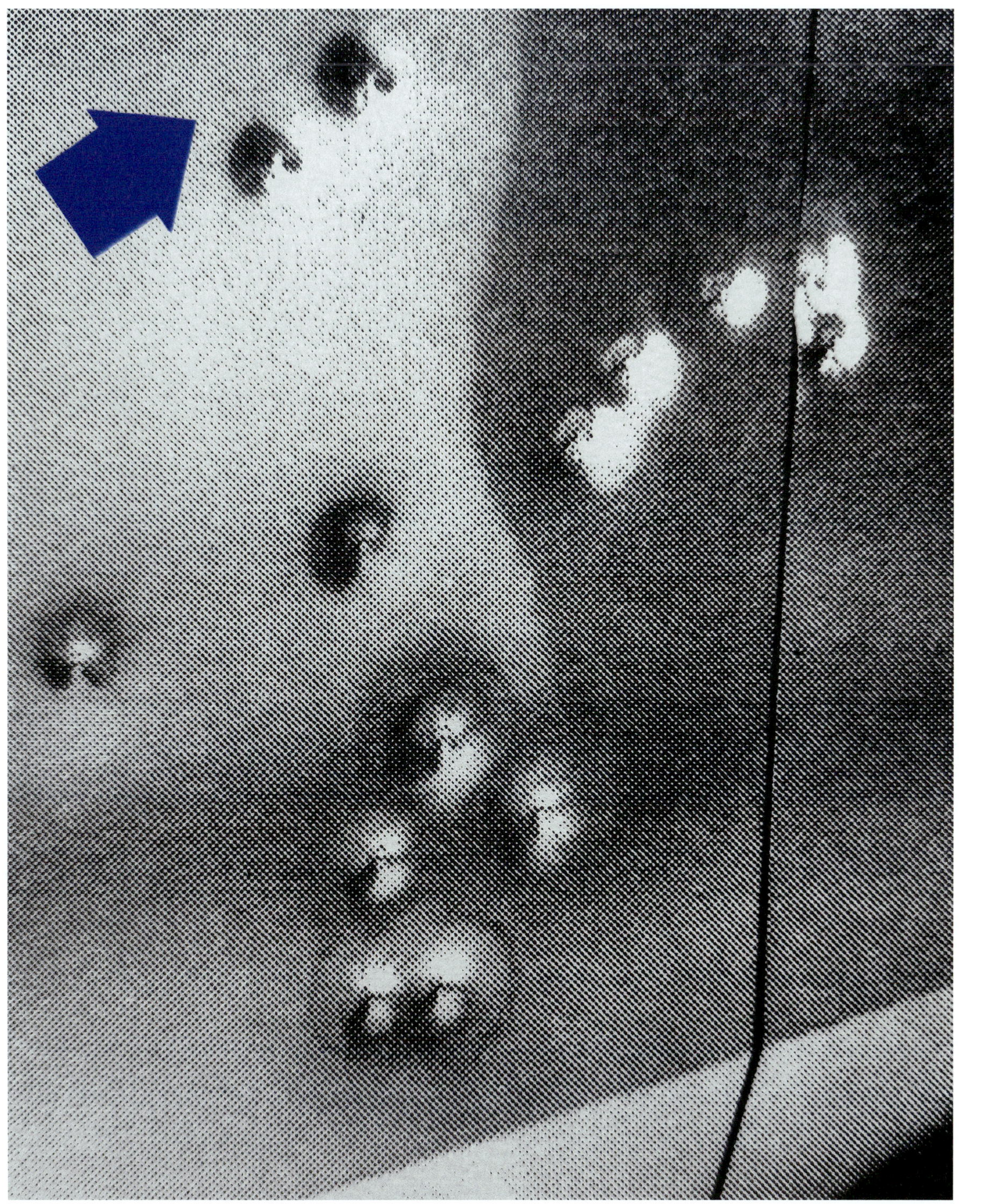

»FUCK EARTH«. DIE BRÜCHIGE FAHRBAHN IN DIE TRAUMWELT DES BEWUSSTSEINS

Lisa Barnard

Als ich gegen Ende der Corona-Pandemie zum ersten Mal ins Lithium Valley reiste, wirkte die Gegend so zerbrechlich wie meine eigene seelische Verfassung. Von San Diego in Südkalifornien fuhr ich durch den Anza-Borrego-Nationalpark zum südlichen Ende des Saltonsees; einem Binnensee, der im Westen von den San Jacinto und Santa Rosa Mountains und im Osten von den Chocolate und Orocopia Mountains eingefasst wird. Die Fahrt führte mich durch wunderschöne Bergpässe mit blühenden Frühlingsblumen hinab in das karge, unwirtliche Imperial Valley. Der Saltonsee liegt in der sogenannten Salton-Senke und ist ein Ort, der von den Träumen seiner Vergangenheit als Freizeitparadies heimgesucht wird: der kalifornischen Riviera, einst Tummelplatz von Frank Sinatra und anderen Schlagerstars der 1950er-Jahre. Im Wind hörte ich noch die melodischen Töne des Promi-Geflüsters und schmeckte die Hoffnungen der Goldsucher:innen in der salzigen, schwefelhaltigen Luft. Parallel löst sich die Region von ihrer Vergangenheit und verwandelt sich in einen technologischen Raum der Zukunft – Schauplatz der neuen technokratischen Ausbeutung durch arrogante Argonauten wie Elon Musk, Jeff Bezos und ihre Gefolgsleute.[1]

Der Saltonsee weint, blutet und schwitzt, während er unter den Folgen von Klimawandel, Spekulationen und landwirtschaftlicher Übernutzung leidet.[2] Seine Vergangenheit lastet schwer: Präzisionstests mit Flugzeugen haben mächtige Atombombenattrappen – »kleine« und »fette«, wie ihre berüchtigten Vorbilder – hinterlassen, die im giftigen Schlamm des flachen, salzigen Gewässers verborgen liegen.[3] Die zerfallenen, bunten architektonischen Überreste postmoderner Schilder, Hotels und Restaurants konkurrieren mit den verlassenen, modernistischen Bunkern der Naval Auxiliary Air Station um Aufmerksamkeit. Geschwindigkeit und Technologie haben sie zu Ruinen der Vergangenheit gemacht – obsolet, seit »Raum und Zeit« neu konfiguriert wurden und die schwindenden Ufer des Saltonsees in eine unaufhaltsame, komplexe Zukunft weisen.[4] Wie Elaine Gan, Nils Bubandt, Anna Tsing und Heather Swanson betonen, werden »anthropogene Landschaften […] von Zukunftsvisionen heimgesucht. Wir sind bereit, Dinge in Schutt und Asche zu legen, Atmosphären zu zerstören und unsere Mitgeschöpfe zu opfern, um Traumwelten des Fortschritts zu erhalten.«[5]

Ich erreichte die Region inmitten eines der für die Gegend typischen Sandstürme. »Am Morgen hing der Staub dicht wie Nebel über der Erde«, wie John Steinbeck so treffend schrieb.[6] Als ich Anfang Januar 2025 zurückkehrte, peitschte der Santa-Ana-Wind durch Los Angeles und

'FUCK EARTH': THE UNEVEN ROAD TO THE DREAMWORLD OF CONSCIOUSNESS

Lisa Barnard

When I first arrived in Lithium Valley towards the end of the COVID-19 pandemic, the area felt as delicate as my state of mind. I drove from San Diego in Southern California, through the Anza-Borrego National Park, to the southern end of the land-locked Salton Sea, a place cocooned by the San Jacinto Mountains and the Santa Rosa Mountains to the west and the Chocolate Mountains and the Orocopia Mountains to the east. I travelled through beautiful mountain passes with blossoming spring flowers, down to the barren, unforgiving Imperial Valley. Situated within the Salton Trough, the Salton Sea is a place haunted by dreams of its recreational past: the California Riviera, the playground of Frank Sinatra and other crooners of the 1950s. I could hear the melodic tones of celebrity whisperings on the wind and taste the expectations of the prospectors in the salty, sulphuric air as the area morphs from the uses of the past into the technological space of the future and the new technocratic exploitation of the arrogant argonauts of Elon Musk, Jeff Bezos, and their cronies.[1]

The Salton Sea weeps, bleeds, and sweats as it suffers from climate change, speculative processes, and agricultural misuse.[2] Burdened by a history of aircraft precision testing, where powerful, faux 'little and fat' nuclear bombs lie hidden within the toxic mud at the bottom of the shallow, salty waters.[3] The jagged, colourful, architectural wreckage of the postmodern signs, hotels, and restaurants compete with the abandoned, modernist bunkers of the Naval Auxiliary Air Station. Speed and technology have made them ruins of the past, obsolete, as 'space and time' have been reconfigured, projecting the receding shores of the Salton Sea into an unstoppable and complex future.[4] As Elaine Gan, Nils Bubandt, Anna Tsing, and Heather Swanson suggest, 'Anthropogenic landscapes are . . . haunted by imagined futures. We are willing to turn things into rubble, destroy atmospheres, sell out companion species in exchange for dreamworlds of progress.'[5]

I arrived in the middle of an omnipresent sandstorm in the area. 'The dust hung like fog', as John Steinbeck famously observed.[6] On this occasion, as I returned in early January 2025, the ferocious wind was the Santa Ana, carrying an apocalyptic and deadly reality to Los Angeles and everything in its path, like 'moths to the flame'.[7] I had never been in such an event, reminiscent only of the fog enveloping the narrow roads of England. My ocular-centric existence became dislocated; the wind was howling, crying perhaps, 'and the sun was as red as ripe new blood.'[8] With diminished senses, my neural networks were confused, my most reliable

brachte eine apokalyptische und tödliche Realität über die Stadt und alles, was auf seinem Weg lag – wie das Licht, dem eine Motte entgegenfliegt.[7] Noch nie hatte ich so etwas erlebt, vergleichbar allein mit dem Nebel auf den engen Straßen Englands. Meine an das Sehen geknüpfte Existenz geriet ins Wanken. Der Wind heulte, schrie geradezu, »und die Sonne war rot wie frisches, reifes Blut.«[8] Die Trübung meiner Sinne ließ meine neuronalen Netzwerke verwirrt zurück, mein sonst so verlässliches Sehvermögen und meine Wahrnehmung lösten sich auf. Autos standen still, gepeitscht von treibendem, durchdringendem Sand. Die Straßen waren gesperrt und für einen Moment schien die Welt stillzustehen. Es war leicht, sich das Ende der Welt vorzustellen.[9]

In der Ära menschlicher Vorherrschaft sind despotische Blicke fest auf das unmittelbare Versprechen von Macht und Profit gerichtet, das in Form von Lithium unter dem Saltonsee verborgen liegt. Und obwohl neue Bergbaumethoden entwickelt werden, um die wachsenden Weiten dystopischer Landschaften – Ursula Le Guin bezeichnet sie als »toten Raum« – zu vermeiden, wird der Abbau des Lithiums die Region weiter verschmutzen und den See schädigen.[10] Viele hoffen, das Direct-Lithium-

Abb. / Fig. 1 Abgestorbene Bäume, Drohnenaufnahme des Saltonsees, Kalifornien / Dead Trees, Drone Footage of the Salton Sea, California

Extraction-Verfahren (DLE) könnte eine Wunderwaffe sein, ein Hoffnungsschimmer in den Rissen des »destruktiven Kapitalismus«. Doch die Geschichte zeigt: Extraktiver Kapitalismus endet niemals gut. Wie Jeff Diamanti sagt: »Jedes Atom, das aus den Tiefen geholt wird, ist längst Spekulationsobjekt und wird abstrakt gehandelt.«[11] In diesem Wettlauf setzen die Hersteller von E-Autos auf die erfolgreiche Skalierung vom Konzept hin zur effizienten Förderung des »weißen Goldes«, das in den Kristallen an den Ufern des Sees glitzert.[12]

»Fuck Earth«, sagt Elon Musk und träumt davon, andere Planeten zu kolonisieren und unseren laut Jeff Bezos »sterbenden Planeten« hinter sich zu lassen.[13] Die meisten von uns werden keine andere Wahl haben, als »unruhig zu bleiben«,[14] tiefergehende Zusammenhänge zu ergründen und Wege zu finden, mit der Verschmutzung durch globale Rohstoffindustrien und landwirtschaftliche Abwässer zu leben, die unsere Flüsse, Seen und Meere vergiften. Wir könnten, wie Anna Tsing vorschlägt, gemeinsam nach der »Möglichkeit des Lebens in kapitalistischen Ruinen« suchen und die »dunkle Ökologie« begrüßen, die auch die Unsicherheit bejaht.[15] Vielleicht sollten wir uns einen freudigen Nihilismus zu eigen machen und jenseits binärer Denkmuster neue Lebensweisen in den Überresten der Moderne

sight and perception dissolved. Cars were motionless, slashed by driving, penetrating sand, roads were closed, and the world, for a moment, stopped moving. It was easy to imagine the end of the world.[9]

In the era of human hegemony, despotic eyes are firmly trained on the immediate promise of power and profits that lie under the Salton Sea, in the form of lithium. And although mining innovations are being explored so as to avoid the ever-expanding, vast swaths of dystopian landscapes – or what Ursula Le Guin refers to as 'dead space' – the process will still pollute the area and the sea will still suffer.[10] Many think, nonetheless, that trials conducted on the Direct Lithium Extraction (DLE) process could be a silver bullet for the area, where hope can

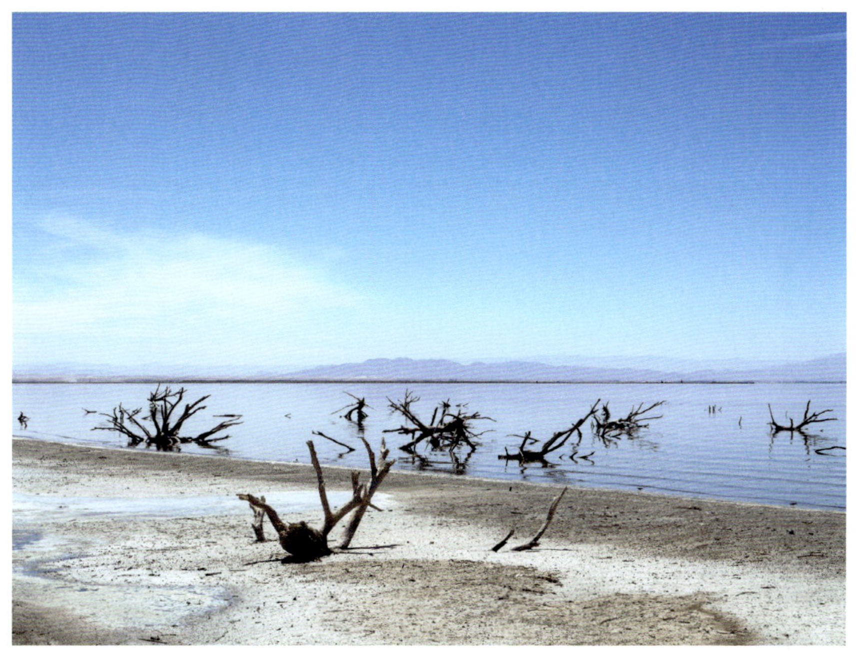

be found in the crack of 'destructive capitalism'. History tells us, that extractive capitalism never ends well, and as Jeff Diamanti suggests, 'each atom of matter dug from the depths has already been speculated upon and tendered for exchange in the abstract'.[11] It's in this arena that manufacturers of electric vehicles are gambling on the successful upscaling, from concept to efficient extraction of the 'white gold' that can also be seen sparkling in the crystals on the shores of the sea.[12]

Elon Musk says we should 'fuck Earth' as he dreams of colonising other planets and leave what Jeff Bezos refers to as a 'dying planet.'[13] Most of us will have no choice but to 'stay with the trouble',[14] dig deep, and discover possibilities of existing with the pollution left by global extractive industries and agricultural runoff that is poisoning our rivers, lakes, and seas. We can collectively seek the 'possibility of life

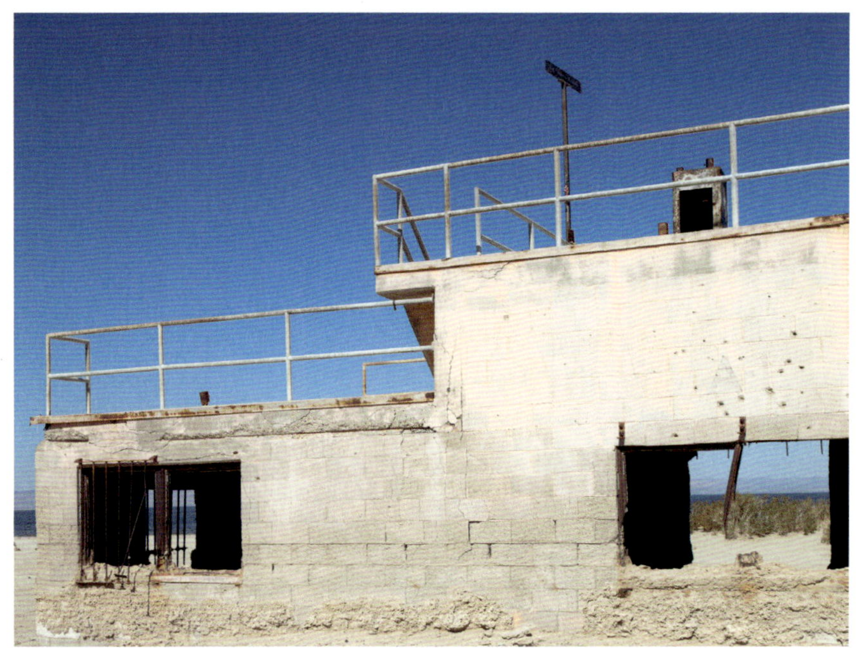

Abb. / Fig. 2 Ruine eines Aussichtsgebäudes in der Testbasis am Saltonsee, 1942 als Salton Sea Naval Air Facility gegründet / Ruin of a Lookout Building at the Salton Sea Test Base, Originally Established as the Salton Sea Naval Air Facility in 1942

finden. Ein solcher Perspektivwechsel könnte weniger objektivierende Interaktionen fördern, insbesondere, wenn wir erkennen, dass Menschen und Nicht-Menschen, Objekte und Technologien sowie Wissenssysteme an der Konstruktion von Bedeutung beteiligt sind.[16] Anders gesagt: Wir könnten von interaktiven Beziehungen, in denen wir eine gewisse Unabhängigkeit zwischen Subjekt und Objekt wahren, zu nicht-hierarchischen Verbindungen übergehen, bei denen Verantwortung gleichmäßiger verteilt ist.

Als die Dunkelheit hereinbrach, flaute der Wind ab. Mücken schwirrten herbei und während sie sich an meinem Blut labten, begann die ein oder andere kalifornische Wüstenfledermaus, die in den nomadischen Palmen nistete, wiederum die Mücken zu jagen. Am Südufer des Saltonsees scheinen abends die Lichter der Geothermiekraftwerke auf. In der Dämmerung erheben sich die Dampfschwaden und schimmern im letzten Licht, während die Turbinen – treu ihrer neu zugewiesenen Aufgabe – unaufhörlich surren. Sie pumpen Lithium in heißer Salzsole an die Oberfläche, wobei das Salz eine alchemistische Verbindung mit der »Dunkelheit« des Schwefels eingeht.[17] Die Auswirkungen der Industrie sind zu hören und zu riechen: In den nahegelegenen Schlammtöpfen brodelt und spuckt es, als ließen sie ihrem Zorn freien Lauf. Der Gestank verendeter Fische, unschuldig vom See vergiftet, ringt mit dem fauligen Geruch zerfallender

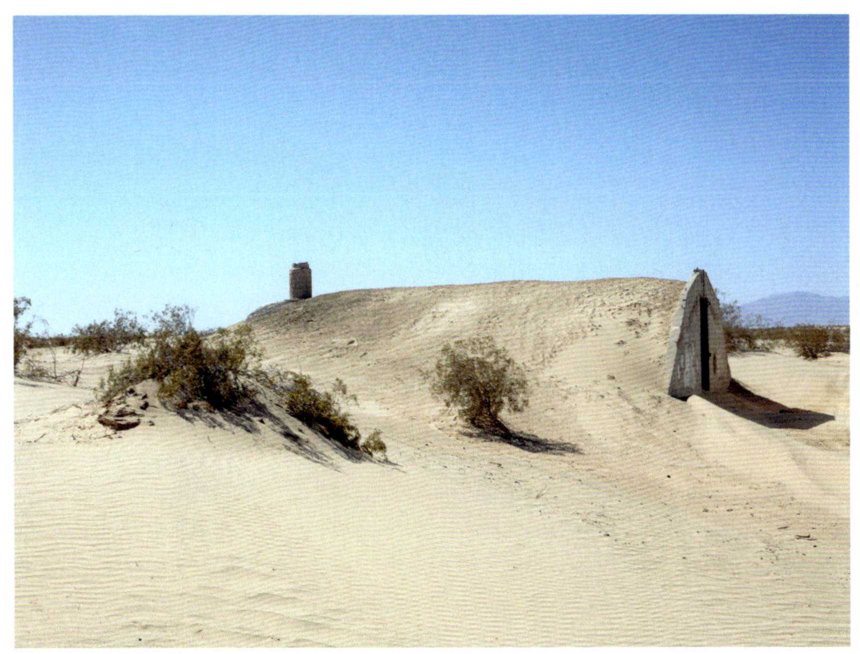

Abb. / Fig. 3 Alter Bunker in der Testbasis am Saltonsee / Old Bunker at the Salton Sea Test Base

in capitalist ruins', as Anna Tsing suggests, and welcome the 'dark ecology' that embraces uncertainty.[15] Maybe we should embrace a joyful nihilism and find new ways of being and living in the vestiges of modernism, outside traditional modes of binary thinking. Such a shift in perspective can lead to less objectifying interactions, particularly considering how humans and non-humans, objects and technologies, and knowledge systems all participate in creating meaning.[16] In other words, a transferal from interactive relationships where we might maintain a sense of independence between subject and object, towards the non-hierarchical, with a more evenly distributed responsibility.

As darkness fell, the wind dropped, mosquitos emerged, and as they fed on me, the occasional Californian pallid bat, roosting in the nomadic palms, started to feed on them. The lights of the geothermal electricity plants punctuate the southern shores of the Salton Sea as the steam billows and shimmers against the fading light, the turbines whir unendingly, with a commitment to their newly designated task. They pump lithium in hot salty brine up from the depths, with salt in alchemic tandem with the shadowy 'darkness' of sulphur.[17] Echoes of industry are heard and smelt in the nearby mud pots, as they bubble, spit, and vent their anger. The scent of the carcasses of dead fish, unjustly poisoned

Algen um die olfaktorische Vorherrschaft, die unter bestimmten Bedingungen das Wasser so tiefrot färben, als würde die Erde bluten.

Seit Aristoteles ist Dunkelheit gleichbedeutend mit Möglichkeiten. Das Dunkle trägt das Potenzial für Licht in sich. Damit etwas sichtbar wird, braucht es Licht – und damit auch Orte ohne Licht, oder wie John Paul Ricco sagt, Öffnungen für das, was jenseits des Lichts liegen könnte, »jenseits der Dichotomien Mensch/Maschine und Mensch/Tier«, eine Zone zwischen Lebendigem und Nicht-Lebendigem.[18] In diesem Raum oder zu dieser Zeit entstehen seltsame Visionen und die Grenzen zwischen Realität und Vorstellung verschwimmen; Geräusche und Gerüche, die aus der Dunkelheit auftauchen, bringen Komplexitäten ans Licht, die normalerweise verborgen bleiben – eine hyperdimensionale Sicht auf die Welt, in der viele Perspektiven gleichzeitig existieren. Die Frage ist, wie wir eine solche Umgebung, das Unfassbare, wahrnehmen und erleben können oder wie wir »Wahrnehmungen der Nichtwahrnehmung« schaffen, die über die »einseitige Modalität des Sehens« hinausgehen.[19] David Chalmers beschreibt die Wahrnehmung als den Ort, an dem der Verstand uns die Welt »präsentiert«. Wahrnehmung ist die Grundlage, wenn wir verstehen wollen, wo das »schwierige Problem« des Bewusstseins liegt. Dieses Problem greift auch Thomas Nagel in seinem sehr anschaulichen Artikel »What Is It Like to Be a Bat?« auf, der weithin als ein Schlüsselmoment im Verständnis von Bewusstsein oder subjektiver Erfahrung, dem sogenannten »Leib-Seele-Problem«, gilt.[20]

Die Fledermaus wird oft verteufelt, vor allem als Überträgerin tödlicher Krankheiten. In der Frühzeit der Pandemie rückte sie als mutmaßliche Hauptakteurin erneut ins Zentrum der Aufmerksamkeit.[21] Meine erste Begegnung mit Fledermäusen hatte ich in Kalifornien – dank der Organisation Los Angeles Bat Rescue – kurz vor Laguna Beach, in einem Haus umgeben von einem Lichtergewirr, wie es nur die Küste bietet. Ein Jungtier schoss mit hoher Geschwindigkeit scheinbar ziellos durch den Raum, wich nur knapp Kollisionen aus und stieß dabei ständig ein hochfrequentes Klicken aus. Die Fledermaus teilt viele unserer Sinne und Bewusstseinsformen: Sehen, Hören und Riechen, allerdings mit einer entscheidenden Ergänzung: die Schall- oder Echoortung. Nagel vermutet, dass ihr Gehirn »dazu bestimmt [ist], die Ausgangsimpulse mit dem darauf folgenden Echo zu korrelieren«, sodass sie Objekte in ihrer Umgebung präzise nach Abstand, Größe, Gestalt, Bewegung und Struktur unterscheiden kann.[22] Mit anderen Worten: Die Fledermaus ist eine komplexe Form von Sehmaschine.

Das Norden-Bombenzielgerät, ein Vorläufer der Objekterkennung bei hoher Geschwindigkeit, steht in berüchtigter Verbindung zum B-29-Bomber Enola Gay.[23] Basierend auf tachymetrischen Messungen konnte es Bombenziele verfolgen, indem es den Abwurfpunkt je nach horizontalen

by the sea, fight for olfactory supremacy, alongside the decomposing algae, that in certain conditions create a colour so deep in red pigment that it is to think that the earth is bleeding.

From Aristotle onwards, darkness has always been equated with possibilities, where the dark has the capacity for light. For something to capture the eye there must be light and, therefore, also places where there is an absence of light, as John Paul Ricco proposes, openings for that which might lie beyond the light, 'beyond the two dichotomies of human/machine and human/animal', a zone between the living and non-living.[18] In this space, or at this time, strange visions occur, and realities are blurred with imaginations, sounds and smells that appear from the dark, unearthing complexities that are ordinarily hidden from view, a hyperdimensional view of the world, where many different perspectives exist simultaneously. The question is, how are we to perceive, experience such an environment, the unfathomable, or create 'perceptions of imperception', where perception requires something beyond the 'single-sense modality of sight'?[19] According to David Chalmers, perception is where the mind 'presents' the world to us and is the foundation of understanding where the 'hard problem' of consciousness lies. Also addressed in an easily accessible paper by Thomas Nagel called 'What Is It Like to Be a Bat?', which is widely cited as a pivotal moment in understanding consciousness or the subjective experience, the mind-body problem.[20]

The bat is often demonised, particularly as a carrier of fatal diseases, and as the suspected main protagonist during the early moments of the pandemic, it was once again destined to take the leading role.[21] My first experience of bats in California was courtesy of the Los Angeles Bat Rescue organisation, just off Laguna Beach, in a house with a riot of light that only the coast can bring. The young pup was flying around the room at great speed, seemingly erratically, only just avoiding collision, whilst all the time emitting a high frequency click. The bat shares with us many of our own perceptive experiences, our conscious experience, that of sight, sound, and smell, but with one key difference, the use of sonar or echolocation as an additional perceptual modality. Nagel suggests that 'their brains are designed to correlate the outgoing impulses with the subsequent echoes', making precise discriminations of objects within range, their distance, size, shape, motion, and texture.[22] In other words, the bat is a complex form of vision machine.

The Norden bombsight was a forerunner to object detection at speed and had an infamous connection to the *Enola Gay* B-29 bomber.[23] It utilised a tachometric design and could track a bomb target, recalculating the release point based on input that included horizontal deviations induced by the minor manoeuvring of aircraft or wind drift.[24] It played an important role in the history of the Salton Sea and was arguably the

Abweichungen durch Flugmanöver oder Winddrift ständig neu berechnete.[24] In der Geschichte des Saltonsees spielte das Norden-Bombenzielgerät eine wichtige Rolle und gilt als erstes Sichtgerät, das den haptischen Raum erfasste. Wie das Teleskop und die unbemannten Luftfahrzeuge der jüngeren Vergangenheit war es in der Lage, unsere Wahrnehmung von Entfernungen und Dimensionen entweder aufzulösen oder zu beschleunigen.[25] Mit seinem apokalyptischen Blick war das unter Verschluss gehaltene Bombenzielgerät ein frühes Beispiel für das, was Joanna Zylinska eine »Wahrnehmungsmaschine« nennt: ein Bestandteil eines multisensorischen Systems, das eine Aufgabe erfüllt und Funktionen im Rahmen einer Operation übernimmt.[26] Dennoch war es auf einen Menschen angewiesen und benötigte einen »Funktionär«. Wie der »Apparat« sollte es den Interessen der Freiheit dienen. Sein Ziel war es, besser zu sehen – schneller und effizienter als ein Mensch.[27] Doch mit der unerbittlichen Kraft seines optischen Auges hatte das Bombenzielgerät verheerende Folgen für die Menschheit. Es führte zu radioaktivem Niederschlag in jedem Atom, trug zur Kontaminierung unserer gesamten Realität bei und veränderte unser Bewusstsein grundlegend.[28]

Abb. / Fig. 4 Sich erholende Fledermaus im Schutzkäfig unter der Obhut von Chumi Paul, Los Angeles Bat Rescue, Altadena, Kalifornien / Recuperating Bat in Protective Cage Under the Care of Chumi Paul, Los Angeles Bat Rescue, Altadena, California

Als ich mich auf den Weg nach Norden machte, rauschten Los Angeles und Magic Mountain mit ihrem endlosen Kreislauf aus Angst und Euphorie an mir vorbei. Die sanfte Wüstenlandschaft wich den berauschenden Düften der industriellen Viehzucht im Central Valley, die sich wie in einem verschwommenen Tanz mit den Gräsern der Prärie vermengen. Die Hauptfigur am nördlichen Ende der Route 5, in der Nähe von San Francisco, ist die mexikanische Bulldoggenfledermaus, ein multisensorisches Wesen. Von Natur aus nomadisch, lebt sie in großer Zahl unter dem Yolo Causeway, der über einem riesigen Überschwemmungsgebiet vor den Toren von Sacramento zu schweben scheint.

Die Straßen von San Francisco sind zu »Laboratorien« geworden, auf denen ethische Fragen rund um das autonome Fahren in Echtzeit erprobt werden.[29] Waymo, ein Unternehmen, das hochgelobte batteriebetriebene Robotaxis der Stufe 4 betreibt, ist in Los Angeles und San Francisco mittlerweile allgegenwärtig.[30] Diese Autos sollen Stadtbewohner:innen mit minimalem Aufwand von A nach B bringen. Eine irritierende, aber dennoch angenehme generisch-künstliche Stimme begrüßt die Fahrgäste und beruhigt sie mit sanften Melodien im Hintergrund, während sie die Kontrolle an die

first vision machine to understand the haptic space; much like the telescope, and more recently Unmanned Aerial Vehicle Systems, it was capable of obliterating or accelerating our experiences of distances and dimensions.[25] With its apocalyptic gaze, the bombsight was shrouded in secrecy, and an early example of what Joanna Zylinska calls a 'perception machine', part of a multisensory system that performs a task and carries out functions as part of an operation.[26] It was still humancentric or in need of a 'functionary', and much like the 'apparatus', it was designed to serve the interests of freedom. Its ultimate goal was to see better – that is, faster and more efficiently than humans.[27] The bombsight had devastating consequences for humanity with its unyielding power contained within its optical eye, the result being a nuclear fallout in every atom, as it contaminated all our reality and changed all consciousness.[28]

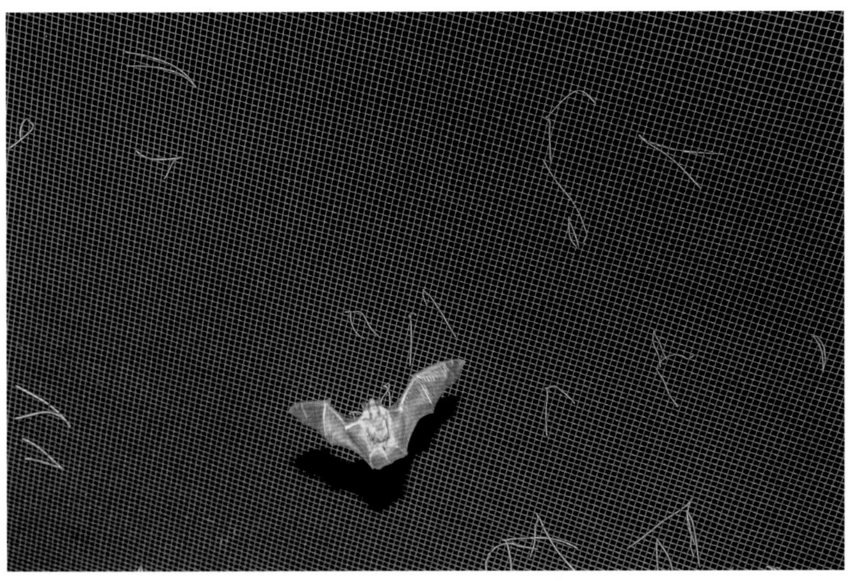

As I head north, Los Angeles and Magic Mountain, with its striated, unending loops of fear and elation, rush by. The smooth desert is replaced by the heady aromas of the industrial cattle farming of the central valley, in a blurred dance with the grasses of prairie land. The lead character at the end of Route 5, close to San Francisco, is the multisensory, Mexican free-tailed bat: nomadic by nature, it resides in vast numbers under the Yolo Causeway, which appears to hover over a vast floodplain just outside Sacramento.

The streets of San Francisco have become 'laboratories' where the morality of the autonomous vehicle is being played out in real time.[29] Waymo is an L4-battery-operated, glorified, automated-vehicle taxi company, now ubiquitous in Los Angeles and San Francisco.[30] The car's main

Maschine abgeben. Insgesamt ist die Fahrt eine ziemlich sterile und geistlose Erfahrung: schmutziger als ein Uber, langweilig und mechanisch. Man kann sich nicht über das Wetter, Politik, die besten Restaurants, Bars, Sehenswürdigkeiten, Promi-Klatsch und so weiter unterhalten. Sie ist ein Beispiel für das, was Rebecca Solnit als die Revolution der Einsamkeit beschreibt, »den großen Rückzug«: Individuen sind zunehmend voneinander und ihrer Umgebung isoliert und in ihren eigenen Gedanken gefangen.[31]

Autonome Fahrzeuge funktionieren vor allem basierend auf Computer-Vision-Algorithmen und modernen Sensoren wie Kameras, LiDAR und Radar (LiDAR nutzt Lichtwellen, Radar elektromagnetische Wellen, ähnlich den Schallwellen, mit denen Fledermäuse ihre Umgebung per Echoortung wahrnehmen). Mit diesen Sensoren erfassen sie fortlaufend Bilder und Umgebungsdaten, um sich fortzubewegen.[32] Sie verarbeiten diese Informationen, um Entscheidungen über das Fahren, Bremsen, Lenken und das Vermeiden von Sachschäden und Unfällen zu treffen – und vor allem, um niemanden zu töten, wie Isaac Asimov bekanntlich betonte.[33] Die Objekterkennung mithilfe von Deep-Learning-Modellen wie YOLO (You Only Look Once) hilft dem Fahrzeug dabei, mehrere Objekte in Echtzeit zu erkennen und deren Muster, Texturen und Formen präzise zu identifizieren. Im Hintergrund ist zwar immer noch ein »Funktionär« präsent, doch im Gegensatz zum Norden-Bombenzielgerät kehrt sich hier das »ursprüngliche Verhältnis *Mensch/Apparat* um, und der Mensch funktioniert in Funktion der Apparate«,[34] das heißt, er verschmilzt gewissermaßen mit ihnen. Geoff Cox weist darauf hin, dass »Algorithmen nicht allein mit magischer (allmächtiger) Kraft wirken, sondern Teil größerer Infrastrukturen und Ideologien« sind.[35] Algorithmisches Lernen und Sehen sind demnach entweder Werkzeuge oder Gefahren für unser Sehvermögen. Stefaan Decostere zeigt, wie stark Technologie unsere Wahrnehmung der Realität verändert hat – ein Phänomen, das Paul Virilio als »Logistik der Wahrnehmung« beschreibt.[36] Decostere zitiert Virilios Warnung in *Die Sehmaschine*: vor einem »Sehen ohne Blick, einer Automatisierung der Wahrnehmung und dem Verschwinden des lebendigen Blicks, der durch die Sehmaschine ersetzt wird«.[37] Autonome Fahrzeuge können tödlich sein, besonders in toten Winkeln oder bei Wahrnehmungslücken, wie zahlreiche dokumentierte Fälle zeigen.[38] Unser Verständnis der Welt beruht nicht allein auf den Informationen, die wir erfassen. Wie der Neurowissenschaftler Anil Seth erklärt, geschieht Wahrnehmung nicht nur dadurch, dass unsere Sinne einfach das Geschehen um uns herum aufnehmen, sondern unser Gehirn ist eine »Vorhersagemaschine«, die kreativ interpretiert.[39] Die Frage lautet also: Werden autonome Fahrzeuge jemals so sicher sein wie menschliche Fahrer:innen? Aktuelle Studien legen nahe, dass sie dies unter den meisten Bedingungen sein werden, nicht jedoch in der Dämmerung – bei schwachem Licht, wenn die Fledermäuse ausfliegen und unergründliche Halluzinationen

preoccupation is to transport city dwellers from A to B with as little fuss as possible. It welcomes you with a disturbing yet pleasant, generic artificial tone, whilst gentle melodic tones in the background are designed to keep you calm as you relinquish control to the machine. Overall, it's a pretty sterile, lowbrow experience, dirtier than an Uber, boring and perfunctory. You can't chat about the weather, politics, where best to eat, drink, tourist destinations, celebrity gossip, etc. It is part of what Rebecca Solnit calls the revolution of loneliness, 'the great withdrawal', where workers and individuals are becoming increasingly isolated from each other and their environments, trapped in their own thoughts.[31]

Automated vehicles (AVs) rely predominantly on computer vision algorithms, and advanced sensors, such as cameras, LiDAR, and radar (LiDAR uses light waves and radar uses electromagnetic waves, similar to the sound waves that bats use when they echolocate), to continuously capture images and environmental data to get around.[32] This information is processed to make the decisions on the act of driving, braking, steering, not damaging property, and, most importantly, not killing anyone or anything, as Isaac Asimov famously pointed out.[33] Object detection, using deep learning models, such as YOLO (You Only Look Once) help the vehicle to detect multiple objects in real time, recognising patterns, textures, and shapes accurately. There is always a 'functionary' hidden in the background, but, unlike the Norden bombsight, the '*human* and *apparatus* are reversed, and human beings operate as a function of the apparatus'[34] – dissolved into the machine, if you will. Geoff Cox suggests that 'algorithms do not act alone with magical (totalising) power but exist as part of larger infrastructures and ideologies'[35] – learning and seeing is therefore either a tool of or a threat to human vision. Stefaan Decostere notes the extent to which technology has changed our perception of reality, what Paul Virilio calls 'logistics of perception'.[36] According to Decostere, Virilio in *The Vision Machine* 'warns against vision without seeing, the automation of perception, the disappearance of the point of view of the living, replaced by the vision machine.'[37] AVs can be deadly, particularly in optical or perceptive blind spots, as a number of recorded events attest to.[38] Understanding the world is not only about information that we experience; as neuroscientist Anil Seth suggests, perception doesn't just come from our senses simply recording what is around us; rather, our brain is a 'prediction machine', both creative and interpretive.[39] So, the question is whether AVs will ever be as safe as human drivers. Current research suggests, yes, in most conditions, but not at dawn and dusk, in low light, the time when bats and unfathomable hallucinations occur, a time of resourcefulness, adventures, and different ways of being.[40] AVs will never be imaginative or experience fully what it means to be human and to understand truly the image of the world.

auftreten, einer Zeit des Einfallsreichtums, der Abenteuer und anderer Lebensweisen.[40] Autonome Fahrzeuge werden niemals kreative Lösungen finden oder vollständig erfahren, was es bedeutet, Mensch zu sein und die Welt so zu verstehen, wie wir es können.

Während ich im Yolo County auf die Brücke zufahre, bricht nach dem heißen Tag die Dämmerung herein. Die Dunkelheit senkt sich über mir herab und die Fledermäuse beginnen ihren Flug über die Feuchtgebiete. Das Flattern ihrer Flügel, ihr Klicken und Schnattern mischt sich mit dem Rattern der Autos mit ihren ungleich laufenden Rädern und dem Klappern der Güter in den unerbittlichen, unaufhörlich dahinrollenden Lastwagen, die über die Brücke donnern. Gelegentlich durchbrechen Sirenen oder Pieptöne von Baufahrzeugen den Lärm, Teil eines endlosen Kreislaufs aus Zerstörung und Reparatur. Der stechende Geruch von Fledermausguano und Kraftstoff mischt sich mit dem süßen Duft der Wildblumen, die in den Feuchtgebieten wachsen, und überfluten meine Sinne in einem letzten Crescendo. Ich fühle mich desorientiert, überwältigt und völlig von der Situation ergriffen, während sich die Fledermäuse hoch am roten Himmel wie Musiknoten in einer Welle formieren – wunderschön, blind für die Komplexität, Widersprüche und Unvorhersehbarkeit unserer Zukunft –, bis sie schließlich in der Dunkelheit der Nacht verschwinden.

1 Vgl. Cory Hewett, »The Race to Extract Lithium Around the Salton Sea Area«, in: *Electrify News*, 8. Mai 2024, https://electrifynews.com/news/batteries/the-race-to-extract-lithium-around-the-salton-sea-area und Ilkhan Ozsevim, »Electric Dreams: Tesla's Gigafactory Network and EV Battery Production Blueprint«, in: *Automotive Manufacturing Solutions*, 17. Juli 2024, https://www.automotivemanufacturingsolutions.com/ev-battery-production/teslas-ev-battery-production-and-global-gigafactory-network/45873.article. Sämtliche in diesem Text zitierten Links wurden zuletzt am 14. Mai 2025 aufgerufen.

2 James Hillman, »The Suffering of Salt« [1979], in: *Salt and the Alchemical Soul*, hg. von Stanton Marlan, Woodstock: Spring Publications 2023, S. 133. Hillman bezeichnet Salz als »Grundlage der Subjektivität« und als »gefühlte Erfahrung«. »Wir tauchen ein in die Erfahrungskomponente dieses Körpers – sein Blut, seinen Schweiß, seine Tränen und seinen Urin –, um unser Salz zu finden. [...] Salz ist das mineralische, unpersönliche, objektive Fundament persönlicher Erfahrung und macht Erfahrung erst möglich.«

3 Während des Zweiten Weltkriegs diente der Saltonsee als Übungsgelände für B-29-Bomber, insbesondere für das Abwerfen von Atombomben auf Japan. Die Bombenattrappen am Saltonsee waren mit Beton gefüllt, um das Gewicht und die Wirkung echter Bomben für militärische Übungen zu simulieren. Informationen von Frank Castner, leitender Bibliothekar und Archivar am Palm Springs Air Museum, Gespräch mit der Autorin 2021.

4 Paul Virilio, *Bunkerarchäologie* [1975], Wien: Passagen 2011. In seiner Arbeit untersucht Virilio die Schnittstelle von Technologie, Geschwindigkeit und Macht am Beispiel verlassener Bunker aus dem Zweiten Weltkrieg. Dabei analysiert er, wie sich unser Verständnis von Raum und Zeit durch die technologische Beschleunigung – insbesondere im militärischen Kontext – verändert.

5 Elaine Gan, Anna Tsing, Heather Swanson und Nils Bubandt, »Haunted Landscapes of the Anthropocene«, in: *Arts of Living on a Damaged Planet*, hg. von dens., Minneapolis: University of Minnesota Press 2017, S. 2.

Driving towards the foot of the bridge at Yolo, dusk emerges from the day's heat, darkness descends, and the anticipated flyout of the bats begins over the wetlands. The sound from the fluttering wings of the clicking and chattering bats build in unison with the rumblings of the cars with their uneven wheels and the clattering of goods in the endless, unforgiving trucks, as they hurtle across the bridge. These sounds are pierced by the occasional siren or beeping from the construction vehicles that are part of an endless loop of destroy and repair. The pungent smell of the bat guano, fuel from the cars, and the sweet scent of the wildflowers, a feature of the wetlands, assault my senses in a final crescendo. I find myself disoriented, overwhelmed, and consumed as the ribbons of bats form like a wave of musical notes, high in the red sky, beautiful and oblivious to the complexity, contradiction and unpredictable of our future, as they finally disappear into the darkness of night.

1 See Cory Hewett, 'The Race to Extract Lithium Around the Salton Sea Area', *Electrify News*, 8 May 2024, https://electrifynews.com/news/batteries/the-race-to-extract-lithium-around-the-salton-sea-area, and Ilkhan Ozsevim, 'Electric Dreams: Tesla's Gigafactory Network and EV Battery Production Blueprint', Automotive Manufacturing Solutions (AMS), 17 July 2024, https://www.automotivemanufacturingsolutions.com/ev-battery-production/teslas-ev-battery-production-and-global-gigafactory-network/45873.article. All links cited in this essay were accessed on 14 May 2025.

2 James Hillman, 'The Suffering of Salt' [1979], in *Salt and the Alchemical Soul*, ed. Stanton Marlan (Spring Publications, 2023), 133. Hillman calls salt 'the ground of subjectivity' and 'felt experience'. 'We descend into the experiential component of this body – its blood, sweat, tears, and urine – to find our salt. . . . Salt is the mineral, impersonal, objective ground of personal experience making experience possible.'

3 The Salton Sea served as a practice ground for B-29 bombers during World War II, specifically for practicing the dropping of atomic bombs on Japan. The faux bombs at the Salton Sea were filled with concrete to simulate the weight and effect of real bombs for military training. Information supplied by Frank Castner, lead librarian/archivist at the Palm Springs Air Museum, in conversation with the author, 2021.

4 Paul Virilio, *Bunker Archeology*, trans. George Collins (Princeton Architectural Press, 1994); originally published as *Bunker archéologie* (Centre Pompidou, 1975). Virilio's work explores the intersection of technology, speed, and power through the lens of abandoned World War II bunkers. He examines how the speed of technology, particularly in military applications, reshapes our understanding of space and time.

5 Elaine Gan et al., 'Haunted Landscapes of the Anthropocene', in *Arts of Living on a Damaged Planet*, ed. Anna Tsing et al. (University of Minnesota Press, 2017), 2.

6 John Steinbeck, *The Grapes of Wrath* (1939; Penguin Classics 2006), 3.

7 See John Paul Ricco, 'Moths to the Flame: Photography and Extinction', in *Capitalism and the Camera: Essays on Photography and Extraction*, ed. Kevin Coleman and Daniel James (Verso Books, 2021), 142–64. See also William Finnegan, 'California Burning', *The New York Review of Books*, 16 August 2018, https://www.nybooks.com/articles/2018/08/16/wildfires-california-burning/: 'We have entered the era of the megafire – defined as a wildfire that burns more than 100,000 acres.'

6 John Steinbeck, *Früchte des Zorns* [1939], München: dtv 2007, S. 9.

7 Vgl. John Paul Ricco, »Moths to the Flame: Photography and Extinction«, in: *Capitalism and the Camera. Essays on Photography and Extraction*, hg. von Kevin Coleman und Daniel James, London und New York: Verso 2021, S. 142–164. Vgl. auch William Finnegan, »California Burning«, in: *The New York Review of Books*, 16. August 2018, https://www.nybooks.com/articles/2018/08/16/wildfires-california-burning: »Wir sind in das Zeitalter der Megafeuer eingetreten – definiert als Waldbrände, die eine Fläche von mehr als 40.000 Hektar erfassen.«

8 Steinbeck 1939/2007 (wie Anm. 6), S. 9.

9 In Anlehnung an Fredric Jameson und Slavoj Žižek hat Mark Fisher bemerkt, es sei »einfacher, sich das Ende der Welt vorzustellen als das Ende des Kapitalismus«. Mark Fisher, *Kapitalistischer Realismus ohne Alternative? Eine Flugschrift* [2009], Hamburg: VSA 2020.

10 Lithium wird aus der Sole gewonnen, die zur Stromerzeugung in den Geothermiekraftwerken des Imperial County ohnehin aus dem Boden gepumpt wird. Vgl. California Energy Commission, »Lithium Valley Vision«, https://www.energy.ca.gov/programs-and-topics/programs/lithium-valley-vision: Laut dem U.S. Geological Survey werden Gebiete als bekannte geothermische Ressourcengebiete (Known Geothermal Resource Areas, KGRA) klassifiziert, wenn »die Aussichten für die Gewinnung von geothermischem Dampf oder damit verbundenen geothermischen Ressourcen auf einem Gebiet gut genug sind, um Ausgaben für diesen Zweck zu rechtfertigen«. Das KGRA Salton Sea am südlichen Ende des Saltonsees gilt als das Gebiet mit der weltweit höchsten Konzentration an Lithium, das in geothermischer Sole enthalten ist.

11 Jeff Diamanti, »Capital Raw Materials«, in: *Worlding Ecologies. Art, Science and Activism Towards Climate Justice*, hg. von Niekolaas Johannes Lekkerkerk und Eva Burgering, Amsterdam und Delft: Valiz 2024, S. 135–143, hier S. 142.

12 2023 unterzeichnete die Ford Motor Company einen Vertrag mit EnergySource Minerals über die Lieferung von Lithiumhydroxid aus dem Saltonsee. Siehe hierzu Janet Wilson, »Ford Signs Deal to Buy Lithium From Near Salton Sea for Electric-Vehicle Batteries«, in: *The Desert Sun*, https://eu.desertsun.com/story/news/environment/2023/05/24/ford-motor-inks-lithium-deal-with-energysource-in-imperial-county/70252788007. Fordismus bezeichnet eine spezifische Phase der wirtschaftlichen Entwicklung im 20. Jahrhundert. Der Begriff wird häufig verwendet, um entweder das von der Ford Motor Company zu Beginn des 20. Jahrhunderts eingeführte System der Massenproduktion oder die typische Form des Wirtschaftswachstums in der Nachkriegszeit sowie die damit verbundene politische und soziale Ordnung im fortgeschrittenen Kapitalismus zu beschreiben.

13 Vgl. Mary-Jane Rubenstein, *Astrotopia. The Dangerous Religion of the Corporate Space Race*, Chicago und London: University of Chicago Press 2024, S. IXf. Vgl. auch Ross Anderson, »Exodus«, in: *Aeon*, 30. September 2014, https://aeon.co/essays/elon-musk-puts-his-case-for-a-multi-planet-civilisation.

14 Vgl. Donna Haraway, *Unruhig bleiben. Die Verwandtschaft der Arten im Chthuluzän*, Frankfurt und New York: Campus 2018. Laut Haraway sind alle, Menschen und Nicht-Menschen, durch ein »tentakuläres Denken« miteinander verbunden. Ihrer Ansicht nach führt das gemeinsame Leben und Sterben auf einer geschädigten Erde zu einem konstruktiven Denken und Problemlösen.

15 Anna Tsing, *Der Pilz am Ende der Welt. Über das Leben in den Ruinen des Kapitalismus*, Berlin: Matthes & Seitz 2018 und Timothy Morton, *Dark Ecology. For a Logic of Future Coexistence*, New York: Columbia University Press 2016. Die von Timothy Morton formulierte dunkle Ökologie ist eine ökologische Theorie, die auf einer objektorientierten Ontologie basiert und neue Denkansätze dazu liefern möchte, wie Menschen mit anderen »Objekten« in der Welt auf bessere, weniger feindselige Weise koexistieren können und sollten. Die Theorie kritisiert anthropozentrische ebenso wie biozentrische Weltanschauungen und will die Dichotomie zwischen Mensch/Natur und Subjekt/Objekt aufheben.

16 Karen Barad verwendet den Begriff »Intra-Aktion« als Ersatz für »Interaktion«, da letzterer vorab festgelegte Körper voraussetze, die dann miteinander interagieren. Intra-Aktion versteht Handlungsfähigkeit dagegen nicht als inhärente Eigenschaft eines Menschen, die von diesem ausgeübt wird, sondern als Kräftedynamik. Vgl. Karen Barad, *Meeting the Universe Halfway. Quantum Physics and the Entanglement of Matter and Meaning*, Durham: Duke University Press 2007, S. 147.

8 Steinbeck, *Grapes of Wrath*, 3.

9 Mark Fisher, citing Fredric Jameson and Slavoj Žižek, famously suggested that it was 'easier to imagine the end of the world than the end of capitalism'. Mark Fisher, *Capitalist Realism: Is There No Alternative?* (Zero Books, 2009).

10 Lithium will be extracted from the brine that is already pumped up from the ground to power the geothermal plants that provide electricity to Imperial County. See 'Lithium Valley Vision', California Energy Commission, https://www.energy.ca.gov/programs-and-topics/programs/lithium-valley-vision: 'According to the U.S. Geological Survey, lands shall be classified as a Known Geothermal Resource Area (KGRA) when "the prospects for extraction of geothermal steam or associated geothermal resources from an area are good enough to warrant expenditures of money for that purpose." The Salton Sea KGRA, located at the southern end of the Salton Sea, is believed to have the highest concentration of lithium contained in geothermal brine in the world.'

11 Jeff Diamanti, 'Capital Raw Materials', in *Worlding Ecologies: Art, Science and Activism Towards Climate Justice*, ed. Niekolaas Johannes Lekkerkerk and Eva Burgering (Valiz, 2024), 142.

12 The Ford Motor Company signed a contract with EnergySource Minerals to obtain lithium hydroxide at the Salton Sea in 2023. See Janet Wilson, 'Ford Signs Deal to Buy Lithium from near Salton Sea for Electric-Vehicle Batteries', *The Desert Sun*, 24 May 2023, https://eu.desertsun.com/story/news/environment/2023/05/24/ford-motor-inks-lithium-deal-with-energysource-in-imperial-county/70252788007. Fordism is a specific stage of economic development in the twentieth century. The term is widely used to describe (1) the system of mass production that was pioneered in the early twentieth century by the Ford Motor Company or (2) the typical post-war mode of economic growth and its associated political and social order in advanced capitalism.

13 Mary-Jane Rubenstein, *Astrotopia: The Dangerous Religion of the Corporate Space Race* (University of Chicago Press, 2024), ix–x. See also Ross Anderson, 'Exodus', *Aeon*, September 30, 2014, https://aeon.co/essays/elon-musk-puts-his-case-for-a-multi-planet-civilisation.

14 See Donna Haraway, *Staying with the Trouble: Making Kin in the Chthulucene* (Duke University Press, 2016). Haraway argues that we are all linked, humans and non-humans alike, through what she terms 'tentacular thinking'. She suggests that living and dying together on a damaged earth will result in more conducive thinking and problem-solving.

15 Anna Tsing, *The Mushroom at the End of the World: On the Possibility of Life in Capitalist Ruins* (Princeton University Press, 2021), and Timothy Morton, *Dark Ecology: For a Logic of Future Coexistence* (Columbia University Press, 2016). Dark ecology is an ecological theory formulated by Timothy Morton, based on an object-oriented ontology and claiming to offer a new perspective on how humans can and should coexist with other 'objects' in the world in a better, less hostile way. It is a critique of both an anthropocentric and a biocentric worldview, aiming to erase the dichotomy between human/nature and subject/object.

16 *Intra-action* is a term used by Karen Barad to replace 'interaction', which necessitates pre-established bodies that then participate in action with each other. Intra-action understands agency not as an inherent property of an individual to be exercised but as a dynamism of forces. See Karen Barad, *Meeting the Universe Halfway: Quantum Physics and the Entanglement of Matter and Meaning* (Duke University Press, 2007), 147.

17 C. G. Jung, 'Sal', in Marlan, *Salt and the Alchemical Soul*, 88: 'Verily, sulphur is the true black devil of hell, who can be conquered by no element save salt alone.'

18 Ricco, 'Moths to the Flame', 158.

19 Joanna Zylinska, *The Perception Machine: Our Photographic Future Between the Eye and AI* (MIT Press, 2023), 73.

20 David Chalmers, *The Conscious Mind: In Search of a Fundamental Theory* (Oxford University Press, 1996), and Thomas Nagel, 'What Is It Like to Be a Bat?', *Philosophical Review* 83, no. 4 (1974): 435–50.

17 C. G. Jung, »Sal«, in: *Mysterium coniunctionis. Untersuchungen über die Trennung und Zusammensetzung der seelischen Gegensätze in der Alchemie*, *Gesammelte Werke*, Bd. 14, Halbbd. 1, hg. von Lilly Jung-Merker und Elisabeth Rüf, Ostfildern: Patmos 2011, S. 214–294, hier S. 216: »Dazu kommt, dass nicht nur der Drache mit dem Teufel / identisch ist, sondern auch der negative Aspekt des Sulphur, nämlich sulphur comburens, wie GLAUBER vom Sulphur sagt, ›ja der rechte schwartze Höllen Teuffel / welcher durch kein Element zu überwunden / als allein durch Saltz.‹«

18 Ricco 2021 (wie Anm. 7), S. 158.

19 Joanna Zylinska, *The Perception Machine. Our Photographic Future Between the Eye and AI*, Cambridge und London: MIT Press 2023, S. 73.

20 David Chalmers, *The Conscious Mind. In Search of a Fundamental Theory*, New York und Oxford: Oxford University Press 1996, und Thomas Nagel, *What Is It Like to Be a Bat? / Wie ist es, eine Fledermaus zu sein?* [1974], übersetzt, herausgegeben und mit einem Nachwort von Ulrich Diehl, Ditzingen: Reclam 2023.

21 David Macdonald, »The Wet Market Sources of Covid-19: Bats and Pangolins Have an Alibi«, Department of Biology, University of Oxford, https://www.biology.ox.ac.uk/article/the-wet-market-sources-of-covid-19-bats-and-pangolins-have-an-alibi.

22 Nagel 1974/2023 (wie Anm. 20), S. 15.

23 Weitere Informationen zur Rolle der Enola Gay bei den Bombenabwürfen auf Hiroshima und Nagasaki sind zu finden in Norman Polmar, *The Enola Gay. The B-29 That Dropped the Atomic Bomb on Hiroshima*, Washington, D.C.: Potomac Books 2004.

24 Weitere Informationen sind auf der Website des Massey Air Museum in Maryland zu finden: https://masseyaero.org/news/Norden.html.

25 Paul Virilio beschreibt das Teleskop als »Modell aller optischen Prothesen und Sehhilfen«, das »das Bild einer Welt [projiziert], die außerhalb unserer Reichweite liegt, und somit eine andere Art und Weise, uns in der Welt zu bewegen; die *Logistik der Wahrnehmung* führt zu einem ungeahnten Transfer des Blickes, sie schafft einen Zusammenstoß von Nahem und Fernem, ein *Phänomen der Beschleunigung*, das unser Bewusstsein von Entfernungen und Dimensionen vernichtet.« Paul Virilio, *Die Sehmaschine* [1988], Berlin: Merve 1989, S. 20.

26 Zylinska 2023 (wie Anm. 19). Für weitere Informationen über Harun Farockis »operative Bilder«, siehe Jussi Parikka, »Operational Images: Between Light and Data«, in: *e-flux journal*, Nr. 133, Februar 2023, https://www.e-flux.com/journal/133/515812/operational-images-between-light-and-data.

27 Zylinska 2023 (wie Anm. 19), S. 97. Für ein besseres Verständnis von Vilém Flussers Analyse des Funktionärs und des Apparats siehe seine Ausführungen in *Ins Universum der technischen Bilder*, Göttingen: European Photography 1985.

28 Ursula K. Le Guin, *Freie Geister. Eine zwiespältige Utopie* [1974], Frankfurt: S. Fischer 2017 deutet auf die allgegenwärtige und heimtückische Natur der nuklearen Katastrophe hin, die alles durchdringt und kontaminiert.

29 Siehe Rebecca Solnit, »Turns Out the Zombie Apocalypse Isn't as Fun as They Said It Would Be: Rebecca Solnit on Our Dangerously Disconnected World«, in: *The Guardian*, 16. November 2024, https://www.theguardian.com/society/2024/nov/16/zombie-apocalypse-dangerously-disconnected-world-rebecca-solnit. Zum Zusammenhang zwischen Moral und autonomen Fahrzeugen siehe F. M. Kamm, *The Trolley Problem Mysteries*, New York und Oxford: Oxford University Press 2015.

30 Für weitere Informationen zu den Stufen des autonomen Fahrens siehe »The 6 Levels of Vehicle Autonomy Explained«, in: *Synopsys*, 15. Februar 2025, https://www.synopsys.com/blogs/chip-design/autonomous-driving-levels.html.

31 Rebecca Solnit, »In the Shadow of Silicon Valley«, in: *London Review of Books*, Bd. 46, Nr. 3, 8. Februar 2024, https://www.lrb.co.uk/the-paper/v46/n03/rebecca-solnit/in-the-shadow-of-silicon-valley.

21 David Macdonald, 'The Wet Market Sources of Covid-19: Bats and Pangolins Have an Alibi', Department of Biology, University of Oxford, https://www.biology.ox.ac.uk/article/the-wet-market-sources-of-covid-19-bats-and-pangolins-have-an-alibi.

22 Nagel, 'What Is It Like to Be a Bat?', 438.

23 For more information on the role of the *Enola Gay* in the Hiroshima and Nagasaki bombings in Japan, see Norman Polmar, *The Enola Gay: The B-29 That Dropped the Atomic Bomb on Hiroshima* (Potomac Books, 2004).

24 More information can be found on the website of the Massey Air Museum in Maryland: https://masseyaero.org/news/Norden.html.

25 Paul Virilio discusses the telescope as being 'that epitome of the visual prosthesis, [which] projected an image of a world beyond our reach and thus another way of moving about in the world, the *logistics of perception* inaugurating an unknown conveyance of sight that produced a telescoping of near and far, a *phenomenon of acceleration* obliterating our experience of distances and dimensions.' Paul Virilio, *The Vision Machine*, trans. Julie Rose (Indiana University Press 1994), 4; originally published as *La Machine de vision* (Galilée, 1988).

26 Zylinska, *The Perception Machine*. For more information on Harun Farocki's 'Operational Images', see Jussi Parikka, 'Operational Images: Between Light and Data', in *e-flux journal* 133 (February 2023), https://www.e-flux.com/journal/133/515812/operational-images-between-light-and-data.

27 Zylinska, *The Perception Machine*, 97. For a greater understanding of Vilém Flusser's analysis of the 'functionary and the apparatus', see Vilém Flusser, *Into the Universe of Technical Images*, trans. Nancy Ann Roth (University of Minnesota Press, 2011); originally published as *Ins Universum der technischen Bilder* (European Photography, 1985).

28 Ursula K. Le Guin, *The Dispossessed* (Harper & Row, 1974), suggests the pervasive and insidious nature of the nuclear holocaust, as it essentially permeates and contaminates all of reality.

29 Cf. Rebecca Solnit, 'Turns Out the Zombie Apocalypse Isn't as Fun as They Said It Would Be: Rebecca Solnit on Our Dangerously Disconnected World', *The Guardian*, 16 November 2024, https://www.theguardian.com/society/2024/nov/16/zombie-apocalypse-dangerously-disconnected-world-rebecca-solnit. For more information on morality and AVs, see F. M. Kamm, *The Trolley Problem Mysteries* (Oxford University Press, 2015).

30 For more information on the levels of driver control of automated vehicles, see 'The 6 Levels of Vehicle Autonomy Explained', Synopsys, 15 February 2025, https://www.synopsys.com/blogs/chip-design/autonomous-driving-levels.html.

31 Rebecca Solnit, 'In the Shadow of Silicon Valley', *London Review of Books* 46, no. 3 (8 February 2024), https://www.lrb.co.uk/the-paper/v46/n03/rebecca-solnit/in-the-shadow-of-silicon-valley.

32 Yuxiao Zhang et al., 'Perception and Sensing for Autonomous Vehicles Under Adverse Weather Conditions: A Survey', *ISPRS Journal of Photogrammetry and Remote Sensing* 196 (February 2023), 146–177.

33 Isaac Asimov first introduced his 'Three Laws of Robotics' in the short story 'Runaround', which was published in the magazine *Astounding Science Fiction* in March 1942.

34 Flusser, *Into the Universe of Technical Images*, 74.

35 Geoff Cox, 'Ways of Machine Seeing: An Introduction', *A Peer-Reviewed Journal About Machine Research* 6, no. 1 (2017), 9.

36 Stefaan Decostere, 'Image, War, Impactology', in *Memory of Fire: Images of War and The War of Images*, ed. Julian Stallabras (Photoworks, 2013), 197.

37 Decostre, *Image, War, Impactology*, 197.

32 Yuxiao Zhang, Alexander Carballo, Hanting Yang und Kazuya Takeda, »Perception and Sensing for Autonomous Vehicles Under Adverse Weather Conditions: A Survey«, in: *ISPRS Journal of Photogrammetry and Remote Sensing*, Bd. 196, Februar 2023, S. 146–177.

33 Isaac Asimovs führte seine drei Robotergesetze erstmals in der Kurzgeschichte »Runaround« aus, die im März 1942 in der Zeitschrift *Astounding Science Fiction* erschienen ist.

34 Flusser 1985 (wie Anm. 27), S. 78.

35 Geoff Cox, »Ways of Machine Seeing: An Introduction«, in: *A Peer-Reviewed Journal About Machine Research*, Bd. 6, Nr. 1, 2017, S. 9–15, hier S. 9.

36 Stefaan Decostere, »Image, War, Impactology«, in: *Memory of Fire. Images of War and The War of Images*, hg. von Julian Stallabras, Brighton: Photoworks 2013, S. 182–203, hier S. 197.

37 Decostre 2013 (wie Anm. 36), S. 197.

38 Cruise, eine Tochtergesellschaft von General Motors, hat sich bereit erklärt, einer Frau, die 2024 in San Francisco von einem selbstfahrenden Robotaxi über den Bürgersteig geschleift wurde, eine Entschädigung in Höhe von 8 bis 12 Millionen Dollar zu zahlen. Die Frau wurde bei einem Unfall mit Fahrerflucht von dem Fahrzeug erfasst und geriet vor das autonome Cruise-Fahrzeug, das sie unter sich einklemmte. Das Auto schleifte sie etwa sechs Meter weit mit, bevor es zum Stillstand kam. Vgl. Summer Lin, »A Woman Was Dragged by a Self-Driving Cruise Taxi in San Francisco: The Company Is Paying Her Millions«, in: *Los Angeles Times*, 16. Mai 2025, https://www.latimes.com/california/story/2024-05-16/woman-gets-millions-after-getting-dragged-by-self-driving-taxi-in-san-francisco.

39 Anil Seth, *Being You. A New Science of Consciousness*, New York: Dutton 2021, S. 80.

40 Mohamed Abdel-Aty und Shengxuan Ding, »A Matched Case-Control Analysis of Autonomous vs Human-Driven Vehicle Accidents«, *Nature Communications*, Bd. 15, Nr. 4931, 2024, https://doi.org/10.1038/s41467-024-48526-4.

38 General Motors' Cruise agreed to pay an eight-to-twelve-million-dollar settlement to a woman who was dragged along the pavement by a self-driving taxi in San Francisco in 2024. She was struck by a hit-and-run vehicle and thrown into the path of Cruise's self-driving car, which pinned her underneath. The car dragged her about twenty feet before coming to a stop. See Summer Lin, 'A Woman Was Dragged by a Self-Driving Cruise Taxi in San Francisco: The Company Is Paying Her Millions.' *Los Angeles Times*, 16 May 2025, https://www.latimes.com/california/story/2024-05-16/woman-gets-millions-after-getting-dragged-by-self-driving-taxi-in-san-francisco.

39 Anil Seth, *Being You: A New Science of Consciousness* (Dutton, 2021), 80.

40 Mohamed Abdel-Aty and Shengxuan Ding, 'A Matched Case-Control Analysis of Autonomous vs Human-Driven Vehicle Accidents', *Nature Communications* 15, 4931 (2024), https://doi.org/10.1038/s41467-024-48526-4.

Selbstporträt, aufgenommen mit einem Helm.ai-System vor dem Facebook-Hauptsitz mithilfe eines semantischen Vollbild-Segmentierungssystems, Menlo Park, Kalifornien / Self-Portrait Recording Made with a Helm.ai System in Front of Facebook Headquarters, Using a Full Scene Semantic Segmentation System, Menlo Park, California

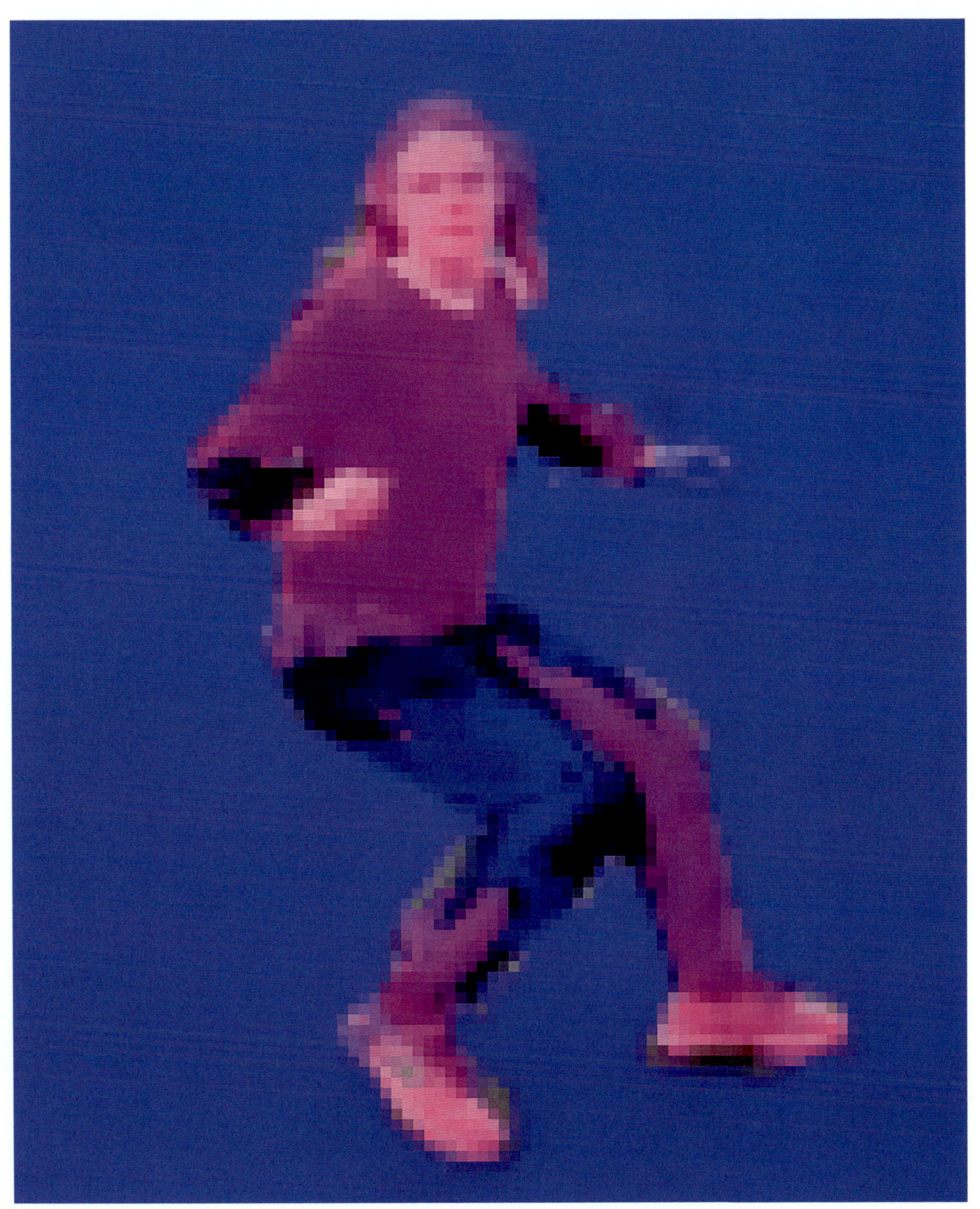

WAHRNEHMUNG, KONTROLLIERTE HALLUZINATION UND DIE INTERPRETATION VON LICHT

Anil Seth

Im Frühjahr 2024, zwanzig Jahre nach meinem letzten Besuch, fuhr ich mit Freunden von San Diego ostwärts in die Anza-Borrego-Wüste, um die Blumen zu sehen. Wir erreichten schließlich die Gegend unweit des Saltonsees, wo die sonst karge Landschaft in einem Meer aus Gelb, Rot, Weiß und Violett erblühte. Es war schwer zu begreifen – und von großer Schönheit.

Wenn wir die Augen öffnen, erscheint uns die Welt, die wir erleben, scheinbar mühelos. Zumindest wirkt es oft so. Doch hinter diesem Gefühl der Mühelosigkeit verbirgt sich ein komplexer neurobiologischer Tanz – ein präzises Zusammenspiel, das jedem bewussten Erlebnis zugrunde liegt, egal ob unser Gehirn nun versucht, die Blumen in einer Wüstenlandschaft zu begreifen, oder ob es sich in das tägliche Ritual des morgendlichen Kaffees einfindet. Wie und warum können materielle, physikalische Prozesse überhaupt ein subjektives Gefühl auslösen? Dieses Rätsel – das »schwierige Problem des Bewusstseins«, wie David Chalmers es nennt – beschäftigt Wissenschaftler:innen seit Jahrhunderten und Philosoph:innen sogar noch länger.[1]

Angesichts der enormen Komplexität des Gehirns ist es unmöglich, dem Reiz von Metaphern zu widerstehen. Ein besonders irreführendes Beispiel stammt aus der Fotografie (obwohl sie nichts dafür kann!): Die Augen gelten als Linsen und das Gehirn als – ja, was eigentlich? Hier beginnt die Verwirrung, hört dort aber noch lange nicht auf. Unsere Augen ähneln in mancher Hinsicht Kameraobjektiven. So fängt die äußere Oberfläche des Auges Licht ein und bündelt es. Die lichtempfindlichen Zellen auf der Rückseite der Netzhaut erinnern ein wenig an die Sensoren einer Digitalkamera, wenn man nicht allzu genau hinschaut. Einige Parallelen setzen sich sogar im Gehirn fort. Moderne Kameras erfassen nicht nur Licht, sondern verbessern die Bildqualität mit raffinierten Tricks wie Farbausgleich und Fokussierung. Auch unser Gehirn betreibt eine Art grundlegende Bildverarbeitung: Während die Augen Signale ans Gehirn senden, passt die Sehrinde die Helligkeit an das Umgebungslicht an und erkennt die Umrisse von Objekten.

Doch dann wird es kompliziert. Im Gehirn gibt es keinen Ort, an dem ein fotoähnliches Bild einem »inneren Beobachter« erscheint, so wie du und ich eine Fotografie betrachten. Die Beziehung zwischen der Welt »da draußen« und unserem bewussten Erleben »hier drinnen« hat kaum etwas mit der Beziehung zwischen der Welt und einem Foto gemein. Fotografien fangen Licht ein, während das Gehirn Licht nutzt, um eine Welt zu erschaffen.

PERCEPTION, CONTROLLED HALLUCINATION, AND THE INTERPRETATION OF LIGHT

Anil Seth

In the spring of 2024, twenty years after my last visit, some friends and I drove out east from San Diego to the Anza-Borrego Desert to see the flowers. We ended up not far from the Salton Sea, where the usually barren landscape was a blaze of yellow, red, white, and purple. It was hard to make sense of, and it was very beautiful.

When we open our eyes, the world we experience appears without any effort on our part. At least that's how it seems, most of the time. But this sense of effortlessness disguises the intricate neurobiological dance within our brains that is responsible for each and every one of our conscious experiences. This is true whether our brains are struggling to make sense of flowers in a desert or settling into the daily rhythm of a morning coffee. And the mystery of consciousness itself – the 'hard problem' of understanding how and why material, physical processes can give rise to any kind of subjective feeling – has been a challenge to scientists for hundreds of years, and to philosophers for even longer.[1]

When faced with the daunting complexity of the brain, it is impossible to resist the lure of metaphor. One especially misleading example of this comes from photography (though photography is not to blame!): the eyes as lenses, the brain as – well, what? This is where the confusion starts, but not where it ends. Our eyes share some properties with camera lenses. The eye's outer surface takes in light and focuses it. And the light-sensitive cells at its back, in the retina, are a bit like the sensors in a digital camera, if you don't look too closely. Some parallels continue even within the brain. As well as sensing light, modern cameras perform various sophisticated tricks to improve image quality, such as balancing colours and adjusting focus. Our brains, too, engage in some basic image processing. As signals stream into the brain from the eyes, the visual cortex adjusts for ambient light, detects where the outlines of objects are, and so on.

But then things get complicated. There is nowhere in the brain where a photograph-like image is presented to an 'inner observer', in the way that you and I can look at an actual photograph. The relationship between the world out there and our conscious experience 'in here' has little in common with that between the world and a photograph. Photographs capture light; brains use light to create a world.

Die klassische Erklärung in Lehrbüchern, wie das Gehirn dies tut – wie es in der Lage ist, die Welt *wahrzunehmen* – lautet etwa so: Die Netzhaut wandelt Licht in elektrische Signale um. Diese Signale durchlaufen verschiedene Bereiche der Sehrinde und gelangen so ins Gehirn. In den primären Arealen des Kortex werden einfache visuelle Merkmale wie Linien und Ränder erfasst, in den mittleren Arealen werden Teile von Objekten erkannt – vielleicht protohafte Gesichter oder tierähnliche Formen. In den höheren Arealen werden vollständige Objekte und andere komplexe Konfigurationen visueller Informationen identifiziert.

So gesehen bedeutet Wahrnehmung im Wesentlichen, sensorische Signale aus der Welt auszulesen – von außen nach innen bzw. von unten nach oben (»bottom-up«). Dies scheint sich mit unserer alltäglichen Intuition zu decken. Meist erleben wir es so, als wären unsere Augen (und Ohren und anderen Sinne) transparente Fenster, durch die die Welt direkt in unseren Verstand strömt.

Doch der Schein trügt. Philosoph:innen und Wissenschaftler:innen streiten zwar noch über Details, doch setzt sich die Erkenntnis durch: Wahrnehmungserfahrungen sind eine Frage aktiver Interpretation und nicht passiver Reaktion. Aus dieser Sicht nimmt der Mensch die Welt eher von innen nach außen wahr als umgekehrt – sie funktioniert eher von oben nach unten (»top-down«) als von unten nach oben (»bottom-up«). Die schon vor Hunderten von Jahren entwickelte Idee besagt, dass das Gehirn ständig vorhersagt, was in der Welt geschieht, und die empfangenen Sinneseindrücke nutzt, um diese Vorhersagen zu aktualisieren.[2]

Genauer gesagt steht das Gehirn ständig vor der Herausforderung, aus sensorischen Signalen den Zustand der Welt – und des eigenen Körpers – zu erschließen. Diese Signale sind von Natur aus verrauscht, mehrdeutig und nicht klassifiziert. Es muss daher gewissermaßen *schlussfolgern*, was geschieht, und unter Bedingungen grundsätzlicher Ungewissheit die »bestmögliche Vermutung« treffen. In der Mathematik nennt man dieses Vorgehen »Bayessche Inferenz«. Meist ist es unmöglich, das Problem exakt zu lösen.

Die Biologie weiß sich zu helfen. Wie sich herausgestellt hat, nutzt das Gehirn eine clevere Methode: Es erstellt und aktualisiert Vorhersagen, um sich der Bayesschen Inferenz anzunähern. Statt die Welt aus den Sinnesdaten »herauszulesen«, passt es seine Kaskade von Top-down-Vorhersagen fortlaufend an und kalibriert sie neu, um die von außen einströmenden Sinnesdaten »wegzuerklären«.

Nach den meisten Deutungen dieser biologischen Theorie erleben wir nicht die Sinnesdaten selbst, sondern die *Vorhersagen*, die diese Daten mit der Welt in Einklang bringen.[3] Das widerspricht unserer Intuition. Die Welt, die wir erleben, entsteht ebenso sehr (wenn nicht sogar stärker) von innen nach außen wie von außen nach innen. Unsere subjektiven Erfah-

The old-school textbook view of how the brain does this – how it is able to *perceive* the world – goes like this. The retina transforms light into electrical signals which, after some initial processing, flow into the brain through various stages of the visual cortex. Early stages of the cortex pick out simple visual features such as lines and edges, middle stages pick out parts of objects – maybe face-like proto-things or animal-like proto-things – and deeper stages detect entire objects and other complex configurations of visual information.

Thought of this way, perception is largely a matter of an outside-in (or 'bottom-up') reading out of sensory signals from the world. This might seem to match our everyday intuitions. For most of us, most of the time, it seems as though our eyes (and our ears and so on) are transparent windows onto a world that pours itself directly into our minds.

But how things seem is not how they are. While the details are still debated by philosophers and scientists, there is a growing recognition that perceptual experience is a matter of active interpretation, not passive response. In this view, perception is more inside-out than outside-in, and more top-down than bottom-up. The idea – which can be traced back hundreds of years – is that the brain is constantly making predictions about what's out there in the world, using the sensory inputs it receives to update these predictions.[2]

In a bit more detail, the brain is continually faced with the challenge of inferring the state of the world (and the body) from sensory signals that are inherently noisy, ambiguous, and unlabelled. It has to *infer* what's going on, to make a 'best guess' under conditions of inherent uncertainty. In mathematics, this is known as 'Bayesian inference', and it's usually an impossible problem to solve exactly.

Biology finds a way. It turns out that the process of making and updating predictions provides a clever method for brains to approximate this process of Bayesian inference. Instead of 'reading out' the world from sensory data, the brain is constantly adjusting and recalibrating its cascade of top-down predictions to try to 'explain away' the sensory data flooding in from the outside.

In most versions of this biological story, *we experience the predictions*, not the sensory data that keeps these predictions geared to the world.[3] This turns our intuitions on their head. The world we experience comes from the inside out, just as much (if not more) than from the outside in. Our subjective experiences of the world – and the body – are 'controlled hallucinations', tuned by evolution not to reflect the world 'as it is', but in ways that have proven to be useful to us in the business of staying alive.

The art historian Ernst Gombrich came very close to this exact idea with his concept of the 'beholder's share', which he developed in

rungen von Welt – unseres Körpers – sind »kontrollierte Halluzinationen«, die die Evolution so angepasst hat, dass sie nicht die Welt zeigen, »wie sie ist«, sondern so, wie sie unserem Überleben dient.

Der Kunsthistoriker Ernst Gombrich kam mit seinem Begriff des »Anteils des Betrachters«, den er Mitte des 20. Jahrhunderts prägte, dieser Idee sehr nahe.[4] Er betonte den Beitrag, den die Betrachtenden zum künstlerischen, ästhetischen Erlebnis leisten. Die impressionistischen Gemälde veranschaulichen dies eindrucksvoll. Künstler wie Monet und Pissarro malten keine detaillierten Szenen – jene Bilder, die wir manchmal zu sehen glauben. Stattdessen verfolgten sie die Stufen der neuronalen Verarbeitung zurück, um das Licht selbst so präzise wie möglich zu malen. Dadurch fordert der Akt des Betrachtens einen größeren Einsatz der Betrachtenden.[5]

Die Algorithmen der künstlichen Intelligenz (KI) eröffnen einen weiteren Resonanzraum. Moderne Computer-Vision-Systeme arbeiten oft mit »generativen« Verfahren, um Inhalte zu erstellen und Bilder zuverlässig zu erkennen und einzuordnen. Diese Methoden hängen eng mit dem Zusammenspiel von Top-down-Vorhersagen und Bottom-up-Vorhersagefehlern zusammen – einem zentralen Prinzip für das Modell des Gehirns als »Vorhersagemaschine«.

Die engen Parallelen zwischen KI und dem Gehirn werfen spannende Fragen auf, vor allem zur Natur des Bewusstseins. Vor gut 50 Jahren veröffentlichte der Philosoph Thomas Nagel einen bahnbrechenden Aufsatz mit dem Titel »What Is It Like to Be a Bat?«.[6] Darin nahm er nicht nur David Chalmers' »schwieriges Problem« vorweg, sondern zeigte auch, dass sich das subjektive Erleben einer Fledermaus stark von dem eines Menschen unterscheidet. Zugleich betonte er, dass es mit ziemlicher Sicherheit *irgendeine Form* subjektiver Erfahrung geben werde. Wie er schrieb, »[ist] es irgendwie«, eine Fledermaus zu sein.

Das wirft die Frage auf: »[Ist] es irgendwie«, ein KI-System zu sein, das ähnlich funktioniert wie das LiDAR-System in selbstfahrenden Autos oder der YOLO-Algorithmus (You Only Look Once), der entwickelt wurde, um unter einer Brücke in Sacramento nistende Fledermäuse zu zählen? Und wenn es dieses Erleben heute noch nicht gibt, wie sieht es dann mit künftigen, ausgefeilteren Versionen solcher statistischen Mechanismen aus?

Diese Fragen werden kontrovers diskutiert. Ich halte es für unwahrscheinlich, dass Berechnungen irgendwelcher Art auch nur den Anschein von Bewusstsein hervorrufen. Es ist vielmehr das Leben selbst, das den Gleichungen des Bewusstseins Feuer einhaucht, nicht die Verarbeitung von Informationen.[7] Das heißt jedoch nicht, dass Computersysteme die Welt nicht auf ihre eigene Weise wahrnehmen können. Sie tun dies nur ohne eine begleitende subjektive Erfahrung. Sie *fühlen* überhaupt nichts, auch wenn sie – dank der Magie großer Sprachmodelle – etwas zu empfinden behaupten.

the mid-twentieth century.[4] Gombrich placed emphasis on that part of an artistic, aesthetic experience that is contributed by the observer, or 'beholder'. The classic Impressionist paintings offer an excellent example. Artists such as Claude Monet and Camille Pissarro didn't paint detailed scenes – the images we sometimes think we see. Instead, they navigated their way back down through the stages of neural processing to paint as closely as possible the light itself, so that the act of viewing engaged more of the beholder's share.[5]

The algorithms of artificial intelligence (AI) provide another resonance. Modern computer vision systems often use 'generative' methods to create content, as well as to recognise and classify images in robust ways. These methods map closely onto the dance of top-down prediction and bottom-up prediction error that is central to the 'prediction machine' view of the brain.

The close parallels between AI and the brain raise many tantalising questions. Perhaps the most significant relates to the nature of consciousness. Just over fifty years ago, the philosopher Thomas Nagel published a landmark essay entitled 'What Is It Like to Be a Bat?'[6] As well as anticipating the 'hard problem' of David Chalmers, Nagel also made the point that the subjective experience of a bat will be very different from that of a human being. But he also argued that – almost certainly – there will be a subjective experience *of some kind* going on. As he put it, there is 'something it is like' to be a bat.

This raises the question: is there 'something it is like to be' an AI system, such as the LiDAR system in a self-driving car or the YOLO (You Only Look Once) algorithm developed to count bats roosting under a bridge in Sacramento? And if not now, what about future, more sophisticated versions of these statistical machinations?

There is no consensus over answers to questions like these. My own view is that computation of any kind is unlikely to be sufficient for even the smallest glimmer of consciousness, and that it is life, rather than information processing, that breathes fire into the equations of consciousness.[7] But this doesn't mean that computational systems can't perceive the world in their own way. They will just do so without there being any accompanying subjective experience. They will not *feel* anything at all, even though – thanks to the magic of large language models – they may say they do.

Thinking about these various interconnected ways of perceiving the world – whether consciously or not – is an opportunity to also think about our own experiential encounters with the worlds we live in, and with our own selves. These days, when technology is running both away from us and towards us ever faster, new ways of perceiving and comprehending our changing worlds are needed, now more than ever. The more we

Das Nachdenken über die verschiedenen, eng verknüpften Arten der Weltwahrnehmung – ob bewusst oder unbewusst – eröffnet die Möglichkeit, auch unsere eigenen Erfahrungsbegegnungen mit den Welten, in denen wir leben, und mit uns selbst zu hinterfragen. In einer Zeit, in der sich die Technologie einerseits immer weiter von uns entfernt und andererseits immer schneller auf uns zukommt, brauchen wir dringend neue Wege, die sich wandelnde Welt wahrzunehmen und zu begreifen. Je mehr wir der Versuchung widerstehen, uns in unsere maschinellen Schöpfungen hineinzuprojizieren, desto klarer werden wir uns als das erkennen, was wir sind: ein Teil der Natur, nicht getrennt von ihr.

ANIL SETH ist Direktor des Sussex Centre for Consciousness Science und Co-Direktor des Programms »Brain, Mind, and Consciousness« am Canadian Institute for Advanced Research (CIFAR). Er ist Autor des Buches *Being You. A New Science of Consciousness* (London: Faber & Faber 2021).

1 Vgl. David Chalmers, *The Conscious Mind. In Search of a Fundamental Theory*, New York und Oxford: Oxford University Press 1996.

2 Vgl. Andy Clark, »Whatever Next? Predictive Brains, Situated Agents, and the Future of Cognitive Science«, in: *Behavioral and Brain Sciences*, Bd. 36, Nr. 3, 2013, S. 181–204.

3 Siehe Anil Seth, *Being You. A New Science of Consciousness*, London: Faber & Faber 2021.

4 Ernst Gombrich, *Kunst und Illusion. Zur Psychologie der bildlichen Darstellung* [1960], Berlin: Phaidon 2002.

5 Anil Seth, »From Unconscious Inference to the Beholder's Share. Predictive Perception and Human Experience«, in: *European Review*, Bd. 273, Nr. 3, 2019, S. 378–410.

6 Thomas Nagel, *What Is It Like to Be a Bat? / Wie ist es, eine Fledermaus zu sein?* [1974], übersetzt, herausgegeben und mit einem Nachwort von Ulrich Diehl, Ditzingen: Reclam 2023.

7 Siehe Anil Seth, »Conscious Artificial Intelligence and Biological Naturalism«, *Behavioral and Brain Sciences*, 21. April 2025, online unter https://doi.org/10.1017/S0140525X25000032 (abgerufen am 2. Juni 2025).

can resist the temptation to project ourselves into our machine creations, the more we'll be able to see ourselves for what we truly are: a part of nature, not apart from it.

ANIL SETH is director of the Sussex Centre for Consciousness Science and co-director of the Canadian Institute for Advanced Research (CIFAR) Program on Brain, Mind, and Consciousness. He is the author of *Being You: A New Science of Consciousness* (Faber & Faber, 2021).

1 David Chalmers, *The Conscious Mind: In Search of a Fundamental Theory* (Oxford University Press, 1996).

2 Andy Clark, 'Whatever Next? Predictive Brains, Situated Agents, and the Future of Cognitive Science', *Behavioral and Brain Sciences* 36, no. 3 (2013): 181–204.

3 Anil Seth, *Being You: A New Science of Consciousness* (Faber & Faber, 2021).

4 Ernst Gombrich, *Art and Illusion: A Study in the Psychology of Pictorial Representation* (Phaidon Press, 1960).

5 Anil Seth, 'From Unconscious Inference to the Beholder's Share: Predictive Perception and Human Experience', *European Review* 273, no. 3 (2019): 378–410.

6 Thomas Nagel, 'What Is It Like to Be a Bat?', *Philosophical Review* 83, no. 4 (1974): 435–50.

7 Anil Seth, 'Conscious Artificial Intelligence and Biological Naturalism', *Behavioral and Brain Sciences*, published online 21 April 2025, https://doi.org/10.1017/S0140525X25000032 (accessed on 2 June 2025).

BIOGRAFIE

LISA BARNARD (* 1967, Vereinigtes Königreich) ist eine Künstlerin, Forscherin und Dozentin, die sich in ihrer fotografischen Praxis mit realen Ereignissen auseinandersetzt und dabei sowohl traditionelle Methoden als auch zeitgenössische bild- und computerbasierte Verfahren nutzt. Ihr Interesse an Ästhetik und an aktuellen Debatten zur Materialität der Fotografie verbindet sie mit politischen Fragestellungen rund um den militärisch-industriellen Komplex, technologische Entwicklungen, neue ökologische Ansätze und Wahrnehmung.

Barnards Werke wurden vielfach in Museen und auf Fotografie-Festivals gezeigt; in Einzelausstellungen unter anderem im Centre de la Photographie Genève, im Fotomuseum Den Haag, bei Images Vevey, dem EXPOSED Torino Foto Festival und The Photographer's Gallery Soho Quarter in London. Sie ist Associate Professor für Fotografie an der University of South Wales und wurde mit verschiedenen Stipendien und Preisen ausgezeichnet, darunter dem Albert Renger-Patzsch-Preis und dem Getty Images Prestige Grant. Sie hat drei Monografien veröffentlicht: *Chateau Despair* und *Hyenas of the Battlefield, Machines in the Garden* (beide erschienen bei GOST Books) sowie *The Canary and The Hammer* (erschienen bei MACK).

BIOGRAPHY

LISA BARNARD (b. 1967, United Kingdom) is an artist, researcher, and teacher whose photographic practice addresses real events using traditional methods, alongside more contemporary visual and computer forms. Her work combines her interest in aesthetics and current debates around the materiality of photography with the political climate within critical projects, centred on the military-industrial complex, new technologies, new ecologies, and perception.

Barnard's work has been exhibited widely in museums and at photography festivals, with solo shows at Centre de la Photographie Genève, Fotomuseum Den Haag, Images Vevey, EXPOSED Torino Foto Festival, and the Photographer's Gallery Soho Quarter in London. She is associate professor of photography at the University of South Wales and has been awarded a number of grants and awards, most notably the Albert Renger-Patzsch Award and the Getty Images Prestige Grant. Barnard has published three monographs: *Chateau Despair* and *Hyenas of the Battlefield, Machines in the Garden* (both published by GOST Books), and *The Canary and The Hammer* (published by MACK).

DANK

Mein besonderer Dank gilt Jack Lander – Assistent, Entwickler von Drohnen- und Bewegtbildinhalten sowie Kollaborationspartner –, dessen Expertise, Intelligenz und Begeisterung für meine Arbeit entscheidend zur Realisierung dieses Projekts beigetragen haben.

Danke an Lauren Bon, Künstlerin und Aktivistin bei Metabolic Studio, die dieses Projekt von Beginn an unterstützt hat. Ihre Freundschaft und unsere Gespräche waren von großem Wert. Ebenso danke ich Richard Nielson für seinen herzlichen Empfang.

Carolyn Drake, deren Freundschaft und Unterstützung unabdingbar für die Realisierung der Nachtsichtaufnahmen war. Danke an Daniel Kish, Gründer von World Access for the Blind, sowie an Anil Seth, Direktor des Sussex Centre for Consciousness Science und Co-Direktor des CIFAR-Programms »Brain, Mind, and Consciousness«.

Weiter danke ich der Fledermausexpertin und Ehrenamtlichen bei LA Bat Rescue, Chumi Paul, deren Engagement inspirierend ist. Amy Spencer. Mary Jean »Corky« Quirk, Koordinatorin bei der Yolo Basin Bat Foundation. Scott D. Osborn, landesweiter Koordinator für Kleinsäugerschutz. Jill Carpenter. Sarah Lagattuta. Jasmyn Phillips »Beach Pebbles«, Captain Bruce Poynter und Evan Trubee – allesamt Expert:innen für den Saltonsee. Max Houghton. Clare Strand. Debi Cornwall. Sandi Wheaton. Jamie Grace. Joshua Garrity und Andrew Mathers vom Transportation Research Center. Vlad Voroninski und Tobias Wessels von Helm.ai. Derek Benson und Nathan Featherstone von EnergySource. Alison Shultz, Kuratorin für Ornithologie am Natural History Museum of Los Angeles County. Frank Castner, Archivar am Palm Springs Air Museum. Ricardo Martinez, Fotoassistent. Kevin Key, Drohnenoperator. Danke an das Taith International Learning Exchange Programme und die University of South Wales für die Unterstützung in der Frühphase des Projekts sowie an die Professor:innen Lisa Lewis und Mark Durden.

Ein großer Dank an Iris Sikking, die mich für diesen Preis nominiert hat, sowie an die Jury: Tomáš Dvořák, Zippora Elders, Hinde Haest, Michelle Henning, Maria-Kyveli Mavrokordopoulou, Boaz Levin, Christiane Riedel und Katharina Täschner – für ihr Vertrauen und die Auszeichnung mit dem renommierten Preis. Danke auch an Ben Livne Weitzman und an Kathy Crocket für die herzliche Begrüßung in Glenkeen Garden in Ballydehob.

Nicht zuletzt danke ich dem großartigen Team von C/O Berlin für ihre Hingabe, Professionalität und Leidenschaft. Und schließlich der unermüdlichen Katharina Täschner, die dieses Projekt als Kuratorin, Autorin, Redakteurin und Kollaborationspartnerin so wunderbar begleitet hat.

ACKNOWLEDGEMENTS

Particular thanks are due to Jack Lander – my assistant, drone, and moving image content creator, and collaborator – whose expertise, intelligence, and enthusiasm for my practice has been pivotal to this project's creation.

Thanks to Lauren Bon, artist and activist from Metabolic Studio, who from the very early stages supported this project. Her friendship and discussions were invaluable. Thanks also to artist Richard Nielson for welcoming me with such enthusiasm.

Carolyn Drake, whose friendship, company, and support were fundamental to the 'night vision' series. The brilliant Daniel Kish, founder of World Access for the Blind. Anil Seth, director of the Sussex Centre for Consciousness Science and co-director of the Canadian Institute for Advanced Research (CIFAR) Program on Brain, Mind, and Consciousness.

Bat expert and LA Bat Rescue volunteer Chumi Paul, whose commitment to bats was inspiring. Amy Spencer. Mary Jean 'Corky' Quirk, program coordinator at the Yolo Basin Bat Foundation. Scott D. Osborn, statewide coordinator for small mammal conservation. Jill Carpenter. Sarah Lagattuta. Jasmyn Phillips 'Beach Pebbles', Captain Bruce Poynter and Evan Trubee, all experts from the Salton Sea. Max Houghton. Clare Strand. Debi Cornwall. Sandi Wheaton. Jamie Grace. Joshua Garrity and Andrew Mathers from Transportation Research Center. Vlad Voroninski and Tobias Wessels from Helm.ai. Derek Benson and Nathan Featherstone from Energy Source. Alison Shultz, associate curator, ornithology, Natural History Museum of Los Angeles County. Frank Castner, librarian/archivist, Palm Springs Air Museum. Ricardo Martinez, photography assistant. Kevin Key, drone operator. Taith International Learning Exchange Programme and the University of South Wales, who both funded the early stages of the project. Professors Lisa Lewis and Mark Durden.

Importantly, thanks to Iris Sikking for nominating me for the *After Nature Prize*, and to jury members Tomáš Dvořák, Zippora Elders, Hinde Haest, Michelle Henning, Maria-Kyveli Mavrokordopoulou, Boaz Levin, Christiane Riedel, and Katharina Täschner for believing in the project and considering me worthy of such a prestigious award. To Ben Livne Weitzman and to Kathy Crocket, who welcomed me to Glenkeen Garden in Ballydehob.

All the team at C/O Berlin, who are brilliant and passionate about what they do. And of course, finally, the indomitable Katharina Täschner, who has been the most wonderful curator, writer, editor, and collaborator.

IMPRESSUM / COLOPHON

Diese Publikation erscheint im Rahmen des *After Nature. Ulrike Crespo Photography Prize 25* anlässlich der Doppelausstellung / This book is published as part of the *After Nature: Ulrike Crespo Photography Prize 25* on the occasion of the double exhibition

Lisa Barnard. *You Only Look Once*

und / and

Isadora Romero. *Notes on How to Build a Forest*

C/O Berlin Foundation
Amerika Haus
Hardenbergstraße 22-24
10623 Berlin, Germany
www.co-berlin.org

27. September 2025 bis 28. Januar 2026 /
27 September 2025 to 28 January 2026

Zweite Station im Crespo Open Space, Frankfurt am Main /
Second venue at the Crespo Open Space, Frankfurt am Main

13. März bis 31. Mai 2026 /
13 March to 31 May 2026

Ausstellungskuratorin / Exhibition Curator
Katharina Täschner

Leihgaben- + Ausstellungsmanagement / Loans + Exhibition Management
Carolin Bollig

PUBLIKATION / PUBLICATION

Herausgeberin / Editor
Katharina Täschner für / for C/O Berlin Foundation

Katalogredaktion / Book Coordination
Katharina Täschner

Buchdesign / Book Design
Naroska

Lektorat / Copyediting
Simon Cowper (EN)

Übersetzungen / Translations
Claudia Kotte (DE)
Simon Cowper (EN)

Fahnenkorrektorat / Proofreading
Cathrin Nielsen (DE)
Tas Skorupa (EN)

Bildbearbeitung / Color separation
Carsten Humme, Leipzig

Papier / Stock
135 g/m² Magno Volume, 330 g/m² Les Naturals

Druck + Bindung / Printing + Binding
Gutenberg Beuys Feindruckerei GmbH, Langenhagen

Erste Auflage / First edition
Oktober / October 2025

Erschienen bei/ Published by
Hartmann Books
Liststraße 28/1
70180 Stuttgart, Germany
info@hartmannprojects.com
hartmann-books.com

ISBN 978-3-96070-127-9

Gedruckt in Deutschland / Printed in Germany

Ein gemeinsames Projekt von / A joint project of

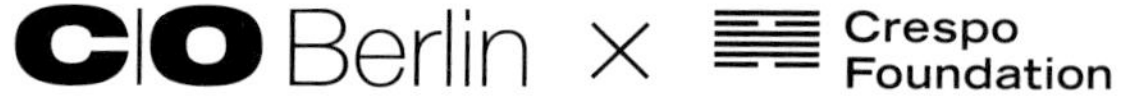

C/O BERLIN FOUNDATION

Vorstand / Executive Board
Stephan Erfurt, Vorstandsvorsitzender / CEO
Dr. Andreas Behr

Programm / Program
Sophia Greiff, Programmleitung + Kuratorin / Head of Program + Curator
Boaz Levin, Programmleitung + Kurator / Head of Program + Curator
Veronika Epple, Junior-Kuratorin / Junior Curator
Katharina Täschner, Kuratorin / Curator

Leihgaben- + Ausstellungsmanagement / Loans + Exhibition Management
Carolin Bollig
Morgan Lacroix
Julian Hemelberg, Assistenz / Assistant

Kaufmännische Leitung / Managing Director
Karin Hänsler

Sponsoring + Fundraising
Louisa Seelis, Leitung / Head
Katharina Schilling

Finanzen / Accounting
Kirsten Mintert, Finanzen + Controlling / Finance + Controlling
Silke Willenborg, Finanzen + Controlling / Finance + Controlling
René Lattusek, Rechnungswesen / Accounting

Bildung / Education
Sibylle Kufus, Leitung / Head
Frauke Menzinger, Künstlerische Leitung / Artistic Direction
Lisa Albrecht, Bildung + Vermittlung / Education

Kommunikation / Commmunication
Beatrice Di Buduo, Leitung / Head
Ksenia Disterhof, Presse- + Öffentlichkeitsarbeit / Press and Public Relations
Paulina Weiß, Digitale Kommunikation + Marketing / Digital Communication + Marketing

Veranstaltungsmanagement / Event Management
Eva Marx

Personal / People + Culture
Kristian Sidenius Lenz, Head of People + Culture

Design
Marc Naroska, Artdirektor / Art Direction
Max Schürmann, Grafik / Design

Office Management + PA für / for Stephan Erfurt
Katja Weinhold

Technik / Tech
Björn Rohde, Leitung / Head
Sebastian Biskup, Technik + Ausstellungsaufbau / Technical Management + Installations

C/O Berlin Friends e.V
Sibylle Kufus, Geschäftsführung / Managing Director

Bookshop
Raluca Blidar, Leitung / Head

Besucher:innen Betreuung + Empfang / Visitor Services
Yanina Raspa, Leitung / Head
Matthias Walendy, Leitung / Head

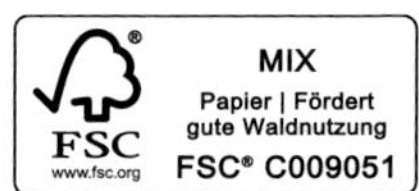
FSC
www.fsc.org
MIX
Papier | Fördert
gute Waldnutzung
FSC® C009051